People, Places, and Material Things:

Historical Archaeology of Albany, New York

People, Places, and Material Things:

Historical Archaeology of Albany, New York

Edited by Charles L. Fisher

NEW YORK STATE MUSEUM
Bulletin 499
2003

The University of the State of New York
The State Education Department

©The New York State Education Department
Albany, New York 12230

Published in 2003

Printed in the United States of America

Copies may be ordered from:

Publication Sales
New York State Museum
3140 CEC
Albany, New York 12230
Phone: (518) 402-5344
FAX: (518) 486-2034
email: nysmpub@mail.nysed.gov

Library of Congress Catalog Card Number: 2002116170

ISBN: 0278-3355

ISSN: 1-55557-143-3

This book is printed on acid free paper.

Table of Contents

List of Figures.. vii

List of Tables xi

Preface xii

Section 1: Introduction and Background

Chapter 1
Introduction to Historical Archaeological Studies of Albany.. 3
Charles L. Fisher

Chapter 2
Thirty Years of Historical Archaeology in the City Of Albany 11
Paul R. Huey

Section 2: People

Chapter 3
Traders or Traitors: Illicit Trade at Fort Orange in the Seventeenth Century.............. 23
Kevin Moody

Chapter 4
Soldiers in the City: The Archaeology of the British Guard House................................ 39
Charles L. Fisher

Chapter 5
Out of the Ashes of Craft, the Fires of Consumerism: A 1797 Deposit in Downtown Albany 47
Matthew Kirk

Chapter 6
Skeletal Analysis of the Human Remains from the Lutheran Church Lot, 1670–1816............................... 57
Shawn Phillips

Chapter 7
Trace Elements and Stable Isotope Analysis of the Human Remains from the Lutheran Church Lot 63
Charles L. Fisher

Section 3: Places

Chapter 8
The Cultural Landscape at the Site of the Lutheran Church Lot and Burial Ground................................. 69
Nancy Davis

Chapter 9
The Garden That Didn't Die: Archaeological Explorations West of the Visitors' Center, Schuyler
Mansion State Historic Site, Albany, New York 83
Lois M. Feister

Table of Contents, *continued*

Chapter 10
From Refrigerator, to Oven, to Down the Drain: Nineteenth-Century Analogs of
Twentieth-Century Household Conveniences in Old Albany 99
J.W. Bouchard

Section 4: Material Things
Chapter 11
Making "Money" the Old-Fashioned Way: Eighteenth-Century Wampum Production in Albany 119
Elizabeth S. Peña

Chapter 12
New Evidence of Wampum Use and Production from Albany, New York...................................... 129
Matthew Lesniak

Chapter 13
Painted Pearlware from the Picotte Site 135
Pegeen McLaughlin

Section 5: Battles and Breakthroughs
Chapter 14
Archaeology, Historic Preservation, and Albany's Past: The Battle over the DASNY Building Project........... 151
Karen S. Hartgen

Chapter 15
From Raritan Landing to Albany's Riverfront: The Path Toward Total 3D Archaeological Site Recording 167
Joel W. Grossman

Contributors 187

List of Figures

Figure 1.1.   Location of Albany and the archaeological sites in downtown Albany discussed in this volume. 5

Figure 1.2.   Early nineteenth-century view of North Pearl Street in Albany by James Eights. The Albany Institute of History and Art, Albany. 8

Figure 2.1.   Detail from a map of the northern parts of New York drawn about 1758 showing the two taverns at "Verberg" west of Albany. 13

Figure 2.2.   Detail from a map of the railroads from Rome to Albany and Troy. 16

Figure 3.1.   1698 Römer Map with Picotte-DEC project area identified. 26

Figure 3.2.   Detail of the 1698 Römer Map with Area 9 of the Picotte-DEC project area identified. 27

Figure 3.3.   Photograph of Area 9 stripped to the early nineteenth-century house floor level. 29

Figure 3.4.   Photograph of reexcavated Test Trench #1 with Feature 133 in profile. 30

Figure 3.5.   Photograph of the location of the eighteenth-century dock relative to Feature 133. 30

Figure 3.6.   Artist's conception of a Dutch Wigwam. Drawing by S. Sherwood. 31

Figure 3.7.   Photograph and plan view of Feature 133 with structural elements exposed by excavation. 32

Figure 3.8.   Photograph of shellfish remains at hearth (Feature 136). 33

Figure 3.9.   Photograph of marked mid-seventeenth-century tobacco pipe fragments. 34

Figure 3.10.   Photograph of seventeenth-century glass trade beads. 36

Figure 3.11.   Photograph of Herkimer diamonds. 36

Figure 3.12.   Photograph of historic lithic tool kit. 37

Figure 4.1.   Detail from Plan of Albany, 1756 and 1757. "N" (the building circled) indicates "Main Guard." The Crown Collection, Series I, Vol. 2, No. 39. New York State Library, Albany. 40

Figure 4.2.   Photograph of 1998 excavations at the pedestrian island in State Street. 42

Figure 4.3.   Section drawing of south wall of excavation. 43

Figure 4.4.   Hand-painted, polychrome creamware bowl, 7 inches in diameter, from the British guard house. 44

Figure 4.5.   Blue hand-painted, 6-inch-diameter pearlware bowl from the British guard house. 44

Figure 4.6.   Revolutionary War period USA button, 7/8-inch diameter, from the British guard house. 45

Figure 4.7.   Cow horn core and skull fragment from the British guard house. 45

Figure 5.1.   Picotte-DEC site location in downtown Albany, New York, shown on a rendering based on Simeon DeWitt's 1794 Map of the City of Albany, with the old Watervliet Street alignment. 48

Figure 5.2.   Ca. 1798 Map of the City of Albany (Albany County Hall of Records). 49

Figure 5.3.   View south of the 1797 house-remains. 50

Figure 5.4.   The excavated pit feature within the western portion of the interior wall. 50

Figure 5.5.   Interior view of excavated wooden privy with a clay-lined bottom. 51

Figure 5.6.   Creamware saltcellar with anthropomorphic foot, recovered from the debris level immediately above the burned floorboards. 51

Figure 5.7.   Tin-glazed enamel plate with Sepharitic letter decorations. 52

Figure 5.8.   Dot, diaper, and basket-weave patterned white salt-glazed stoneware plate, recovered from the pit feature within the house. 52

Figure 5.9.   Whieldon-ware or "cauliflower-ware" tea server, recovered from the pit feature within the house. 53

Figure 5.10.   Copper alloy, cross pendant, recovered from beneath the burned floorboards. 54

Figure 5.11.   Red calumet pipe fragment engraved "Johannes De Graef Syn" (*syn* meaning "his" in Dutch). 54

Figure 6.1.   Photograph of New York State Museum archaeologists excavating Burial 1 under shelter by artificial light. 57

Figure 6.2.   Facial reconstruction created upon the cast of the adult female skull from Burial 1. Gay Malin, New York State Museum. 58

Figure 8.1.   South Pearl Street and the location of the archaeological features found during the investigation. 72

Figure 8.2.   Profile of the east wall of Burial 1 excavation showing the location of the pollen column. 73

Figure 8.3.   Pollen types and percentages based on total pollen sums for each major soil stratum of the Burial 1 east wall profile (Kelso 1999). 74

Figure 8.4.   Bar chart of the percentage of total tree pollen found in each stratum. 76

Figure 8.5.   Bar chart of the percentage of pine pollen found in each stratum. 76

Figure 8.6.   East wall profile showing time periods assigned to the soil strata as determined by index artifacts present. 77

Figure 8.7.   Detail of the 1698 Col. Wolfgang Römer Map of Albany showing the Lutheran Church (circled) and the Rutten Kill bridge. 78

Figure 9.1.   Photograph of Schuyler Mansion, Albany. New York State Office of Parks, Recreation and Historic Preservation. 84

Figure 9.2.   Plan of the archaeological test units excavated in 1986 and 1994. 85

Figure 9.3.   Detail of 1794 DeWitt Map of Albany (Gibbons and Scott 1977:34). 86

Figure 9.4.   View of a specialty garden, ca. 1768 (Diderot 1959:Plate 10). 87

Figure 9.5.   Plan of the postholes found during the 1994 excavations. 91

Figure 9.6a.   Photograph of posthole and post remains (Catalog No. 753) in Trench 6. 92

Figure 9.6b.   Section drawing of posthole and post remains (Catalog No. 753) in Trench 6. 92

Figure 10.1.   Project location and excavation areas at Picotte-DEC office building site, 597–643 Broadway, Albany. 100

Figure 10.2.   Albany in the late seventeenth century (Römer 1698). 101

Figure 10.3.   Plan of the City of Albany about the year 1770 (Yates 1770). 102

Figure 10.4.   Map of the City of Albany (DeWitt 1794). 103

Figure 10.5.   Map of the City of Albany from original survey (Sidney 1850). 104

Figure 10.6.   City Atlas of Albany, New York (Hopkins 1876). 105

Figure 10.7.   Excavation Areas 6 and 7 showing the Samuel Stevens and James Kidd houses. 108

Figure 10.8.   The Stevens house kitchen. 109

Figure 10.9.   The Stevens house kitchen and second-floor drains and other wastewater features. 110

Figure 10.10.   The Stevens house cold room. 111

Figure 10.11.   The Stevens house cold room and kitchen plumbing details. 111

Figure 10.12.   The Stevens house freshwater cistern and lead water supply pipe. 112

Figure 10.13.   Ad for kitchen ranges and bathing apparatus (Hoffman 1849–50). 113

Figure 11.1.   KeyCorp site scatter plot, showing wampum bead distribution. 123

Figure 11.2.   KeyCorp site scatter plot, showing wampum debris distribution. 123

Figure 11.3.   Stages of wampum production from the KeyCorp site, collection of the New York
                 State Museum. 124

Figure 11.4.   Wampum production tools from the KeyCorp site, collection of the New York
                 State Museum. 125

Figure 12.1.   Picotte-DEC site plan featuring excavation areas that yielded wampum beads
                 or evidence of wampum production. 130

Figure 12.2.   Area 1 site plan. 131

Figure 12.3.   Wampum waster with drill mark, from Area 1. 132

Figure 12.4.   Area 2 site plan. 132

Figure 12.5.   Wampum beads from Area 2, Unit 2.1. 133

Figure 13.1.   Plan of the Picotte-DEC site showing excavation areas. 136

Figure 13.2.   Detail of the 1794 DeWitt Map of the City of Albany. 137

Figure 13.3.   Site plan of Areas 11 and 12 showing the location of Units 12.2, 12.4, 12.5, and
                 12.6 containing ceramic deposits. 138

Figure 13.4.   Profile of Units 12.2 and 12.4 showing the relationship among the 35 Montgomery
                 Street foundation, the nonburned ceramic (pearlware) deposit, and the 1797 fire level. ... 139

Figure 13.5.   A variety of the painted pearlware patterns recovered from the Picotte-DEC
                 ceramic deposits. 141

Figure 13.6.   Examples of imperfections in the painted pearlware pieces. 143

Figure 13.7.   Pattern 4 base motifs with corresponding painters' marks. 144

Figure 13.8a.   Pattern 41 base motifs with painters' marks. 145

Figure 13.8b.   More Pattern 41 base motifs with painters' marks. 146

Figure 13.9.   Examples of painted pearlware fragments from the 7 Hanover Square site in
                 New York City. Courtesy of the William Duncan Strong Museum of Anthropology,
                 Columbia University. 147

Figure 14.1.   Detail from the Römer Map of 1698 showing the location of the DASNY project site. 154

Figure 14.2.   Seventeenth-century deposits in blue and brown clay located during the initial
                 backhoe testing. 156

Figure 14.3.   Seventeenth- or early eighteenth-century red bricks from the initial testing. 156

List of Figures, *continued*

Figure 14.4.   Early trade goods, glass beads, shell beads and an early English pipe bowl recovere during the initial testing. 157

Figure 14.5.   Evidence of shell bead production, a cut conch and two shell beads. 158

Figure 14.6.   Native American pitted stone recovered in the initial testing. 158

Figure 14.7.   Tin-glazed enameled-wares recovered in the initial testing. 159

Figure 14.8.   Imported yellow Dutch bricks from Trench 5B. 160

Figure 14.9.   Decorative cut stone from the façade of Bleeker Hall, recorded in initial study. 160

Figure 14.10. Sample of faunal materials from the initial testing, including oyster, cow, bird, and fish remains. 161

Figure 14.11. Intact foundations exposed during mitigation, probably from the late eighteenth or early nineteenth century, along Broadway. 162

Figure 14.12. Looking south to Maiden Lane showing broad areas of the archaeological mitigation. 162

Figure 14.13. Excavation techniques during the archaeological mitigation. 164

Figure 14.14. Archaeological mitigation in the northeast portion of the site exposing a unique seventeenth-century drainage feature. 165

Figure 15.1.   Locations of sites discussed in this chapter. 168

Figure 15.2.   View of Raritan Landing 1979 excavation of the EPA impact corridor. 170

Figure 15.3.   Photomosaic of overlapping bipod image segments within Raritan Landing construction corridor. 172

Figure 15.4.   Detail of 1983 custom-built overhead camera suspension system. 173

Figure 15.5.   Grossman and Associates 1992 HAZMAT archaeological team excavating under fixed and heated winter shelters at the West Point Foundry. 174

Figure 15.6.   Single-camera photogrammetric Rolleimetric system over exposed 1863 Civil War gun-testing platform at West Point Foundry. 176

Figure 15.7.   Near-overhead Rolleimetric perspective image of exposed iron and wood cannon-testing platform discovered at West Point Foundry. 177

Figure 15.8.   Final scaled AutoCAD plan and profile record of excavated Civil War cannon-firing platform drawn from Rolleimetric photos. 177

Figure 15.9.   Rolleimetric view looking southeast toward the Hudson River showing two-block-long excavation in Albany, New York. 178

Figure 15.10. View toward the southern section of excavation. 179

Figure 15.11. Three-dimensional Cyra LIDAR scanner equipment and technical support team mapping exposed bulkhead features. 181

Figure 15.12. Field view of portable LIDAR scanner and technicians suspended over the wooden bulkhead structures. 182

Figure 15.13. Detail of one section of vertical eighteenth-century wooden log bulkhead. 183

Figure 15.14. Computer "screen shot" of raw 3D laser-radar scan of vertical wooden bulkhead elements. 184

List of Tables

Table 4.1.   Type and number of ceramic sherds recovered from two strata excavated at the British guard house. 44

Table 6.1.   Summary of burials. 58

Table 7.1.   Summary of trace element analysis. 65

Table 8.1.   Latin and vernacular names of plants discussed in the text. 75

Table 8.2.   Latin and vernacular names of seeds discussed in the text. 79

Table 9.1.   Posthole and post remains uncovered during excavations for the Schuyler Mansion Visitors' Center addition project. 90

Preface

Charles L. Fisher

The past decade has been a period of archaeological activity in Albany, New York, unlike any other in the city's history in terms of the size and quantity of investigations that were completed. Although the results of these studies have been, and will continue to be, the subject of numerous professional and public presentations, student research, and cultural resource management reports, they tell a larger story when they are considered together. The objective of this volume is to present some of the results of recent archaeological excavations in Albany to archaeologists and others with an interest in the material remains of this city's past.

This volume began as a series of papers presented at the Annual Conference on New York State History held at Hartwick College in Oneonta in June 1999. The positive response from the audience encouraged the production of this volume. The symposium was organized by Karen S. Hartgen at the request of Stefan Bielinski and titled "Uncovering Albany's Past: Archaeology, History, and Urban Redevelopment." It included papers by Tricia Barbagallo, J.W. Bouchard,

Charles L. Fisher, Paul R. Huey, and Pegeen McLaughlin. Versions of the latter four are contained here. James Gibb provided a commentary for the session at Hartwick College and offered helpful suggestions to the authors.

Papers concerning archaeology in Albany and initially presented in January 2000 at the Society for Historical Archaeology Annual Meeting in Quebec, the October 1999 meeting of the Council for Northeast Historical Archaeology in St. Mary's City, Maryland, and the New York State Archaeological Association meeting in April 1999 were sought from the authors for inclusion here. Additional chapters were requested from scholars with ongoing research based upon Albany material.

I want to thank the contributors for their efforts in bringing their data to the surface and permitting their inclusion in this volume. Particularly helpful were the comments of Rebecca Yamin and an anonymous reviewer. The concise and alliterative title of the final section was one of Rebecca's many ideas that I regret was not mine.

Section 1

Introduction and Background

CHAPTER 1

Introduction to Historical Archaeological Studies of Albany

Charles L. Fisher

The tension between urban and rural life has been a feature of the American social and political landscape since the initial European colonization. The founding fathers debated the existence of the moral virtues necessary for a republic to survive. Many viewed these essential characteristics as being exhibited by independent, self-sufficient, rural farmers. Cities, in contrast, were viewed as "sores upon the body" by revolutionaries who wanted a new political order based upon an idealized rural society distinct from the immoral, corrupt system of the old world (Fries 1977).

Early America was a rural society in which only 1 in 20 people lived in communities with a population of more than 2,500 at the end of the eighteenth century. Yet cities were crucial centers of commerce and innovation.

> American cities were important far beyond their size; streams of goods, people, livestock, information and ideas flowed between them and the villages and farms. They were settlements of merchants and artisans, laborers and mariners, teamsters and boatmen, places where goods were bought and sold, moved and made . . . Cities were noisier, dirtier and more unhealthy than rural communities, but far more exciting, more anonymous, quicker-paced and immersed in cash and trade. They were the focal points of culture as well as commerce. (Larkin 1988:9)

The chapters in this volume derive from efforts to carry out archaeological research *of* the city, rather than merely conduct excavations *in* the city that ignore the urban context. Pointed out by Bert Salwen in 1973, this distinction marked a change in the orientation of archaeologists away from trying to find unspoiled areas within the bounds of urban areas where earlier sites could be studied. Today many historical archaeologists, in contrast, focus their investigations on the complexity of the cultural landscape and the alterations that have created the modern city.

Albany is an excellent subject for historical archaeology of the city. It is one of the oldest European cities in North America. A permanent settlement was established in 1614 on Castle Island, and continuous settlement began in 1624 with the establishment of Fort Orange. Within a very short period after its founding, this Dutch West India Company trading fort was in conflict with the surrounding settlement of Rensselaerswyck, established in 1630. By the 1650s the major streets of the town of Beverwyck—Broadway, State Street, and Pearl Street—were laid out to the north of Fort Orange and surrounded by a protective palisade. After the English took over the colony from the Dutch in 1664, a new fort was constructed, and the town walls were repaired and expanded several times before the American Revolution.

Albany's position as an inland port at the gateway to the natural western transportation corridor of the Mohawk Valley enabled the Dutch and their Iroquois allies to control the fur trade. During the eighteenth century, this strategic location turned Albany into the military headquarters for numerous expeditions against the French in Canada. Following the American Revolution, Albany was the starting point for traveling west on the Inland Navigation Canal and later, the Erie Canal, turnpikes, and railroads. Throughout its history Albany expanded and rebuilt to accommodate the constant immigration.

A theme present throughout this volume reflects a

People, Places, and Material Things: Historical Archaeology of Albany, New York edited by Charles L. Fisher, New York State Museum Bulletin 499, © 2003 by the University of the State of New York, New York State Education Department, Albany, New York. All rights reserved.

hallmark of modern historical archaeology as the study of the emergence of the modern world through the expansion of European culture and its relationship to indigenous peoples (Deetz 1977; Orser and Fagan 1995). This is the representation of everyday life in the past: the people, their material things, and the places associated with them that have not played a significant role in traditional historical interpretations. Knowledge of the past that is based only on those events written about at the time is very limited and is inherently elitist; it frequently obscures the population majority and focuses on those few who wrote or participated in activities deemed valuable enough to record. Modern scholars are aware of the need to consider every available source of information in their efforts to develop a detailed picture of individuals' daily lives, how they interacted with others, and how they constructed the world around them.

Archaeologists interpret artifacts in their context as primary documents in revealing past lives. Although some archaeologists have advocated the "reading" of artifacts, the messages they carry are different from those of written documents (Hodder 1986). This difference communicated by artifacts, or the "small things forgotten," makes them important entry points to understanding life in the past (Deetz 1977). Day-to-day life, however, was never static, and the detailed description of archaeological context is necessary to place material things in time and space, which is essential to infer the specific messages artifacts carry regarding their meaning to the people who made and used them.

That early Albany was a multicultural community is continually revealed in new ways by archaeological evidence. There is no single, unified past of the city that can be revealed by a single individual or group; rather, there are many pasts described by the multiple voices of the former inhabitants. The illegal traders outside Fort Orange, the persecuted religious minority, cottage industrialists, soldiers, servants, and even a middle-class lawyer are among the subjects of archaeological studies included here. Although historic documents have provided names for some of these individuals, the silence of documentary records regarding their daily lives begs for archaeological exploration.

The material things that were created, used, exchanged, and discarded by the people of Albany at specific places are the primary sources of these archaeological studies. Places in the landscape of historic Albany may be considered as larger material objects created for a variety of reasons. Gardens, yards, cemeteries, military structures, pottery dumps, and the development of the waterfront have come to light through archaeological investigations that provide new perspectives on daily life: the structures that surrounded the occupants of the city and the way that the urban environment was created and then shaped people's lives. The places that are referred to in the studies presented here are shown within the current city of Albany on Figure 1.1.

Following the initial chapters that provide a brief overview of the history of Albany and a history of archaeology in Albany, the book is organized under the topics related to daily life in the past: people, places, and material things. Chapters in the final section deal with "battles" and breakthroughs or challenges that archaeologists in Albany have faced in the process of investigating this city.

In Chapter 3 Kevin Moody presents the results of the excavation of an illegal trader's shelter during the early seventeenth-century settlement of Fort Orange. Although historical documents contain evidence of the trader's existence, the archaeological excavations at this site have provided details of lives that were unknown previously. The specific construction method and location of this shelter reveal a strategy of deceit that promised considerable wealth.

British soldiers in the colonies have been subject to numerous studies, but their material conditions revealed by excavations in Albany have provided a different perspective, presented in Chapter 4. They appeared to have been well supplied and integrated into the urban economy through craftwork and the production of nonmilitary items.

In Chapter 5 Matt Kirk describes the change from craft to mass-produced goods in an Albany household. The 1797 fire provided evidence for the division of material objects into those used before and after the fire. This, in turn, provided the basis for an evaluation of continuity and change in the organization of production and consumption.

Direct evidence of the colonial inhabitants of Albany is provided in Chapters 6 and 7. Shawn Phillips describes the physical remains of individuals excavated from the Lutheran Church lot. Under the rules of the Dutch West India Company, the Lutheran minority was prohibited from worshiping in public but was allowed to establish a church and cemetery of its own at this location in the 1670s, during the period of English rule. As revealed by this study, the poor health of these people depicts a daily life of physical

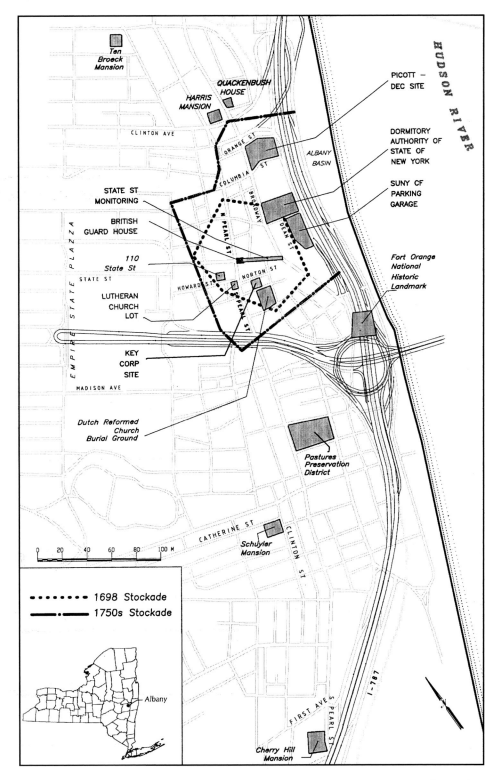

Figure 1.1. Location of Albany and the archaeological sites in downtown Albany discussed in this volume.

pain and hard labor. The trace element analysis of these individuals produced additional evidence of physical problems and potential avenues for the future study of social distinctions among them. The investigation reported here does not reveal a single history of this religious minority but indicates different health conditions that may have resulted from social or sexual inequality within this community.

Chapter 8 continues the analysis of the Lutheran Church lot from the perspective of the cultural landscape. Nancy Davis employs environmental data from several sources to obtain details of the creation, maintenance, alterations, and even neglect of this location during the colonial period.

The meaning of formal gardens in the eighteenth century has been a subject of considerable discussion in modern historical archaeology. In Chapter 9 Lois M. Feister describes archaeological investigations for a new Visitors' Center at Schuyler Mansion State Historic Site that discovered evidence of the formal gardens constructed during the eighteenth century. Material remains of the gardens were uncovered and examined, despite subsequent urban development that appeared to have destroyed them. The gardens are viewed as artifacts that demonstrated the power and knowledge of the Schuylers.

In Chapter 10 J.W. Bouchard uses archaeological information of nineteenth-century "conveniences" to show how a specific house worked. The Stevens house was much more than a shelter for the family and their servants. It was a place that communicated ideas about the owner, his family, their social standing, and their success to the surrounding community.

The next three chapters emphasize new information concerning two types of material things that have been important to archaeological studies of Albany, shell beads and pottery. The production, use, and meaning of wampum changed during the early history of Albany, which emphasizes the importance of the archaeological context in understanding specific places. The results of Elizabeth Peña's important research that documented this change is contained in Chapter 11. Chapter 12 by Matt Lesniak contributes new evidence of eighteenth-century wampum production in Albany from recent excavations that continue to support Peña's interpretation. In Chapter 13 Pegeen McLaughlin presents the archaeological evidence of an unusual pottery deposit. In addition to interpreting this feature, she discusses individual painting styles discovered on these ceramics and opens a new avenue for future analysis.

The final section of this volume contains two chapters that focus on positive and negative aspects of doing archaeology in Albany. The struggle over the treatment of the important Broadway–Maiden Lane archaeological site is described by Karen Hartgen in Chapter 14. The public outcry over the construction at this site in the absence of a plan for professional archaeological excavations and the subsequent legal battle was a pivotal moment for archaeology in Albany. Most of the studies included in this book may be considered the results of this conflict; it is unlikely they would have been carried out to such an extent without the example of public concern displayed for the Broadway–Maiden Lane site.

In Chapter 15 Joel Grossman offers his solution to the need for fast and accurate field recording of complex archaeological features. New methods of archaeological field documentation of the historic Albany waterfront, which was uncovered in excavations for a parking garage, were employed when the construction schedule prohibited traditional archaeological techniques. This innovative work was carried out during 1999 and holds considerable promise for new understandings of this massive, historic development of the Albany waterfront when the analysis is completed.

Historical Context for Archaeology of Albany

Each chapter in this volume uses historical information to interpret the material evidence encountered in excavation. The contributing archaeologists recognize the possible contradictions between documents and material things and realize the necessity of critical evaluation of both types of sources. The interdisciplinary approach to the archaeological record is essential to the construction of a context that enables cultural interpretations. A common historical background is presented here for the period covered by the archaeological studies. This is not intended as complete but is presented to aid readers unfamiliar with the general historical overviews of the city, such as those by Barbagallo (1997), Bielinski (1991, 1996), Hackett (1991), Kenney (1976), McEneny (1981), Merwick (1980, 1990), Munsell (1850, 1871, 1876), Rink (1986), Van Laer (1918), Warren (1997), Weise (1884), and Wilcoxen (1984).

In September 1609 Henry Hudson encountered native people at the mouth of the river that is now known by his name. It is clear from the journals of his voyage that he was not the first European visitor to this area. The Native Americans, familiar with Europeans, brought tobacco to the sailors in exchange for knives and beads. In the vicinity of Catskill, about 62 kilometers (100 mi) north of modern New York City, Hudson again encountered friendly Native Americans who traded tobacco, corn, and pumpkins to the Europeans. As he continued to sail north, more native people brought food, tobacco, and pelts to trade for beads, knives, and axes.

The construction of Fort Nassau in 1614 at Castle Island was an effort to establish the Dutch trading system at a permanent place. This fort was built immediately south of the current city line where the Normanskill entered the Hudson River. The Normanskill Valley provided a route to the Mohawk River to the west of Albany. Both Iroquois and Mohicans had access to the trading post.

Conflict between these native peoples, however, soon involved the Dutch settlers. Only 2 years after the construction of Fort Orange in 1624, the Mohawk defeated a Mohican war party that included seven Dutchmen. The Mohawks and the Dutch negotiated a resolution, and the event resulted in a strengthened trading relationship between the Dutch and the Iroquois. By 1628 the Mohawks appeared to have won their struggle with the Mohicans, who were forced to the east side of the Hudson River and no longer could control trade between Fort Orange and the west.

The early history of Albany may be viewed as the product of two seventeenth-century conflicts in colonialism. One was that between two European countries, the Netherlands and Great Britain, over control of North American resources. Albany was the name the British gave to the Dutch town of Beverwyck in 1664 when the Dutch colony of New Netherland was surrendered to the English. The second conflict was the earlier one between the trading interests of the Dutch West India Company and the settlement objectives of the patroon of the colony of Rensselaerswyck, established in 1630.

In 1644 Isaac Jogues recorded the two settlements at the site of modern Albany.

> First, a wretched little fort, named Fort Orange . . . which the Company of the West Indies has reserved for itself . . . There is, secondly, a Colony sent thither by that Renselaers, who is its Patron. This colony is composed of about a hundred persons, who live in 25 or 30 houses built along the River . . . All their houses are merely of boards, and are covered with thatch. There is as yet no masonry, except in the chimneys . . . They have found some very suitable lands, which the savages had formerly prepared. (1996:31)

The presence of the company trading post within the patroonship created several problems within the colony. These two institutions were in conflict over their competing jurisdictional claims, as well as their "incompatible" goals (Wilcoxen 1984:10). The West India Company's economic interest was in the fur trade, which was dependent upon maintenance of the monopoly and good relations with the Native Americans. In contrast, the patroonship required clearing land for permanent settlement and agriculture. These activities had direct negative impacts on the company's trading activities, because they eliminated the habitats necessary for fur-bearing animals and created land-use conflicts with the natives. In addition, the new settlers found it difficult to resist participating in the lucrative fur trade, thus diverting profits from the West India Company.

Beverwyck was established as a planned and palisaded community in 1652. The defense of Fort Orange was endangered by the illegal construction of houses just outside the fort. Beverwyck replaced these houses at a greater distance from the fort, off two major roads that are currently recognized as Broadway and State Street. The first reference to the fortification of the community outside of Fort Orange was in 1659 (Wilcoxen 1984:4).

Jasper Danckaerts described the city of Albany in 1680 as

> nearly square, and lies against the hill, with several good streets, on which there may be about eighty or ninety houses . . . [Fort Orange] is now abandoned by the English, who have built a similar [fort] behind the town, high up on the declivity of the hill, from whence it can command the place. From the other side of this fort the inhabitants have brought a spring or fountain of water, under the fort, and under ground into the town, where they now have in several places always fountains of clear, fresh, cool water. The town is surrounded by palisades, and has several gates corresponding with the streets. (1996:205)

Albany was acknowledged with a city charter in 1686. The charter protected the land rights of the citizens of Albany, who were given the right to deal with the Native Americans and establish a market. As a result Albany monopolized both the fur trade and regional agriculture. A census in 1697 indicated a population of 714 people and 175 households within the walled town.

> However, the count omitted the garrison soldiers (at least fifty more men), some prominent

residents (including two former mayors), and made no note of the number of slaves or of the Native American fur traders who seasonally stayed in permanent huts built outside the city walls. (Warren 1997:2)

The renewed armed conflict between the French and the British in the mid-eighteenth century resulted in the development of Albany as a military headquarters. Large numbers of troops gathered at Albany in preparation for the campaigns against the French in Canada between 1755 and 1759. Numerous military structures were built throughout the city. The area within the city wall was enlarged to include many of these soldiers and refugees who fled the dangerous frontier for the protection of Albany. A Scottish officer's daughter in Albany described the town shortly after the end of the French and Indian War as "a kind of semi-rural establishment; every house had its garden, well, and a little green behind" (Grant 1903:76).

By the end of the eighteenth century, the growth of Albany was no longer restricted to the walled town. The city expanded along the river and grew rapidly as canals, turnpikes, and railroads increased the traffic through Albany. In 1844 Wilson (1845:109) noted

that the city had been demolishing the clay hills of west Albany during the past 20 years and filling the deep ravines that cut through the upper part of the city. By 1847, for example, the Rutten Kill ravine was filled, which enabled building on additional lands within the town. The grading over of the Rutten Kill took about 3 years and employed 250 men and 60 teams (Munsell 1857 (8):175).

By the mid-nineteenth century, the population of Albany was approximately 50,000. The transformation of the city into divided business, manufacturing, and residential districts was noticed by the artist James Eights, who recreated a number of views of the old city of Albany from memory. These scenes include streetscapes of early nineteenth century Albany and evidence the mixture of Dutch and English architectural styles in Albany at that time (Figure. 1.2).

The archaeology presented in this volume is the result of the late twentieth-century development of Albany. Highway construction, new utility installations, new public buildings, and private developments have destroyed large portions of the city's historic structure and archaeological remains. At the same time, these activities have provided opportunities for scholars to

Figure 1.2. Early nineteenth-century view of North Pearl Street in Albany by James Eights. The Albany Institute of History and Art.

investigate the material evidence of the creation of the city. The role of Albany as the center of state government and its location on both north-south and east-west transportation corridors continue to influence the growth and development of the city today. The preservation of the archaeological records and artifacts from the studies reported in this volume will enable future students of Albany to investigate their past with new methods and new perspectives.

References Cited

Barbagallo, T.A. 1997. The City Evolves, 1800–1930. In *A Historical Orientation to Albany, New York*, pp. 5–11. Annual Conference of the National Council on Public History, Albany.

Bielinski, S. 1991. How a City Worked: Occupations in Colonial Albany. In *A Beautiful and Fruitful Place: Selected Rensselaerswijck Seminar Papers*, edited and indexed by N.A. McClure Zeller, pp. 119–136. New Netherland Publishing, New York State Library, Albany.

_____. 1996. The Jacksons, Lattimores, and Schuylers: First African-American Families of Early Albany. *New York History* 77(4):373–394.

Danckaerts, J. 1996. Journal of a Voyage to New York and a Tour in Several of the American Colonies in 1679–1680. In *Mohawk Country, Early Narratives About a Native People,* edited by D.R. Snow, C.T. Gehring, and W.A. Starna, pp. 193–220. Syracuse University Press, Syracuse, N.Y.

Deetz, J. 1977. *In Small Things Forgotten: The Archeology of Early American Life.* Anchor Press, Doubleday, Garden City, N.Y.

Fries, S.D. 1977. *The Urban Idea in Colonial America.* Temple University Press, Philadelphia.

Grant, A. 1903. *Memoirs of an American Lady.* Dodd, Mead and Company, New York.

Hackett, D.G. 1991. *The Rude Hand of Innovation: Religion and Social Order in Albany, New York 1652–1836.* Oxford University Press, New York.

Hodder, I. 1986. *Reading the Past: Current Approaches to Interpretation in Archaeology.* Cambridge University Press, Cambridge.

Jogues, I. 1996. Novum Belgium and an Account of Rene Goupil [1644]. In *Mohawk Country, Early Narratives About a Native People,* edited by D.R. Snow, C.T. Gehring, and W.A. Starna, pp. 29–37. Syracuse University Press, Syracuse, N.Y.

Kenney, A.P. 1976. *Albany, Crossroads of Liberty.* Albany Institute of History and Art, Albany, N.Y.

Larkin, J. 1988. *The Reshaping of Everyday Life, 1790–1840.* Harper & Row, New York.

McEneny, J.J. 1981. *Albany: Capital City on the Hudson.* Windsor Publications, New York.

Merwick, D. 1980. Dutch Townsmen and Land Use: A Spatial Perspective on Seventeenth-Century Albany, New York. *William and Mary Quarterly* 37(1):53–78.

_____. 1990. *Possessing Albany, 1630–1710: The Dutch and English Experiences.* Cambridge University Press, New York.

Munsell. J. 1850–59. *Annals of Albany*, Vols. 1–10. J. Munsell, Albany, N.Y.

_____. 1871. *Collections of the History of Albany from Its Discovery to the Present Time*, Vol. 4. J. Munsell, Albany, N.Y.

_____. 1876. *Men and Things in Albany Two Centuries Ago.* Joel Munsell's Sons, Albany, N.Y.

Orser, C.E., Jr., and Fagan, B.M. 1995. *Historical Archaeology*. HarperCollins College Publishers, New York.

Rink, O.A. 1986. *Holland on the Hudson: An Economic and Social History of Dutch New York.* Cornell University Press, Ithaca, N.Y.

Salwen, B. 1973. Archeology in Megalopolis. *Research and Theory in Current Archaeology*, edited by C.L. Redman, pp. 151–163. John Wiley & Sons, New York.

Van Laer, A.J.F. (editor). 1918. *Early Records of the City of Albany and the Colony of Rensselaerswyck.* Originally translated by J. Pearson. State University of New York, Albany.

Warren, J. 1997. Founding and Birth of the City, 1609–1800. In *A Historical Orientation to Albany, New York*, pp. 1–4. Annual Conference of the National Council on Public History, Albany.

Weise, A.J. 1884. *History of the City of Albany.* E.H. Bender, Albany, N.Y.

Wilcoxen, C. 1984. *Seventeenth Century Albany: A Dutch Profile* (Rev. ed.). Albany Institute of History and Art, Albany, N.Y.

Wilson, S. 1845. *Albany City Guide.* Compiled and published by S. Wilson, Albany, N.Y.

CHAPTER 2

Thirty Years of Historical Archaeology in the City of Albany, New York

Paul R. Huey

Background History of Albany

The historical record of permanent Dutch settlement in the area of New York State that is now the City of Albany begins with the construction of Fort Nassau in 1614 on Castle Island, today the location of the Port of Albany in the south part of the city. This was close to where Henry Hudson, sailing for the Dutch East India Company in 1609, had anchored the ship *Half Moon*. The Dutch had quickly recognized that the upper Hudson Valley, with its access to the Iroquois Indians to the west, would be a source of immense wealth and profit through the fur trade. Floods forced the abandonment of Fort Nassau in 1618, and a new company, the Dutch West India Company, in 1624 replaced it with the construction of Fort Orange on the riverbank to the north. The surrounding Colonie of Rensselaerswyck was established in 1630, and there was soon friction between officials of the Colonie and the traders in Fort Orange. Illegally built houses just north of Fort Orange were on land claimed by the West India Company, and in 1652 Peter Stuyvesant, the Dutch governor, included them within a new town that he laid out and called Beverwyck. Present Broadway, running north and south, and State Street, running westward up the hill, constituted the earliest streets of this town. Physically outside and separate from but under the jurisdiction of Fort Orange, the town of Beverwyck itself soon was surrounded with a palisade wall for protection from the Indians. The English arbitrarily took possession of Fort Orange and Beverwyck in 1664, during a time of peace. Beverwyck was renamed Albany. Fort Orange was renamed Fort Albany but was abandoned in 1676, and a new fort was built on the hill in present State Street.

Governor Dongan granted the city a charter in 1686. This charter confirmed the city's jurisdiction over a strip of land that extended 16 miles from the Hudson River northwest toward Schenectady, and Albany was given a monopoly of the fur trade with the Iroquois. During the eighteenth century, Albany became a British military headquarters in the ongoing war against the French in Canada, and the stockade wall around the city was not removed until shortly before the Revolutionary War. After 1790 Albany developed and expanded rapidly north and south along the river. The city continued to grow with the arrival Irish, German, Italian, and other immigrants, and by 1850 a diversity of turnpikes, canals, railroads, and steamboats provided direct links with Buffalo, Montreal, Boston, and New York City. Albany today is still a major crossroads of the Northeast.

Early Archaeology in Albany

Many discoveries of archaeological remains occurred in Albany as development and new construction continued in the city throughout the nineteenth century. Most discoveries were viewed as objects of curiosity rather than as sources of information, however. One of the first attempts to use archaeology for research was by Cuyler Reynolds, the City Historian, in 1926. He announced that a major historical discovery would occur during the new construction of the Port of Albany on Castle Island, proving that the first fort there was not Fort Nassau, built in 1614, but rather a French fort built in 1540. There is no known basis for such a hypothesis, and it is not known what, if anything, Cuyler Reynolds actually found (Huey 1988b:55).

Twenty-seven years later, one of the earliest ar-

People, Places, and Material Things: Historical Archaeology of Albany, New York edited by Charles L. Fisher, New York State Museum Bulletin 499, © 2003 by the University of the State of New York, New York State Education Department, Albany, New York. All rights reserved

chaeological projects in which artifacts were deliberately excavated from a site within the City of Albany occurred as the construction of the New York State Thruway passed through the Pine Bush area. It was said that in all the miles across the state covered by the Thruway, "[no] other piece of terrain so wild and unpopulated" was penetrated by the new highway (Roseberry 1952). The Pine Bush area is within the 16-mile strip of land originally granted by Dongan to the city in 1686 and called the Liberty of Albany. In 1953 in an area of the Liberty of Albany once called the Verebergh, two colonial English coins were excavated from a tavern site near the Thruway construction. The coins, dated 1749 and 1728, seemed to verify the site of the Verebergh Tavern, where British troops were stationed in the 1750s (Roseberry 1953). The tavern thus appears on some of the maps drawn by soldiers on powder horns of the period. The extent of the city's irregular boundaries today represent only a fraction of the original Liberty of Albany, but the city still owns the preserved site of the Verebergh Tavern.

In 1953 and 1954 two avocational archaeologists, William D. Mohr and Edward Brooks, excavated a part of the Verebergh Tavern site. They uncovered a large collection of artifacts in addition to several features. East of the site the location of the stables was also identified. The artifacts included a deadly "dum-dum" bullet that was made probably by the soldiers stationed there, as well as thimbles, lead bale seals, buckles, scissors, iron knives, and many buttons. An article by Lois Feister on the ceramics was published in 1975, but the collection deserves further study (Cornell 1982:36; Feister 1975). The "dum-dum" bullet is nearly identical to one found in a Revolutionary War campsite at Inwood on Manhattan (Calver and Bolton 1970:76, 79 [Plate III, #2]).

Bartholomew Pickard, an English soldier from Leicestershire, evidently established a tavern at Verebergh as early as 1704, and the city rented the lot to him in 1717. By that time there was a second tavern, nearby, operated by Isaac van Valkenburgh; the city leased it with 16 acres to Van Valkenburgh in 1719 (Figure 2.1) (Pickard 1991:140–141; Feister 1975:2; Munsell 1856:61, 80; ACHOR 1719). Following the end of Van Valkenburgh's lease, the city evidently leased his 16 acres at the Verebergh to Daniel McMichael in 1753. McMichael's widow continued to operate the McMichael tavern as late as 1773 (ACHOR 1753; Munsell 1865:213; Feister 1975:3). Bartholomew Pickard, meanwhile, in 1723 had become one of the patentees of the Stone Arabia Patent

in the Mohawk Valley, and in 1732 the city conveyed apparently his former tavern at the Verebergh to 32-year-old Volkert Douw, Jr. (Munsell 1858:62; 1859:19). Douw was part of a wealthy Albany family, and his cousin Volkert owned interests in at least two distilleries in the city, probably along the south side of Fox Creek. A third cousin, Petrus, lived at Wolvenhoeck (Douw's Point) on the east side of the Hudson River, where rescue excavations in 1971 revealed remains of still another eighteenth-century distillery (Talcott 1973:67–70; Pelletreau 1899:208). A traveler in 1752 noted at the Verebergh "only two houses, kept for the entertainment of passengers. They were alone, but did not harmonize" (Hawley 1850:1034–1035). Volkert Douw had died by 1766, and in 1768 the Douw tavern was leased to Anthony D. Bradt (Munsell 1865:169, 194, 196). In 1808 the Verebergh Tavern was described as "formerly kept by Mr. Douw," and it was said "the house and buildings are in good repair" (Smith 1808). The excavations of 1953 and 1954 evidently occurred at this site, because the artifacts indicate an occupation continuing through the nineteenth century. The building was torn down about 1890 (Omwake 1961:12).

Early in the 1960s federally funded urban renewal projects soon had a major negative impact on archaeological sites in downtown Albany. In north Albany, the historic Albany Arsenal designed by Philip Hooker and built in 1799 was one of many structures lost. This writer and a friend, Dean Calamaras of East Greenbush, a business major at Junior College of Albany, carefully monitored the destruction, took photographs, and watched for archaeological features. One day in March 1962, on a recently cleared lot adjacent to Van Woert Street, Calamaras made a curious discovery. In an area about 20 feet square and less than a foot in depth were concentrated at least 90 complete or nearly complete tobacco pipe bowls and between 600 and 700 pipe stem fragments. The pipes were Dutch and were all molded with the name of the maker, Peter Dorni of Gouda (Calamaras 1962). Similar Dorni pipes had been found by Mohr at the Verebergh Tavern site, and those pipes had inspired H. Geiger Omwake (1961) to publish an article on Dorni pipes. Omwake correctly concluded that Dorni pipes dated from the nineteenth century, and the Dorni pipe deposit near Van Woert Street probably represents a shipment of broken pipes discarded by a merchant. Irish immigrants and railroad workers settled the area, but Edward M. van Alstyne, son of a successful Albany hardware merchant, had acquired the

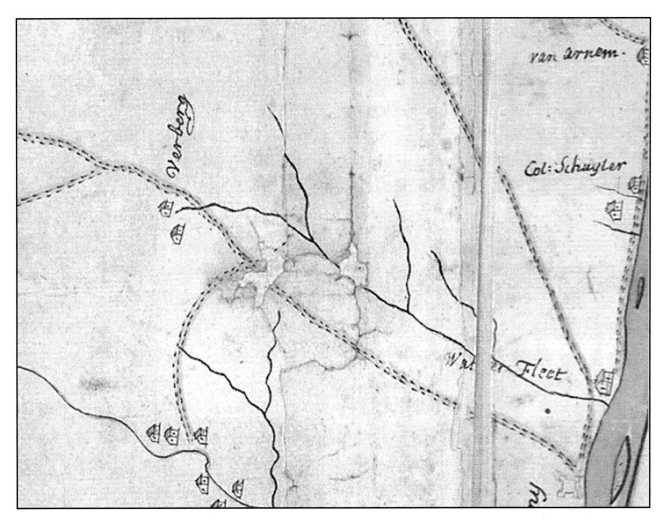

Figure 2.1. Detail from a map of the northern parts of New York drawn about 1758 showing the two taverns at "Verberg" west of Albany. Library of Congress Geography and Map Division, call number G3800 1758 .M3 Vault.

lot where the pipes were found in 1853. It passed from Van Alstyne to James Welsh in 1870 (ACHOR 1853; Munsell 1869:359; ACHOR 1870; Van Alstine 1974:38).

Archaeological Rescue and Research Projects Through 1980

Congress passed the Federal Historic Preservation Act of 1966 in response to the many losses of historic sites and buildings nationwide, and this law was to have a major impact on archaeology. It protected archaeological sites that were listed on the National Register of Historic Places, and in New York State the National Register and State Historic Sites programs were assigned to the newly established State Historic Trust. The Historic Trust soon initiated a program of

archaeological research at State Historic Sites, but relatively few other sites were listed on the National Register, and rescue archaeology of threatened sites was not a priority.

In 1968 the New York State Historic Trust contracted with J. Glenn Little, an archaeologist in Virginia, to conduct a survey of the grounds at Schuyler Mansion State Historic Site in Albany. In the fall of 1968 he excavated test squares and trenches to determine where eighteenth-century soil strata remained undisturbed and to locate the walls of various outbuildings that once stood adjacent to the Schuyler Mansion, built in 1762 outside the colonial city area. This work revealed the foundation walls of the two symmetrical flanking rear wings of this Georgian mansion (Little 1974; Gibbons and Stott 1977:81, 84–85). Unfortunately the contractor subsequently lost all the artifacts that were found. Nevertheless, this work in 1968 represents probably the first systematic, professional historical archaeology in the City of Albany.

In 1969 the Historic Trust, surviving today as the historic preservation program of the New York State Office of Parks, Recreation and Historic Preservation, established its own permanent, professionally staffed historical archaeology program. The Trust continued with the excavations at Schuyler Mansion in Albany in 1969. This time the work was conducted along the front wall of the mansion, where deep foundation repairs were necessary. Valuable interpretive information about the original ground surface levels and early drainage systems in front of the house was rescued (Wallace 1969; Gibbons and Stott 1977:69, 75). The artifacts, such as an air-twist wineglass stem, provided valuable information about the mansion's eighteenth-century furnishings. These very objects were, after all, once in Schuyler Mansion and were undoubtedly used by Philip Schuyler himself.

Meanwhile, the construction of arterial highways in downtown Albany prompted new preservation issues. Many historic buildings were lost, but the historic Quackenbush House was saved. As major construction of deep sewers continued in the area from the Quackenbush House southward to the former railroad yard behind Union Station, this writer was able to monitor the trenching in September and October 1969. The trenches revealed buried walls of buildings, along Montgomery Street between Columbia and Steuben Streets, for example. These blocks were near the colonial waterfront of Albany, and there were also deeply buried deposits of thousands of late eighteenth-century pottery sherds possibly representing shipments of imported ware that were broken and discarded by merchants (Huey 1998).

Interstate 787 was soon under construction through this area, and its proposed route southward would take it directly across and through the original site of Fort Orange on lower Broadway. This writer, from documentary research, had determined the original location of Fort Orange, built in 1624 and abandoned in 1676, but proposals in 1966 to conduct test excavations at the site had been denied. In 1970, however, the New York State Department of Transportation offered to conduct a test excavation that October for the Historic Trust. As of 1970, no archaeological evidence from the seventeenth-century Dutch colonial period before 1664 in Albany had yet been carefully excavated and recovered. Other than

from vague references in the Dutch records that had been translated and published, the types of furnishings, utensils, and other artifacts that the Dutch had brought with them to Fort Orange and Beverwyck remained unknown.

On October 20, 1970, the first test excavation was dug, and soon the first seventeenth-century Dutch beads, pipe stems, Westerwald stoneware, and tin-glazed Dutch majolica were found. The excavations were expanded while construction work on the new highway moved temporarily to another area. The archaeological excavations continued through the entire winter of 1970–1971, until March, and there was sufficient time to excavate carefully the narrow portion of the site that would be impacted by the highway.

The discoveries that winter helped inspire a great awakening of interest in the seventeenth-century Dutch and in the archaeology of Albany. Because so many Dutch deeds and other records had been translated and published, thanks to the work of Joel Munsell, Jonathan Pearson, and Arnold J.F. van Laer, it was actually possible to identify which part of the fort was uncovered. Moreover, the artifacts demonstrated a previously unsuspected level of high refinement in the material culture imported by the Dutch. Except for the deer bones, wampum, and Indian pottery fragments, the broad assemblage of delicate glassware, ceramics, clay pipes, beads, and architectural fragments was virtually indistinguishable from collections that had been excavated from the yards of prosperous seventeenth-century houses in Dutch cities and towns such as Amsterdam and De Rijp. It was immediately clear that the Dutch at Fort Orange had spared no effort in importing and recreating their Old World way of life, and this new interpretation was also soon to be accepted by historians (Huey 1988a, 1988b:61–62; 1991:330–333; Fisher 1997:7; Goodfriend 1999:10, 17).

The Fort Orange excavations also demonstrated a problem inherent in the Federal Historic Preservation Act of 1966. Because Fort Orange had not been listed on the National Register, the site was not legally protected during the planning and construction of the highway. In May 1971 President Nixon signed Executive Order 11593. This required the identification and protection of not only those historic sites and structures already listed on the National Register, but also those that are eligible or appear to qualify for nomination to the National Register. Henceforth surveys would be required in advance of federally funded or licensed projects in order to identify cultural resources that might be affected and were eligible for nomination.

In Albany, meanwhile, other excavations occurred, revealing artifacts and features from both the seventeenth and eighteenth centuries. The Niagara Mohawk Power Corporation in 1972 and 1973 installed electrical conduits in deep trenches under upper Broadway, State Street, and South Pearl Street, and these excavations were carefully watched. Extensive archaeological data were recorded, but many other data were lost. Under State Street, remains of wooden conduits associated with seventeenth-century artifacts were probably from Albany's gravity-fed water system installed in 1678. This may be the oldest such municipal water system in North America. Above this early water pipe were foundations of a British guard house of the 1750s at the junction with South Pearl Street. Under South Pearl Street, the sloping bank of the Rutten Kill ravine was revealed, together with wooden privies behind the house that was the birthplace of Philip Schuyler in 1733. At the foot of State Street, stone walls were found from the Dutch Reformed Church that stood there until 1806, and under Broadway were wooden cellars and drains probably from either the original market house or from other British military structures that stood in the street (Huey 1988b:62; 1991:333–334; Fisher 1997:7–11).

Meanwhile, the City of Albany Bureau of Cultural Affairs under Bob Arnold conducted excavations at the Quackenbush House in 1973 and 1974. Approximately 65,000 artifacts were recovered. At the same time, Don Rittner began excavation of the Isaac Truax, Sr., Tavern site in the Pine Bush area in the west part of Albany, the original "Liberty of Albany." Located west of the Verebergh, this tavern was built sometime between 1756 and 1767. The faunal remains found at the site suggest a diet including passenger pigeon, beef, mutton, lamb, pork, venison, deer, rabbit, and shellfish. An unusual artifact from the site is a silver shoe buckle made by Charles Oliver Bruff of New York City between 1765 and 1783. In 1979 the excavations continued with work at the site of the Isaac Truax, Jr., Tavern, a short distance away (Roseberry 1952; Crupi 1973; Rittner 1974; Fowler 1979; Jones 1982).

Archaeological testing and then extensive excavations occurred at Schuyler Mansion State Historic Site in 1976 and 1977. Directed by this writer, the work covered a large area to the rear of the mansion, where a new parking lot was to be constructed. Results included the discovery of a brick drain system at the site of Schuyler's barn. An early nineteenth-century roadbed of broken red sandstone running uphill from the mansion also was found. More information on eighteenth-century furnishings was generated, and trash deposit areas were defined (Anon. 1977; Feister 1995:3–48).

Artifacts of the nineteenth and early twentieth centuries occupied the attention of New York State museum archaeologists under Phil Lord in 1978 during development of the riverfront park between Interstate 787 and the Hudson River. This work required the excavation of fill that had been deposited about 1903 in the old Albany Basin, built in 1825. Bottles of all types were found, including many that represented Albany businesses of the late nineteenth century. Other bottles represented goods imported from England and elsewhere (Anon. 1979). A year later Karen Hartgen directed testing for a proposed new storm sewer in the Pastures Preservation Historic District in south Albany. Deposits of wood chips and shavings were found, apparently associated with the construction of many of the buildings in the district in the late eighteenth and early nineteenth centuries. There were also remains of nineteenth-century privies, foundation walls, and a single layer of seventeenth-century bricks. Additional work in 1980 revealed an extensive and interesting deposit of early nineteenth-century trash east of South Pearl Street (Laden 1979; Hartgen Archeological Associates, Inc. 1981; Fisher 1997:13).

Archaeological Rescue and Research Projects After 1980

The New York State Historic Preservation Act of 1980 established a State Register of Historic Places and gave archaeological sites protection at the state level the same as was formerly provided only by federal legislation. The review process was extended to cover the impacts of state-sponsored as well as of federally sponsored projects.

Important research projects of the 1980s in Albany included the work at sites outside the area of the original stockaded town. Hartgen Archeological Associates, Inc., for example, conducted research at Cherry Hill mansion in present southern Albany from 1980 to 1984. Cherry Hill was built in 1787 by Philip van Rensselaer, but the site survey and excavations beginning in 1980 revealed artifacts of an earlier date. It was concluded that the site had indeed been the location of an earlier building, the home of Hitchin Holland as early as the 1750s (Hartgen Archeological Associates, Inc. 1980, 1984). This work was funded with matching federal grants administered by the state.

Other important discoveries occurred in the Pine Bush area of Albany beginning in 1982 as plans were developed to improve Exit 24 of the Thruway. New York State Museum archaeologists directed by Donald Cornell tested an embankment believed to have been the roadbed of New York State's first railroad, the Mohawk and Hudson Rail Road that ran between Schenectady and Albany in 1831 (Figure 2.2). Their excavations confirmed the presence of a rare survival of early railroad technology: the stone blocks instead of wood ties upon which the rails were laid. In 1986 the New York State Museum continued its work in this area with important new discoveries at the Verebergh.

A second tavern site, which had previously eluded discovery, was found across the creek from the Douw tavern. It is believed to have been the one established as early as 1704 by Bartholomew Pickard, leased to Isaac van Valkenburgh in 1719, and occupied until about 1790. An intact well was discovered associated with artifacts consistent with those dates. The mean ceramic date for the site is 1755 (Cornell 1982; Vaillancourt 1986).

From 1986 through 1994 the Bureau of Historic Sites of the New York State Office of Parks, Recreation and Historic Preservation conducted another series of projects at Schuyler Mansion State Historic Site. This work, directed by Lois Feister, was done in an area proposed for a new visitors' center, and the excavations revealed evidence of Schuyler's formal gardens on the south side of the mansion (Chapter 9, this volume). The gardens are shown on Simeon DeWitt's

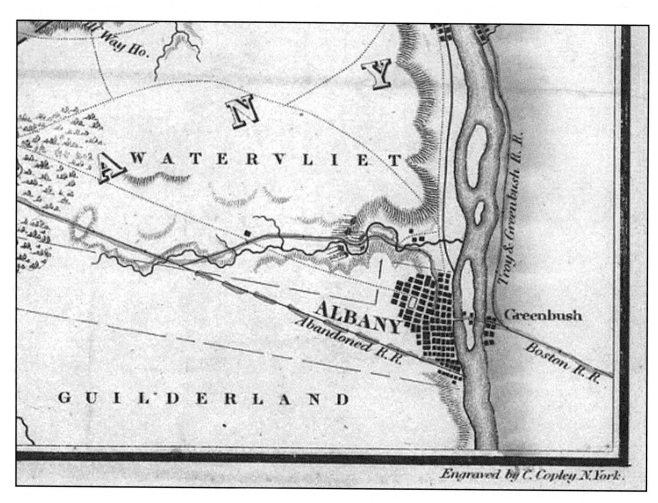

Figure 2.2. Detail from a map of the railroads from Rome to Albany and Troy by one of the engineers who assisted in the construction, published in 1846 by Levi Williams, civil engineer, showing the "Abandoned R.R." that ran from Albany to Schenectady. Library of Congress Geography and Map Division, call number G3802.M6P3 1845 .W5 RR 260.

map of 1794, and Feister (1998) found the outlines of large rectangular planting beds cut into the dense natural clay. Schuyler Mansion, like the house originally at Cherry Hill, was a mansion outside the original stockaded town of Albany. A third mansion outside the original town, the Ten Broeck Mansion, was to the north and built in 1798. In 1994 Hartgen Archeological Associates, Inc., conducted excavations there prior to foundation repairs. They found the outline of an early door that had been cut into the foundation, and they found a buried wall from a previous structure (Peña 1994).

Only since 1980 have the most extensive and informative excavations occurred within the area of the colonial town of Beverwyck and Albany. This has included the excavation of complete blocks of the colonial town previous to modern development projects. Testing by Hartgen Archeological Associates, Inc. (1983) for a new office building east of South Pearl Street between State and Norton Streets revealed fill deposited between 1842 and 1845 into the original Rutten Kill ravine. West of South Pearl Street, in 1986, soil borings for the proposed Albany Civic Center revealed additional information about the location of this ravine. At the same time, testing along South Pearl Street north and south of Beaver Street revealed locations of early features and deposits (Fisher 1997:13).

East of South Pearl Street and south of Norton Street, excavations in 1986 at the KeyCorp site by Hartgen Archeological Associates, Inc., revealed the remains of a house built probably as early as 1647 by Volkert Jansen Douw and converted into the Reformed Church almshouse in 1685. The excavations at this site in 1986, coinciding with Albany's bicentennial celebration, produced a wealth of information about colonial poor relief and the material culture of almshouses. Extensive evidence of wampum making from shells suggests that the almshouse functioned as a workhouse (Chapter 11, this volume). The archaeology of hospitals and almshouse sites is a fascinating subject of growing interest and significance (Huey 1991). In addition, excavations at the nearby Dutch Reformed Church burial ground, shown on the 1695 map of Albany, commenced (Hartgen Archeological Associates, Inc., 1986; Fisher 1997:14). Collamer & Associates continued the work through the winter of 1986–1987.

Other blocks in the old city were soon to be developed. In September 1987 the block west of upper Broadway between Maiden Lane and Steuben Street was tested. This work, in a block located in the heart of the oldest part of Albany, revealed a number of seventeenth- and eighteenth-century artifacts and probable features, but the results were inconclusive and disappointing (Collamer & Associates, Inc. 1988). Similar frustrating results occurred in 1987 at the proposed location of the new 110 State Street office building. Cultural strata dating from the seventeenth century were located but subsequently lost, but further work has been done in the area with great success in 1997 and 1998, revealing eighteenth- and nineteenth-century features (Hartgen Archeological Associates, Inc. 1997a, 1997b, 1998b).

There was also success in 1987 with the initial testing in the area east of upper Broadway north of Columbia Street where the Fox Creek originally was located. This was an area occupied by tanneries and shoemakers in the colonial period, and it was near the waterfront (Hartgen Archeological Associates, Inc. 1987). The area eventually became the Picotte site, where further testing by Hartgen Archeological Associates, Inc., in the fall of 1997 was followed by extensive and very productive excavations in 1998 (Chapters. 3, 5, 10, 12, 13, this volume). The two entire blocks east of Broadway from Columbia Street north to Water Street, future location of an office building for the New York State Department of Environmental Conservation, were outside the colonial Albany stockade wall. The buildings in these blocks were destroyed by the fire of 1797, but in the nineteenth century the area contained buildings including the first home of the Albany Academy for Girls, the Third Presbyterian Church, residences of tradesmen, and many commercial and industrial establishments (Hartgen Archeological Associates, Inc. 1998a). The excavations revealed important seventeenth- and eighteenth-century deposits and structural remains, including remains perhaps from a mid-seventeenth-century pre-Beverwyck structure built by a trader close to the original riverbank. On the west side of Broadway north of Columbia Street, meanwhile, testing in 1988 revealed seven mid-nineteenth-century privies, all but one of which dated between about 1830 and 1865 (Wehrwein 1988; Hartgen Archeological Associates, Inc. 1988).

In 1988 the City of Albany, with the support of the Historic Albany Foundation, adopted new rules protecting archaeological resources. A new Historic Resources Commission was set up, but its jurisdiction was limited only to the original stockaded area of the colonial city (Gesensway 1987, 1988).

Major issues of the 1990s included the development of another block of the colonial city and an attempt to avoid doing thorough archaeology (Chapter 14, this volume). The controversial Dormitory Authority building project was in the block east of Broadway between Maiden Lane and Steuben Street, ultimately excavated in 1996 and 1997 by Collamer & Associates to reveal interesting features and produce many artifacts from as early as the seventeenth century (Hartgen Archeological Associates, Inc. 1996).

Work in 1998 by the New York State Museum under Charles Fisher has revealed burials from the Lutheran church under South Pearl Street (Chapters 6, 7, 8, this volume). At the same time Hartgen commenced excavations on the colonial Albany waterfront east of Dean Street south of Maiden Lane, future location of the State University of New York 600-car parking garage (Hartgen Archeological Associates, Inc. 1998c). A succession of quay walls was uncovered, representing the waterfront locations from about 1760 to 1790, and the construction is reminiscent of the quay walls and warehouses excavated on the Roman waterfront of London. The 300-foot section of the eighteenth-century waterfront that was exposed consisted of stacked logs and vertical wood pilings; farthest inland from it was found a line of pilings believed to represent an Albany stockade line constructed along the river about 1750.

Noteworthy discoveries at nineteenth-century sites include the excavation in 1989 by the New York State Museum of 30 graves dating about 1890 to 1900 from the cemetery of the Albany County Almshouse (LoRusso and Van Wagenen 1990:14, 19, 42–45). In 1990 Hartgen investigated a tunnel and other features at the Quackenbush Pumping Station of the Albany Water Works, built in 1873 (Hartgen Archeological Associates, Inc. 1990). Nearby, also on Broadway, Stephen Oberon (1998) investigated a privy and other features near the O'Brien Federal Building, site of the Harris Mansion built in 1813 or 1814. Ira Harris, whose daughter Clara and Major Henry Rathbone were the tragic couple associated with Lincoln's assassination, purchased the house in 1836 (ACHOR 1836; Gerber 1970:242; Huey 1992).

Significance and Interpretation

A result of archaeology in Albany during the past 30 years has been the first solid evidence of Dutch colonial material culture, representative of the Dutch Golden Age of the seventeenth century. It is now recognized that indeed the New Netherlanders brought their culture with them from the Netherlands, but the archaeological evidence may indicate a greater degree of cultural transplantation by the determined Dutch than even historians have been willing to admit (Goodfriend 1991:9–10, 17). It has become increasingly apparent that in general for the eighteenth century, not to mention the seventeenth century, "a great deal of revealing material about the shared world of goods and cultural ties that bound the colonies to the mother country has come to light" (Lawson 1993:223). The archaeology of Albany is also providing the resources for future meaningful comparisons with colonial Dutch settlements elsewhere, such as at Cape Town, South Africa. The transplantation of Dutch culture to other colonies may have been significantly different from the situation with New Netherland, and the reasons and the results should be explored further.

There are now many archaeological collections from previous excavations in Albany. Many sites have been destroyed as the city continues with the normal process of urban development and rebuilding, but the archaeological collections will survive as permanent resources rescued from those sites for future research and interpretation. Not only is there seventeenth- and eighteenth-century material, but there is also material for the study of urbanization and economic change through the nineteenth century. Graduate students and other scholars must be encouraged to use it. One topic in need of further study and for which there are excellent resources is the number and variety of excavated colonial tavern sites. Even at Fort Orange, a dump found in the south moat is believed to have come from a nearby tavern (Huey 1988a:472–474). Historians of Albany and the colonial Dutch, such as Merwick, Bielinski, Armour, Kinney, Goodfriend, and others have already provided many hypotheses worthy of further examination and testing, and it is time to make greater use of their work as well.

References Cited

ACHOR (Albany County Hall of Records). 1719. City of Albany lease to Isaac van Valkenburgh, May 3. (Book 5, p. 453). Albany County Hall of Records, Albany, N.Y.

———. 1753. City of Albany lease to Daniel MacMichael, April 13. (Book 6, p. 456). Albany County Hall of Records, Albany, N.Y.

_____. 1836. Deed from J. Willard and M. Willard to Ira Harris, April 11. (Book 54, p. 149). Albany County Hall of Records, Albany, N.Y.

_____. 1853. Deed from Fonda et al. to Edward M. van Alstyne, March 1. (Book 122, p. 30). Albany County Hall of Records, Albany, N.Y.

_____. 1870. Deed from Harris Parr to James Welsh, April 7. (Book 232, p. 448). Albany County Hall of Records, Albany, N.Y.

Anon. 1758. *Map of the Northern Parts of New York*. Library of Congress Geography and Map Division, call number G3800 1758. M3 Vault.

Anon. 1977. Site of Schuyler Barn Located. *The Times Record,* Troy, N.Y., July 7, p. 2.

_____. 1979. Cultural Resources Survey Report: PIN 1075.02, Riverfront Park Lagoon Excavation Area, Albany County. Division of Historical and Anthropological Services, New York State Museum, Albany.

Calamaras, D.G. 1962. Letters to Paul R. Huey, March 19, March 25. Copies in Archeology Unit files, Bureau of Historic Sites, New York State Office of Parks, Recreation and Historic Preservation, Peebles Island, Waterford.

Calver, W.L., and Bolton, R.P. 1970. *History Written with Pick and Shovel*. The New-York Historical Society, New York.

Collamer & Associates, Inc. 1988. Stage 1A & 1B Cultural Resources Investigation, 532–554 Broadway, City of Albany, Albany County, N.Y.

Cornell, D.G. 1982. Cultural Resource Survey Report: PIN 1528.30, Thruway Access Study, Exit 24 Vicinity, Albany County. Prepared for the New York State Department of Transportation. Archeological Field Services (Highway Salvage) Unit, Division of Historical and Anthropological Services, New York State Education Department, Cultural Education Center, Empire State Plaza, Albany.

Crupi, J. 1973. Mayor Corning "Digs in" for the Dig. *The Knickerbocker News-Union Star,* Albany, December 21, p. B-3.

Feister, L.M. 1975. Analysis of the Ceramics Found at the Vereberg Tavern Site, Albany County, New York. *Man in the Northeast* 10:2–20.

_____. 1995. A Synthesis of Archeology at Schuyler Mansion State Historic Site, Albany, New York, Prior to the 1994 Visitor Center Addition Project. Bureau of Historic Sites, New York State Office of Parks, Recreation and Historic Preservation, Peebles Island, Waterford.

_____. 1998. The Garden That Didn't Die: Archeological Explorations West of the Visitors' Center, Schuyler Mansion State Historic Site, Albany, New York, 1986 and 1994. Bureau of Historic Sites, New York State Office of Parks, Recreation and Historic Preservation, Peebles Island, Waterford.

Fisher, C.L. 1997. Cultural Resources Survey Report: Archaeological Background Study of PIN 1753.58.121, Pearl Street from McCarty Avenue to Livingston Avenue, City of Albany, Albany County, New York. Anthropological Survey, New York State Museum, Albany.

Fowler, B. 1979. Rocky's Lofty Goals Are Biting the Dust. *Albany Times-Union*, Albany, August 24, p. 20.

Gerber, M. 1970. "Old Albany," Vol. 1. (Author: 55 Sycamore St., Albany, N.Y.).

Gesensway, D. 1987. Tougher Historic Law Eyed. *Times Union,* Albany, October 12, pp. B-1, B-2.

_____. 1988. Historic-Site Rules Reviewed: Vote Possible Tonight. *Times Union,* Albany, March 21, pp. B-1, B-8.

Gibbons, K.L., and Stott, P.H. 1977. *Schuyler Mansion: A Historic Structure Report*. New York State Parks and Recreation, Waterford.

Goodfriend, J.D. 1999. Writing/Righting Dutch Colonial History. *New York History* 80(1):4–28.

Hartgen Archeological Associates, Inc. 1980. A Report on the Archeological Test Excavations at Historic Cherry Hill, Albany, New York.

_____. 1981. Limited Archeological Investigations of Selected Areas, East Side of South Pearl Street and School 15, South End Urban Renewal Project No. 2 (The Pastures), Infill Housing, City of Albany, Albany County, New York.

_____. 1983. Archeological Investigations at the Proposed Site of the 80 State Street Project, Albany, New York. Submitted to Hershberg and Hershberg.

_____. 1984. Report on the Archeological Excavations at Historic Cherry Hill (1982–1984).

_____. 1986. Dutch Reformed Church Burial Ground, c. 1656–1882: Key Corp Parking Garage, Beaver St. & Hudson Ave., City of Albany, Albany County, New York.

_____. 1987. Literature Review and Archeological Survey, Norstar Financial Center, Albany, New York.

_____. 1988. Literature Review and Archeological Survey, 602 Broadway Project, Albany, New York.

_____. 1990. Archeological Recording and Monitoring at the Quackenbush Pumping Station, Albany Water Works and Quackenbush Square Courtyard.

_____. 1996. Phase 1A Literature Review and Phase 1B Archeological Investigations, Dormitory Authority of the State of New York Office Building, Broadway and Maiden Lane, City of Albany, New York.

_____. 1997a. Phase 1A Archeological Resources Assessment: The 110 State Street Office Building Project (102-110 State Street), City of Albany, Albany County, New York.

_____. 1997b. Phase 1B Archeological Field Reconnaissance: The 110 State Street Office Building Project (102-110 State Street), City of Albany, Albany County, New York.

_____. 1998a. Phase II Site Evaluation: The Picotte-DEC Office Building Site, 597-643 Broadway, City of Albany, Albany County, New York.

_____. 1998b. Phase 1A Archeological Resources Assessment: The 40 Howard Street Project, City of Albany, Albany County, New York.

_____. 1998c. Phase 1 Literature Review, Archeological Sensitivity Assessment, and Archeological Field Reconnaissance: SUNY 600 Car Parking Garage, City of Albany, Albany County, New York.

Hawley, G. 1850. Rev. Gideon Hawley's Journey to Oghquaga, (Broome Co.). In *The Documentary History of the State of New-York,* edited by E.B. O'Callaghan, Vol. 3, pp. 1031–1046. Weed, Parsons & Co., Albany.

Huey, P.R. 1988a. *Aspects of Continuity and Change in Colonial Dutch Material Culture at Fort Orange, 1624–1664.* Doctoral dissertation, University of Pennsylvania, Philadelphia. University Microfilms International, Ann Arbor, Mich.

_____. 1988b. The Archeology of Colonial New Netherland. In *Colonial Dutch Studies: An Interdisciplinary Approach,* edited by E. Nooter and P.U. Bonomi, pp. 52–77. New York University Press, New York and London.

_____. 1991. The Archeology of Fort Orange and Beverwijck. In *A Beautiful and Fruitful Place: Selected Rensselaerswijck Seminar Papers,* edited by N.A. McClure Zeller, pp. 327–349. New Netherland Publishing, New York State Library, Albany.

_____. 1992. Memorandum to Diana S. Waite, May 22. Copy in Archeology Unit files, Bureau of Historic Sites, New York State Office of Parks, Recreation and Historic Preservation, Peebles Island, Waterford.

_____. 1998. Narrative Report on Archeological Investigations in Albany, New York, September and October 1969. Bureau of Historic Sites, New York State Office of Parks, Recreation and Historic Preservation, Peebles Island, Waterford.

Jones, K.M. (editor). 1982. Collectors' Notes: A Tory Shoe Buckle. *Antiques* 121(2):496–497.

Laden, G.T. 1979. Limited Archaeological Investigation of Selected Test Areas, South End Urban Renewal Project No. 2 (The Pastures) Storm Sewer, City of Albany, Albany County, New York. Karen S. Hartgen and Associates, North Greenbush, N.Y.

Lawson, P. 1993. Review of *The Blackwell Encyclopedia of the American Revolution,* edited by J.P. Greene and J.R. Pole. *The William and Mary Quarterly* (3rd Series) 50(1):221–224.

Little, J.G. 1974. Preliminary Archaeological Testing: Schuyler House. Prepared for New York State Parks and Recreation, Division for Historic Preservation, by Contract Achaeology, Inc., Alexandria, Va.

LoRusso, M.S., and van Wagenen, K. 1990. A Cultural Resource Survey Report of Wadsworth Center for Laboratories and Research, Summer Boiler Project and Virus Building Demolition, City of Albany, Albany County, for the New York State Office of General Services. Division of Research and Collections, New York State Museum, Albany.

Munsell, J. 1856. *The Annals of Albany,* Vol. 7. J. Munsell, Albany, N.Y.

_____. 1858. *The Annals of Albany,* Vol. 9. Munsell and Rowland, Printers, Albany, N.Y.

_____. 1859. *The Annals of Albany*, Vol. 10. Munsell and Rowland, Printers, Albany, N.Y.

_____. 1865. *Collections on the History of Albany*, Vol. 1. J. Munsell, Albany, N.Y.

_____. 1869. *The Annals of Albany*, Vol. 1. Joel Munsell, Albany, N.Y.

Oberon, S.J. 1998. Phase II Cultural Resources Survey Site Evaluation Phase, Site of Proposed Playground Improvements, Leo F. O'Brien Federal Building, City of Albany, Albany County, New York.

Omwake, H.G. 1961. Peter Dorni White Kaolin Pipes. *Archeological Society of New Jersey Bulletin* 18/19:12–15.

Pelletreau, W.S. 1899. *Abstracts of Wills on File in the Surrogate's Office, City of New York*, Vol. 7, 1766–1771. *Collections of the New-York Historical Society for the Year 1898*. Printed for the Society, New York.

Peña, E. 1994. 1994 Archeological Investigation at Ten Broeck Mansion, City of Albany, Albany County, New York.

Pickard, F.C. 1991. English Ancestry of Bartholomew Pickard. *New York Genealogical and Biographical Record* 122:135–142.

Rittner, D. 1974. Letter to Erastus Corning, June 4. Copy in Archeology Unit files, Bureau of Historic Sites, New York State Office of Parks, Recreation and Historic Preservation, Peebles Island, Waterford.

Roseberry, C.R. 1952. New Highway to Parallel Forgotten 'King's Highway.' *Sunday Times Union, Pictorial Review*, Albany, May 4, p. 5.

_____. 1953. 18th Century Coins Turn Up at Old Tavern Sites. *Times Union,* Albany. Copy of undated clipping in Archeology Unit files, Bureau of Historic Sites, New York State Office of Parks, Recreation and Historic Preservation, Peebles Island, Waterford.

Smith, D. 1808. For Sale, a Fifteen Years' Lease. *The Albany Gazette,* November 14, 25(2293):3.

Talcott, S.V. (compiler). 1973. *Genealogical Notes of New York and New England Families.* Genealogical Publishing Co., Inc., Baltimore.

Vaillancourt, D.R. 1986. A Cultural Resources Survey Report of PIN 1528.30, Rapp Road Monitoring Project, Albany County, New York. Division of Historical and Anthropological Services, New York State Museum, Albany.

Van Alstine, L. 1974. *Van Alstyne-Van Alstine Family History*, Vol. 1. U. Grant Stevenson, 230 West 1230 North, Provo, Utah.

Wallace, D.D. 1969. Archeological Excavations at the Southeast and Southwest Corners of Schuyler Mansion State Historic Site, 1969. New York State Historic Trust, Albany.

Wehrwein, P. 1988. Developer Wants to Expand in Albany: Broadway Office Site Would Have Nearly 200,000 Square Feet. *Times Union,* Albany, September 7, p. B-4.

Williams, L. 1846. *Map of the Railroads from Rome to Albany and Troy.* Library of Congress Geography and Map Division, call number G3802. M6P3 1845. W5 RR 260.

Section 2

People

CHAPTER 3

Traders or Traitors: Illicit Trade at Fort Orange in the Seventeenth Century

Kevin Moody

Introduction

From the outset, the Dutch West India Company's (WIC) monopsony over the fur trade in New Netherland was frequently and flagrantly challenged by independent traders at Fort Orange. A monopsony exists when there is one party with the exclusive right to purchase a specific commodity. In New Netherland the commodity was furs, and the WIC was the only legitimate purchaser. Unfortunately the company had neither the means nor the mechanism to enforce this right. By 1640 the company capitulated to these traders and opened trade to everyone except its own "public servants" (O'Callaghan 1853:112–123). Eight years later Peter Stuyvesant reversed the policy. He not only reasserted the company's exclusive right to engage in the fur trade, but he also threatened to confiscate or destroy the property of the independent traders (Huey 1988:49). By 1648 there were at least eight traders housed along the Hudson River north of Fort Orange (Fernow 1883:92). The great flood of 1648 destroyed most of these houses; the one that survived, along with others rebuilt, were subsequently demolished under Stuyvesant's orders.

The remains of a wood-lined pit feature were exposed during the 1998 excavation by Hartgen Archeological Associates, Inc., on at the Picotte–New York State Department of Environmental Conservation (DEC) office building site in downtown Albany (Figure 1.1). Initial evaluation of the artifact assemblage from the feature and the soils that sealed it suggest that the deposit was in place by about 1650. The wooden feature is the remnant of one of the trader's houses destroyed by flood or demolished in 1648. Examples of the early artifacts are illustrated in this chapter, and the early New Netherland archives, maps, and other documents are discussed in support of this interpretation.

Environmental Setting

Area 9, located in the southeast quadrant of the Picotte-DEC project area, originally encompassed the natural bank of the Hudson River where it overlooked a small sheltered cove or backwater formed by the confluence of the Fox Creek with the Hudson River (Figure 3.1). The area consisted of a low terrace or terraces that dropped off sharply to the east and northeast to the Hudson River channel and rose more gradually to the south and west to a narrow band of alluvial flats that extended from the Fox Creek south to the Normanskill. The average elevation of Area 9 was 6 to 13 feet (2–4 m) above sea level, making the area prone to cyclical flooding. It is reasonable to conclude that Area 9 was not conducive to, or suitable for, agricultural purposes or prolonged human occupation until the late eighteenth century when the natural land forms were extensively modified.

Despite the obstacles to prolonged human occupation during prehistoric and early historic times, Area 9 possessed certain natural features that would have encouraged short-term or seasonal occupation of the land. The shallow cove, which formed its eastern boundary, would have provided an ideal habitat for shellfish, bait fish, game fish, and a wide variety of migratory water fowl. In addition, the river and its environs would have supported an abundance of plant life that was edible or otherwise exploitable.

The low terrace paralleled the shoreline and would have provided an advantageous site from which to exploit these resources while also affording some protection from the prevailing winds. Situated below the

People, Places, and Material Things: Historical Archaeology of Albany, New York edited by Charles L. Fisher, New York State Museum Bulletin 499, © 2003 by the University of the State of New York, New York State Education Department, Albany, New York.

Site Location (Römer 1698)

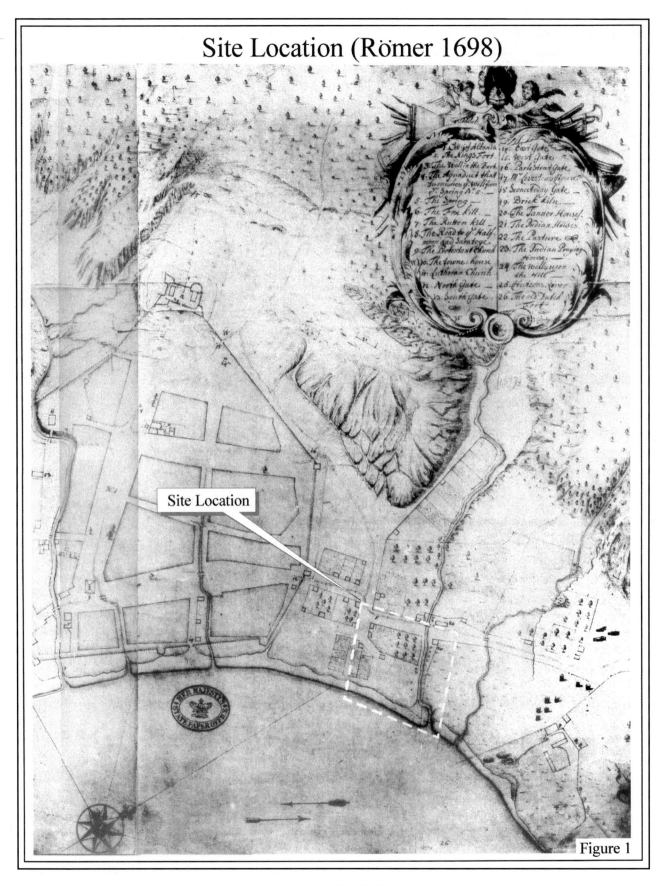

Figure 3.1. 1698 Römer Map with Picotte-DEC project area identified.

Area 9 Location (Römer 1698)

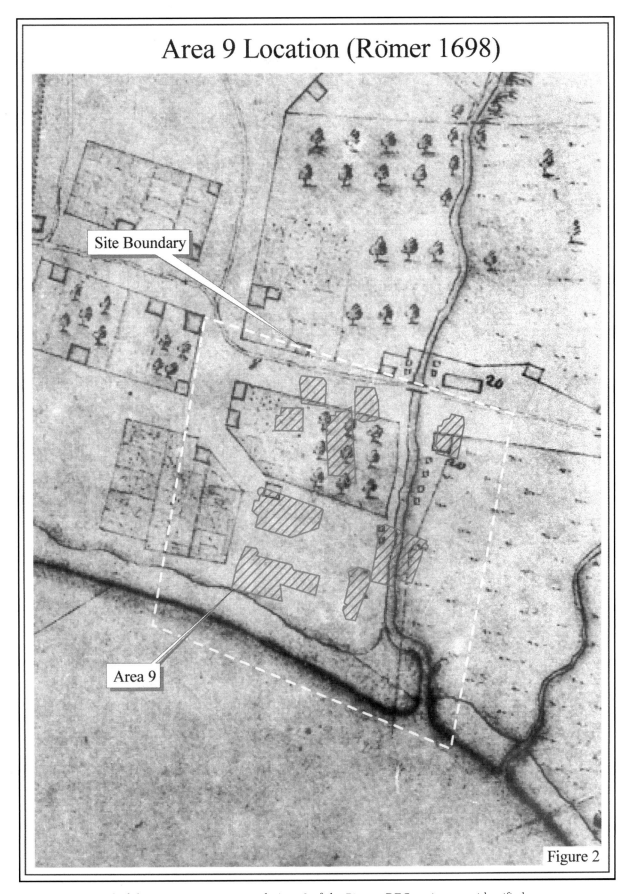

Site Boundary

Area 9

Figure 2

Figure 3.2. Detail of the 1698 Römer Map with Area 9 of the Picotte-DEC project area identified.

crest of the riverbank, the terrace provided a secluded vantage point from which to observe movement along the river and along the trails that followed the Fox Creek valley from the Hudson River into the Pine Bush, and on to the Mohawk Valley (Figure 3.2). Undoubtedly prehistoric populations exploited these features of Area 9 to their advantage.

Historical Background

After European contact in the seventeenth century, the location and topography of Area 9 relative to the location of Fort Orange made the area desirable for other activities, particularly trade between the Native American populations and the recent Dutch immigrants who were prohibited from engaging in this trade at Fort Orange. The archaeological evidence recovered during the excavation of the Picotte-DEC site indicates that both groups used Area 9 intensively during the second quarter of the seventeenth century for that purpose.

Although contractually prohibited from engaging in the fur trade, many Dutch colonists flagrantly and frequently violated the prohibition. Violations occurred within the confines of the fort, but many of these illicit traders recognized quickly that establishing trade sites outside the fort would allow them to intercept Native Americans before they reached the fort. Initially these trading sites appear to have expanded concentrically from the fort (Huey 1984:63–85). Following the defeat of the Mohicans at the hands of the Mohawks in 1628, the more favorable trading sites were located north and the west of the fort, closer to the confluence of the Mohawk River with the Hudson River. The most desirable of these illicit trading sites were located at the eastern terminus of the trails that led west into the Mohawk and Schoharie Valleys. From 1628 until 1643 the more adventurous of the illicit traders appeared to have played a game of trade leapfrog. They established trade sites that progressed steadily northward as they sought to best their competitors.

The situation was complicated further when Killiaen van Rensselaer founded Rensselaerswyck in 1630. Like the original colonists brought over by the Dutch West India Company to settle Fort Orange, Van Rensselaer was forbidden from engaging in the fur trade by the terms of his patroonship (Huey 1988:31; Van Laer 1908:137–153). He and his agents succumbed to the lure of the lucrative fur trade and established a trading house directly outside the north gate of Fort Orange in the 1630s (Huey 1988:39).

In 1639 the Dutch West India Company recognized the impossibility of enforcing its ban on trade and opened the market to all of its colonists except those employed by the company. For the next 4 years, competition between the Fort Orange traders was intense. It was brought to an abrupt end in 1643 when Van Rensselaer's agent Arent Van Curler established a permanent trading post at Schuyler Flats, 5 miles north of Fort Orange (Van Laer 1908:660). At the same time, he placed a ban on private traders, forbidding them from entering his land.

The death knell for the independent traders at Fort Orange sounded in 1648 by an act of nature and an act of politics. The great flood of 1648 destroyed virtually every structure associated with the settlement of Fort Orange, including at least eight traders' houses located north of the fort. It was the appointment of Peter Stuyvesant as Director General of the West India Company, however, that sealed their fate. Not only did he reassert the Dutch West India Company's monopoly over the fur trade, he also banned construction of all buildings within a cannon shot of Fort Orange, which translated to a distance of 3,000 feet (915 m) from the fort (Huey 1988:49). Van Rensselaer, through his agents, fought Stuyvesant on both points, but the independent traders lacked the financial resources and the political clout to take on such an adversary. The last of the independent trader houses north of Fort Orange was demolished in 1648.

Within this historical framework, the evolution of Area 9 in the seventeenth century may be reconstructed from the archaeological evidence.

Archaeology of an Illicit Trader's House

During the last week of October 1998, Area 9 was mechanically stripped to a mid-nineteenth-century occupation level, a process that required the removal of 10 to 13 feet (3–4 m) of fill overlying the floors and foundation of the last dwelling to occupy the site (Figure 3.3). Associated with these dwellings was a variety of outbuildings, wells, cisterns, and utility surfaces that were mapped, photographed, and then systematically excavated.

At the same time Area 9 was stripped, Test Trench 1 and Test Trench 201 from earlier surveys were reopened to allow a more thorough examination of the stratigraphic sequences. Careful troweling and firsthand examination of the Test Trench 1 profiles re-

Figure 3.3. Photograph of Area 9 stripped to the early nineteenth-century house floor level.

vealed a remarkable and intriguing feature that had gone undetected during the first two surveys, because it was 13 feet (4 m) below grade and was only represented by a thin outline of wood mold (Figure 3.4). The depth of these deposits prohibited close examination during the previous investigation.

The remains of the seventeenth-century trader's house consisted of a rectangular wood-lined pit that had been excavated into the natural bank of the Hudson River. The structural remains of an eighteenth-century dock made of stacked pine logs were exposed in the same trench, less than 7 feet (2 m) east of the wood-lined pit (Figure 3.5). The proximity of the eighteenth-century dock demonstrates just how close the trader's house was to the water's edge. The stratified deposits that overlaid the collapsed house contained mid-seventeenth-century material, thus establishing its antiquity.

More convincing evidence of the feature's antiquity came from the fact that the three archaeological deposits that overlaid the collapsed structure contained material and artifacts from the mid-seventeenth century. More important, the nature of the assemblage indicated that the feature was the remains of a seven-teenth-century dwelling.

In the seventeenth century, this structure would have been described as a hut, a hovel, a cabin, a dugout, or a wigwam, depending on the chronicler (Carson et al. 1981). Technically these structures would all fall into the category of earth-fast constructions, meaning that they were all built directly on the ground, without masonry footings or foundation. They were intended to provide temporary shelter. Contemporary accounts of Fort Orange describe the original dwellings as "hutts of Bark" (Huey 1988:26).

Of the various definitions available, the term *wigwam* best describes the structure. Wigwams were based on the Native American bark wicciup, which was a partially subterranean dwelling with a pole-framed superstructure, sheathed with bark. The Dutch wigwam was a modified wicciup that employed European framing techniques, incorporated finished lumber, and was joined with nails (Figure 3.6). Apparently variation reflected the needs, the means, and the initiative of the builder. This structure seems to have been carefully built, given its precarious location and temporary function.

The construction of this wigwam is noteworthy for

Figure 3.4. Photograph of reexcavated Test Trench 1 with structure (Feature 133) in profile.

Figure 3.5. Photograph of the location of the eighteenth-century dock relative to structure (Feature 133). Logs of dock visible in upper left corner of photograph.

Figure 3.6. Artist's conception of a Dutch wigwam. Drawing by S. Sherwood.

a number of reasons. One, it was a strongly built post-and-beam structure that seemed to reflect its builders' concern for durability. Two, it was constructed of finished dimensional lumber rather than rough timbers or logs. The sheathing was affixed to the outside of the posts, so the subterranean portion of the structure had to have been prefabricated and then set in place. There is no builder's trench to accommodate in situ construction. Finally, nails were used rather than wooden treenails, dowels, or pegs. The care with which it was built seems unjustified, given the obvious threat of flooding.

In terms of its dimensions, the structure was 9 feet (2.8 m) wide, which is approximately 8.75 Rhineland *voets,* along its east-west axis. The north and south walls were not exposed during the excavations, but since the feature continued north of Trench 1 and south of Units 9.5 and 9.6, it had to have been at least 10 feet (3 m) long. The remnants of the wall posts, which supported clapboards lining the pit, were 5 feet, 3 inches (1.6 m or 5 Rhineland *voets*) in length. When the structure collapsed or was demolished, the

walls fell inward and against each other near the center of the feature (Figure 3.7).

The most valuable information gained from the structural remains of the house was its mode of construction. Evidence from the relationship of the sections of the vertical wall posts and the depth of the pit to the seventeenth-century ground surface indicate the trader's house rose, minimally, 3 feet (0.9 m) above the ground surface of the river bank and only 2 feet (0.6 m) below it (Figures 3.4 and 3.7). Paul Huey has excavated and reported wood-lined pit features from the seventeenth century in the Albany area, including the 1643 Van Curler house at Schuyler Flatts and the 1654 Van Doesburgh house at Fort Orange (Huey 1987:15–21). Huey identified these features as wood-lined cellar holes, based on the fact that both were completely subterranean, excavated to a depth of 4 to 6 feet (1.2–1.8 m) and both were located within the footprint of a larger superstructure.

In contrast, the trader's house was a semisubterranean house, with most of the structure extending above the ground. The footprint of the subterranean

Figure 3.7. Photograph and plan view of structure (Feature 133) with structural elements exposed by excavation.

portion and the superstructure were one and the same. The wigwam excavated at the Picotte-DEC site is the only known example of this building type in Albany.

The wigwam was supported by 8-inch by 8-inch (0.20 x 0.20 m) hewn sleepers aligned north-south and spaced 8.8 feet (2.7 m) on center. The floorboards were hewn or sawn planks, probably 1 or 1.25 inches (2.5 or 3 cm) in thickness and ranged from 8 to 12 inches (20–30 cm) in width. It seems likely that there were joists running under the floorboards, perpendicular to the sleepers, although there was no conclusive evidence of this in the archaeological record except for nails running through the floorboards. The boards themselves were not removed to preserve as much of the structure as possible for future exposure and analysis.

Wall construction consisted of vertical, 4-inch by 4-inch by 60+-inch (10 x 10 x 150 cm) hewn or sawn posts spaced 35 inches (90 cm) on center and (probably) joined to an 8-inch by 8-inch (20 x 20 cm) sill or sleeper by mortise, tenon, and tusk. Whip or sash-sawn clapboards 1- to 1.25-inch (2.5–3 cm) thick of various widths were affixed to the vertical posts with wrought nails. The clapboards were not intended to function as exterior sheathing. The sheathing was proba-

bly made of bark sheets, thus creating a Dutch wigwam.

Because the house was more than 2,300 feet (700 m) north of the fort and was built on a steep slope barely 6 feet (2 m) above sea level, it seems unlikely that any of the original inhabitants of Fort Orange would have built a permanent dwelling in such an inconvenient and precarious location. On the other hand, the structure was probably not visible from the fort while affording an excellent vantage point to observe and intercept traffic along the river and trails running north and west from it. These advantages would have outweighed the disadvantages to a trader.

The wigwam probably collapsed within a few years of its construction, almost certainly due to flooding and the slumping of the very plastic clay into which it had been dug. Following the collapse of the wigwam, its remnants were quickly encapsulated and formed a shallow basin that was filled with rubble from the collapsed structure and the refuse of its occupants. The natural contours of the site that existed prior to the time of the wigwam's construction were reestablished and the site was reoccupied. The individuals who reoccupied the site after 1650 were not Dutch entrepreneurs but Native Americans. Apparently the trade relationship between an illicit Dutch trader and his Native American partners continued after the wigwam was destroyed. The site appears to have gained special significance to one or both parties.

The Native American encampment and the trading session, which likely transpired within it, represent the last use of the site during the seventeenth century. Evidence of the reoccupation of the Dutch wigwam site by Native Americans consisted of a hearth, designated Feature 136, and a unique group of artifacts associated with its construction and use (Figure 3.8).

Feature 136 conformed in shape and size to a Native American hearth. It was a basin-shaped pit lined with a combination of quartzite cobbles and Dutch bricks, apparently salvaged from the rubble of the former wigwam. It seems only proper that this multicultural hearth was used to prepare a multicultural feast. Within the hearth and scattered on the ground surface surrounding it was evidence of the meal, as well as the activities that occurred in its aftermath. The faunal analysis indicated that the feast consisted of several hundred freshwater mussels, freshwater fish that included bullhead and sturgeon, and a variety of game, including bear, duck, and deer (Pipes 2002). Pumpkins or squash were also consumed, but with the exception of some beef (represented by a cow head),

and the obligatory alcohol provided by Dutch traders, all the food consumed at the hearth, including the dog, was probably provided by the Native Americans.

Artifacts

More than 300 diagnostic artifacts were recovered from the deposits associated with the wigwam, the hearth built in its rubble, and the overlying deposit that sealed them both. The actual time period that transpired between the initial construction of the wigwam and the sealing of the hearth was probably less than a decade. In addition, the artifact assemblages recovered from the three deposits were so similar in terms of quantity, quality, and variety that they were virtually indistinguishable. Therefore, these assemblages were analyzed and interpreted as a single entity, indicative of the common trading activity that was the raison d'etre for the creation of each.

Of the various activities implicit in the assemblage, tobacco smoking was best represented, based on the number of kaolin pipe fragments recovered. Eighty-five measurable pipe stems were recovered. When subjected to Binford's formula, the mean date for the assemblage was 1646 (Binford 1962). Eight stems

Figure 3.8. Photograph of shellfish remains at hearth (Feature 136).

and the one complete bowl recovered were all marked with decorative motifs and/or maker's marks frequently found on mid-seventeenth-century colonial sites and early historic Native American sites. Four stems were impressed with the fleur-de-lis motif in various patterns, all of which had analogs in the seventeenth-century Fort Orange deposits (Huey 1988:737–738) and in several seventeenth-century Mohawk sites (Snow 1995; Tanner 1995:35) (Figure 3.9). Three stem fragments and the complete bowl bore the heel mark EB in an impressed circular cartouche, with the same analogs previously cited. It is significant to note that the majority of the Mohawk analogs to these artifacts were recovered from sites occupied between 1635 and 1646 (Snow 1995: 300–360).

The most unusual of the marked pipe fragments recovered was a stem piece from a Sir Walter Raleigh pipe. These pipes, depicting a crocodile regurgitating Raleigh because he tasted so bad after smoking, were manufactured in the Netherlands during the seventeenth century (Brongers 1964:46). Although hundreds of these pipes have been recovered from seven-teenth-century sites in Europe, only eight sites in North America had produced examples of this rare artifact prior to this excavation in 1998. Three of the sites were within a mile (1,600 m) of this site; another example was recovered from Schuyler Flatts, 4 miles (6,437 m) to the north.

A Sir Walter Raleigh pipe was found at Fort Orange in a deposit dating before 1640 (Huey 1988:572). Another example recovered locally was from a feature discovered under Riverside Avenue in Rensselaer in the 1970s, which was identified as a Native American hearth; a third was recovered from the Van Curler house at Schuyler Flatts (Feister, personal communication 2002). Two additional examples have been recently recovered from the Peter Bont Quackenboss house, less than 650 feet (200 m) north of the trader's house.

The remaining North American examples, reported prior to 1998, were more widespread. One was recovered in Quebec City from a deposit associated with the French occupation, while others were found in Native American contexts. The best documented example of these was recovered from a mid-

Figure 3.9. Photograph of marked mid-seventeenth-century tobacco pipe fragments.

seventeenth-century Native American grave in Rhode Island (Turnbaugh 1992:117). The other two were recovered at Oneida, New York, and New Brunswick, Canada, from deposits presumed to have a Native American affiliation, but their provenience has been questioned (Walker 1972).

The recovery of a Sir Walter Raleigh pipe fragment from the wigwam was significant, because it helped date the construction and occupation of the structure. For whatever reason, these pipes were never popular in the colonies, and only slightly more popular among the Native Americans. Given the popularity of anthropomorphic motifs on Native American tobacco pipes during this period, the apparent disinterest in the Raleigh pipes is difficult to explain. Perhaps the allegorical allusion to the evils of smoking was not lost on either group.

The consumption and storage of food and drink were activities well represented in the trader's house assemblage. Ceramics comprised the second largest artifact group and contained 73 diagnostic sherds. The 29 delft sherds and the 12 Dutch majolica sherds formed 56 percent of the sample but contained the fewest identifiable vessel forms. It is likely that most of the delft and majolica vessels were tableware.

Redwares formed 23 percent of the sample, and from the 17 sherds recovered 2 vessel forms and 3 vessels were identified. One was a colander. The other 2 were milk pans, which were common seventeenth-century kitchenwares.

There were three sherds each (4 percent) of Frechen, Westerwald, white-bodied earthenware, and a green-glazed buff earthenware. Proportionately, these groups provided the largest number of vessels in the assemblage, and all are associated with the storage or consumption of spirituous drink. The Frechen sherds came from three different Bellarmine or Bartman jugs. These vessels were first produced in the sixteenth century, and they continued to be popular in the seventeenth century (Noël Hume 1969:55–57). The applied medallions, which typify these jugs, are often temporally diagnostic. Two of the sherds have partial medallions, but, as yet, neither has been identified. One hopes analogs will eventually be found in other collections. The other vessel form identified was a Westerwald tankard. This early stoneware was very popular in the seventeenth century.

Just 8 glass sherds were recovered from the seventeenth-century deposits, but each represented an identifiable vessel. Four case bottles and 2 wine bottles were represented, along with 2 Roemer prunts.

These decorative glasses are an archetype for seventeenth-century sites. All 8 glass vessels were clearly associated with storage or consumption of alcohol. As 12 of the 14 ceramic and glass vessels represented in the assemblage are associated with alcohol use, the imbibing of strong drink was obviously one of the major activities that occurred at the site.

The third largest artifact group in the assemblage falls into the category of personal or clothing items. This was the most diverse of the artifact groups represented and perhaps the most interesting in terms of the activities implied. Clothing fasteners included 14 hand-headed pins, 2 eyes from hook-and-eye closures, an aglet or lace tip, and 2 shanked cast metal buttons with an elaborate basket-weave motif. With the exception of the pins, which appear to be a copper alloy of a very reddish bronze rather than the more common golden brass, these closures have analogs in several collections recovered from seventeenth-century Dutch sites in Albany County and from a protohistoric Native American site in Rensselaer County (Huey 1984:74–78). In addition, analogs to these items exist in collections recovered from numerous Mohawk sites occupied between 1635 and 1646 (Snow 1995:371).

Next to clothing fasteners, trade beads were the most frequently recovered item in the personal or clothing group. Eight glass trade beads representing six bead types were recovered from the site. All were seventeenth-century tube beads, and all but one fit within the Kidd bead typology, as Type Ib (Kidd and Kidd 1970) (Figure 3.10). The anomaly is a tube bead made from an opaque red glass that appears to be a spiral-wound wire bead. The form and manufacturing technique are not uncommon, but application of a single strand of glass to the bead's surface is unusual. If the appliqué was intentional, then the bead has no known analog. Karlis Karklins, an expert on glass trade beads, examined the bead and suggested that it was a common tube bead flawed during manufacture (personal communication 2000). In either case, the form and color of the bead indicate that it was contemporaneous with the rest of the assemblage, which dates to the mid-seventeenth century.

The remaining items in the personal or clothing group include two finely made marbles and two small quartz crystals. Both items were of particular interest, not because of their uniqueness but because of their presumed function and the activities implied by each. Marbles are normally considered toys, but adults probably used these as gaming pieces, because they

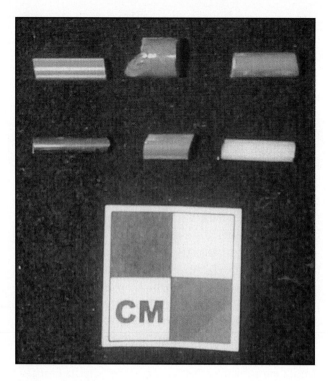

Figure 3.10. Photograph of seventeenth-century glass trade beads.

Figure 3.11. Photograph of Herkimer diamonds.

were carefully crafted from stone or stoneware (Huey 1988:451–454). Gaming equates with gambling, particularly on seventeenth-century Dutch sites, so gambling can be added to the list of activities in which the wigwam's occupants were engaged.

The two quartz crystals, known locally as Herkimer diamonds, probably served a more noble function. While these crystals are occasionally found in historic deposits, they also have been found on Native American sites in all cultural phases (Murphy and Luedtke 2000). That they have special significance to Native Americans has been documented since European contact. In the seventeenth century Roger Williams recorded that Native Americans carried crystals as good luck (Turnbaugh 1992:117). George Hamell suggests that these crystals were imbued with an ideological value and were symbolic of light and brightness (1983:3). It was believed that among the Iroquois items like crystal and shell would convey well-being and other life-enhancing forces to the owner (Peña 1990:31). More recently Murphy and Luedtke (2000) have suggested that crystals may have been used by Native Americans to sanctify important sites, in much the same manner that wampum was exchanged among Native Americans to establish the significance and sincerity of their agreements. The presence of quartz crystals at the wigwam site seems indicative of the significance placed on the site and the activities that occurred here (Figure 3.11).

All of the items in the personal or clothing artifact group were valued trade items, as were most of the artifacts that were recovered from the wigwam site. A copper alloy coin, identified as a Dutch half duit was recovered from the deposit sealing the hearth feature. The coin has been as frustrating as it has been fascinating. Research shows that it was minted in the Province of Gelterland, Killean Van Rensselaer's ancestral home, and the first two digits of the date prove that it was minted during in the seventeenth century (Scholten 1953:39). Unfortunately the last two digits are illegible, thus depriving us of a precise *terminus post quem* for the site.

A coin virtually identical to this, but with a complete date of 1633, was recovered from a seventeenth-century deposit at Schuyler Flatts (R. Brustle, personal communication 2000). Coins of any sort are conspicuous by their absence from most seventeenth-century sites, as Peña and others have established (Peña 1990:50–51). The recovery of two identical coins from two deposits on two sites established for the same purpose prior to 1650 is worthy of note, even if coincidental.

The last artifact group to be discussed is unusual if not unique, given its context. This group of artifacts is a historic lithic tool kit. In addition to 17 traditional lithic tools, which included 3 bifacial blades, 9 utilized flakes, a graver, and 2 modified projectile points; there were 8 whole or fragmentary gunflints. Some were in the process of manufacture, some were exhausted, but all appeared to have been reused or reworked for some purpose. At least 3 of the gunflints were made of European flint, and because there were flakes of the same material recovered from the same deposits, the logical conclusion is that gunflints were modified at the site. The traditional lithic tools were obviously made and used by Native Americans, but they may have been manufactured elsewhere or were manufactured prior to construction of the wigwam. The modified gunflints postdate it or are contemporaneous with it, thus leading to the conclusion that the site was functioning very early in the historic period, before lithic technology had been supplanted by metal tools (Figure 3.12).

Interpretation

The artifact assemblage could be interpreted as the product of a seventeenth-century Dutch colonial household, similar in many respects to the assemblages recovered from deposits at Fort Orange, Schuyler Flatts, and the Van Buren farm (Huey 1984). On the other hand, the same assemblage could be attributed to any number of historic Iroquois sites in the Mohawk Valley, based solely on the artifacts (Snow 1995). Both interpretations are substantially correct, because the Dutch built the wigwam, and Native Americans built the hearth, which supplanted it. More important, both groups contributed the artifact assemblage.

Numerous activities that occurred at the site were identified as the separate artifact groups were discussed. Conspicuous among these were the smoking of tobacco, drinking alcoholic beverages, feasting, and gambling. If considered independently, and viewed with the cultural biases of twentieth-century

Figure 3.12. Photograph of historic lithic tool kit.

society, each of these activities might be considered licentious or antisocial, at the very least. In the seventeenth century, however, these activities were not only acceptable but were in keeping with protocol for establishing the proper milieu for social interaction. Trade was the impetus to the site's creation and evolution, but trade did not take place in a social vacuum. Each party had social and economic expectations and obligations that had to be met, and apparently both the Dutch colonists and their Native American counterparts were satisfied with the results of their meetings here, because they returned to the site. Rarely does the archaeological record capture the essence of the acculturation process so clearly.

References Cited

Binford, L.R. 1962. A New Method of Calculating Dates from Pipe Stem Fragments. *Southeastern Archaeological Conference Newsletter* 9(1):19–21.

Brongers, G.A. 1964. *Nicotiana Tobacum: The History of Tobacco and Tobacco Smoking in the Netherlands.* Theodorus Nienmeyer, Groingen, Netherlands.

Carson, C., Barka, N.F., Kelso, W.M., Stone, G.W., and Upton, D. 1981. Impermanent Architecture in the Southern American Colonies. *Winterthur Portfolio* 16(2/3):135–178.

Hamell, G.R. 1983. Trading in Metaphors: The Magic of Beads. In *Proceedings of the 1982 Glass Trade Bead Conference,* edited by C.F. Hayes III, pp. 5–28. Research Records No. 16, Rochester Museum and Science Center, Rochester, N.Y.

Huey, P.R. 1984. Dutch Sites of the Seventeenth Century in Rensselaerswyck. In *The Scope of Historical Archaeology,* edited by D. Orr and D. Crozier, pp. 63–85. Laboratory of Anthropology, Temple University, Philadelphia.

_____. 1987. Archaelogical Evidence of Dutch Wooden Cellars and Perishable Wooden Structures at Seventeenth and Eighteenth Century Sites in the Upper Hudson Valley. In *New World Dutch Studies Dutch Arts and Culture in Colonial America 1609–1776,* edited by R.H. Blackburn and N.A. Kelley, pp. 13–35. Albany Institute of History and Art, Albany, N.Y.

_____. 1988. *Aspects of Continuity and Change in the Colonial Dutch Material Culture at Fort Orange, 1624–1664.* Doctoral dissertation, University of Pennsylvania, Philadelphia. University Microfilms International, Ann Arbor, Mich.

Kidd, K.E., and Kidd, M.A. 1970. A Classification System for Glass Beads for the Use of Field Archaeologists. In *Canadian Historic Sites: Occasional Papers in Archaeology and History,* No. 1. National Historic Site Services, Ottawa, Ont.

Murphy, J., and Luedtke, B. 2000. The Stone Tools from Magunco. Paper presented at Annual Meeting of Society for Historical Archaeology, Quebec City.

Noël Hume, I. 1969. *Artifacts of Colonial America.* Random House, New York.

O'Callaghan, E.B. 1853. *Documents Relating to the Colonial History of the State of New York,* Vol. 1. Weed, Parsons and Co., Albany.

Peña, E.S. 1990. *Wampum Production in New Netherlands and Colonial New York: The Historical and Archaeological Context.* Doctoral dissertation, Boston University. University Microfilms International, Ann Arbor, Mich.

Pipes, M. 2002. Faunal Report: Illegal Dutch Trader's House. Analysis performed for Hartgen Archeological Associates, Inc., Rensselaer, N.Y.

Römer, Col. W.W. 1698. *Map of Albany.* New York State Archives, Albany.

Scholten, C. 1953. *The Coins of the Dutch Overseas Territories 1601–1948.* J. Schulman, Amsterdam, Netherlands.

Snow, D.R. 1995. *Mohawk Valley Archaeology: The Sites.* The Institute for Archaeological Studies, State University of New York at Albany.

Tanner, T. 1995. Who Walked Lot 18 Site? *William M. Beauchamp Chapter, NYSAA* 7(1):1–9.

Turnbaugh, W.A. 1992. Post Contact Smoking Pipe Development: The Narragansett Example. In *Proceedings of the 1989 Smoking Pipe Conference: Selected Papers,* edited by C.F. Hayes III, pp. 113–124. Rochester Museum and Science Center, Rochester, N.Y.

Van Laer, A.J.T. (editor and translator). 1908. *Van Rensselaer Bowier Manuscripts.* The University of the State of New York, Albany.

Walker, I. 1972. Sir Walter Raleigh Pipes. *Quarterly Bulletin of the Archaeological Society of Virginia* 24(4):161–164.

CHAPTER 4

Soldiers in the City: The Archaeology of the British Guard House

Charles L. Fisher

Introduction

In 1972 archaeologist Paul Huey made a fascinating discovery while monitoring an electrical line installation beneath State Street in Albany, New York. He recorded a single course of stone from the base of the northeast corner of the foundation of a mid-eighteenth-century British guard house (Figure 1.1). The British guard house on State Street was part of the British fortifications of Albany constructed during the French and Indian War, the North American portion of the European conflict known as the Seven Years War (Figure 4.1). Military maps of the 1750s show the structure in the center of State Street midway up the hill toward the fort. Huey noted that most of the stone foundation was removed, probably for reuse in the city's postwar building boom.

In 1998 archaeologists from the New York State Museum returned to this location when the New York State Department of Transportation undertook a major project aimed at the reconstruction of Pearl Street. To place a drainage line beneath the busy intersection of State and Pearl Streets, the excavation of a jacking pit and a receiving pit was required. These large, deep excavations were placed within the pedestrian island in the center of State Street on both sides of Pearl Street and provided the space necessary to drive, or jack, the drain line beneath the intersection without disrupting traffic on the street surface. Careful planning in advance of construction enabled archaeological excavation of a location adjacent to the east side of the historic guard house remains discovered in 1972.

The objective of the 1998 excavation was the recovery of material remains of British soldiers during the brief period they occupied this site in the mid-eighteenth century. No other occupation was historically documented at this site, although an earlier seventeenth-century wooden drain was discovered in 1972 beneath the site. The artifacts are of interest to the interpretation of the British soldiers in North America during the war. The material remains from the soldiers in the city may be combined with those from numerous forts, camps, and battlefields to provide a more complete picture of daily life during this conflict.

The 1998 excavations produced the expected material remains from this period and new evidence of subsequent activities at this location before and during the Revolutionary War. The site was abandoned by the end of the Revolutionary War, as evident by the absence of any later cultural material.

The presence of the British guard house in the center of this fortified town, the continued use of the site after the end of the French and Indian War, and the presence of material items from the Revolutionary War period may be viewed as the result of the specific social relationships existing in Albany during this period. Because the construction and use of the guard house was the product of British-colonial interactions in Albany, a discussion of these relationships is relevant to the meaning of this archaeological site.

The Social Context of the Guard House

In 1676 the English built a new fort on the hill to the west overlooking Albany to "defend and command the whole town" (Merwick 1990:266). This fort replaced the deteriorated Dutch Fort Orange and signaled the English control over the town. The

People, Places, and Material Things: Historical Archaeology of Albany, New York edited by Charles L. Fisher, New York State Museum Bulletin 499, © 2003 by the University of the State of New York, New York State Education Department, Albany, New York. All rights reserved

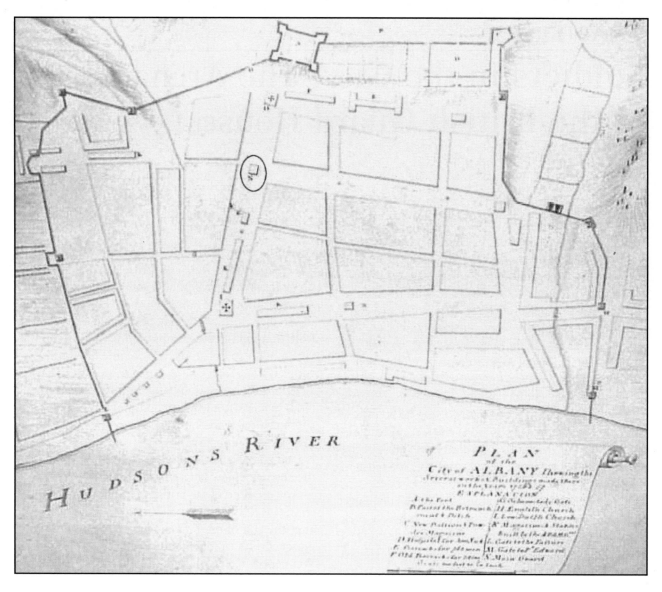

Figure 4.1. Detail from Plan of Albany, 1756 and 1757. "N" (the building circled) indicates Main Guard. The Crown Collection, Series I, Vol. 2, No. 39. New York State Library, Albany.

British military presence in Albany must be considered as a police force, as well as a defensive one. As early as 1687 the English considered the residents of Albany to have "a turbulent disposition" (Merwick 1990:266).

Although illegal, the Dutch in Albany continued to trade with the French and their native allies. Based upon frequent stories that their possessions appeared in Albany shops following bloody raids, New Englanders believed that Dutch traders encouraged native raids on their villages. In 1749 Peter Kalm noted "the hatred which the . . . [New Englanders] bear against the people of Albany is very great, but that of the Al-banians against the English is carried to a ten times higher degree" (Merwick 1981:391).

The location of Albany made it the logical selection as the headquarters for the expeditions against French Canada in the 1750s. The military buildup included the construction of a new city wall and numerous buildings including guard houses, barracks, a hospital, stables, magazines, and storehouses. These buildings were placed on public land within the streets to minimize conflicts with the townspeople.

As many as 1400 officers and soldiers were moved into the already doubly occupied Dutch homes. During the winter of 1756, Albany's tightly circumscribed world was composed of seventy-five acres filled with 335 households and a teeming population of more than 4000 natives, refugees, and soldiers. (Hackett 1991:33)

The British military was aware of the numerous problems between the townspeople and the many soldiers from New England coming to Albany. In 1755 William Johnson was informed that a camp to the north of town "would be a good location, and better than having the troops near the town where it will be impossible to keep them out, and from making beasts of themselves" (Huey 1988:124).

Recent research has suggested that the well-known words to the song "Yankee Doodle" composed in the military camps around Albany during this period reflect the negative attitudes the colonial allies had of each other. The lyrics are a result of the English-colonial conflict during this period (Carola 1999; Murray 1999). The term *yankey,* for example, was a derogatory Dutch term used for describing the New Englanders, while *doodle* derived from the Dutch word for simpleton or fool.

Warren Johnson passed through Albany in 1760 on his way to visit his brother Sir William Johnson in the Mohawk Valley. He expressed dislike of most things Dutch he encountered in Albany, from the "dirty, nasty streets" to the women and children smoking tobacco in public. He voiced disgust at the lack of stone paved streets, which he attributed to the Dutch not wanting to wear their cartwheels down (Johnson 1996).

The end of the war began a new series of problems between the British and the inhabitants of Albany. In 1763 fences around the storehouse on the site of Fort Orange were pulled down "in a riotous manner" (Huey 1988:127). In 1765 the magistrates of Albany requested that the British army remove their warehouses from the city. General Gage responded by requesting an alternative site, such as the former site of Fort Orange. The city, however, did not own this land that belonged to the Dutch Reformed Church (Huey 1988:127).

A number of military buildings were sold in October 1765, including the old barracks, wagon house, king's stables, and old provision shed (Huey 1988:128). The north wall of the city was no longer necessary and the British planned to take it down to use the stone for a new warehouse. Although the warehouse was never built, the stone was used in the construction of the new waterfront.

In 1766 a company of British troops from the Seventeenth Regiment stationed in Albany was called out to protect the stores when a mob assembled and began to destroy the storehouse and rob the provisions. The British were unsuccessful in their efforts to construct a new storehouse in Albany.

Some scholars have suggested that the city leaders did not want the British military present, because this would have interfered with their trade (Huey 1988; Kenney 1969). The army would have occupied an economically advantageous location and brought in sutlers who would have competed with Albany merchants.

Mob action by the local Sons of Liberty was a reaction to the new taxes imposed on the colonies to help England pay for the victory over the French. The opposition to these taxes resulted in riots that were led by members of the wealthiest families in the colonies (Morgan and Morgan 1995:192).

An analysis of another mob action in Albany in 1766 that involved the Sons of Liberty demonstrated that the "Sons" were nearly all young adults, Dutch, and closely related to the town magistrates (McAnear 1947). When it was rumored that Henry Van Schaack was about to accept the position of deputy to the stamp tax collector, he was summoned to confront a mob at Thomas Williams' Inn in Albany and swear he would not accept the job. He went to the mayor for protection, because there were between 200 and 300 troops in the garrison that could have been used to maintain order. Instead, he was told to obey the mob. The following night his house was badly damaged by a rioting mob that included Stephen van Rensselaer, the patroon of Rensselaerswyck, and John van Alen, an assistant in the Albany Common Council and surveyor to the patroon.

Lieutenant Governor Cadwallader Colden wrote that the City of Albany was the scene of the "most unaccountable riots," which he attributed to the spread of mob action with the return of colonial delegates from a general congress in New York City (Colden 1853).

The British were troubled by difficulties within the military as well. The daughter of a Scottish officer, Anne Grant, observed a mutiny in 1765 at the guard house on State Street. While she was staying at the Schuyler house, located on the southeast corner of State and Pearl Streets, she recorded "an impressive spectacle" at the guard house in the middle of the street, directly in front of the Schuyler house.

There was a guard extraordinary mounted in honor of Sir Jeffrey; at the hour of changing it all the soldiery in the fort assembled there, and laid down their arms, refusing to take them up again. I shall never forget the pale and agitated countenances of the officers; they being too well assured that it is a thing preconcerted; which was actually the case, for at Crown Point and Quebec the same thing was done on the same day. Sir Jeffrey came down, and made a calm dispassionate speech to them, promising them a continuance of their privileges till further orders from home, and offering pardon to the whole, with the exception of a few ringleaders, whose lives, however, were spared. (1903:92–93)

The cause of the discontent, however, she attributed to the soldiers finding themselves treated with a coldness, amounting to aversion by the people of the country; who now forgot past services, and showed in all transactions a spirit of dislike bordering on hostility to their protectors, on whom they no longer felt themselves dependent. (91–92)

Although the war between the French and British was over with the treaty of 1763, the traditional social conflicts within the community intensified. Archaeological evidence of the continued British presence in Albany that resulted from this tension and the subsequent American occupation of a British military building that marked the violent upheaval of the political order was observed during excavations at the intersection of Pearl and State Streets.

Archaeological Evidence

The 1998 excavation was within a pedestrian island in the center of State Street (Figure 4.2). Archaeologists monitored a test excavation to establish the location of existing utilities and the presence and depth of undisturbed historic deposits. The southern half of the proposed excavation area, which was disturbed previously by the installation of a storm drain and a layer of cement placed over an electrical conduit for protection, prevented examination of a 1-meter-wide corridor across the central section of the island. The test excavation in the northern portion, however, exposed an eighteenth-century deposit at a depth of 1.5 meters below the street surface. Archaeological excavations commenced after power equipment was used to remove the pavement and the modern deposits above the historic deposit.

Archaeological evidence in the form of the strati-

Figure 4.2. Photograph of 1998 excavations at the pedestrian island in State Street facing east.

graphic record was expected to demonstrate either a continuous deposition from the middle to the late eighteenth century or several discrete episodes of deposition represented by discontinuities, such as a layer of debris from the construction or destruction of the guard house. Material remains of known manufacturing dates were important to the stratigraphic analysis.

Five 1-meter-square excavation units were placed from west to east across the undisturbed northern portion of the proposed drainage structure installation pit. These units identified a single eighteenth-century deposit. Artifacts were recovered from a shallow, narrow, trench that was present in the westernmost excavation unit at approximately the center of the guard house and continued downhill to the east almost 5 meters (Figure 4.3). This trench was well defined at the west, uphill side and more difficult to delineate at the east or downhill side. It appears to have been constructed to drain runoff water from the State Street hill east around the guard house and control it in a single trench downhill.

The soil adjacent to the trench did not contain artifacts. Only a single soil deposit was present as two layers of trench fill, with finer soils observed above coarser sand. This was a result of gradual and continuous deposition throughout the short occupation period of the site, because artifacts and artifact assemblages were similar in both strata (Table 4.1). For example, the most recent ceramic types in this collection, eighteenth-century pearlware and creamware, were recovered from both strata. A blue hand-painted pearlware bowl was reconstructed from sherds found in both Stratum II and Stratum III. The different soil textures noted in excavation appear to be the result of complex particle sorting caused by the water running through the ditch, rather than two temporally distinct deposits.

The trench contained material remains from the soldiers' occupation of the guard house. These remains reflected a domestic occupation resulting from the soldiers' "off duty" lives. A small number of military items were recovered, including four gunflints, the lower jaw of a musket hammer, a sling swivel, a small fragment of a D-shaped iron canteen lid or base, and lead shot and casting waste. The majority of the material consisted of a wide variety of faunal remains, glass, and ceramics. The last included white salt-glazed stonewares, redwares, English tin-glazed earthenwares, coarse salt-glazed stonewares, and sherds of creamware that indicate the guard house occupation continued after the 1763 treaty that ended

the war. A polychrome hand-painted creamware bowl was recovered, probably discarded in the late 1760s or early 1770s (Figure 4.4). A similar bowl is on display at the Wadsworth Atheneum in Hartford, Connecticut, and is associated with a date of manufacture of 1770.

Important evidence of continued use of the site included sherds of blue, hand-painted pearlware in the chinoiserie style, which was not available in North America until the Revolutionary War period (Figure 4.5). This bowl is very similar to ones found in excavations at New Windsor Cantonment near Newburgh, New York, which was the site of the Continental Army's last encampment during the winter of 1782 and 1783.

One of the most recent objects in the archaeological deposit was a "USA" button of the Continental Army, additional evidence of the reoccupation of this site during the Revolutionary War (Figure 4.6). Buttons of this type appear in Continental Army camp sites in the Hudson Valley in the 1780s, although they may be as early as 1777, the year that the Continental Congress began to identify military equipment with these initials. These buttons signify the important role of the Continental Army in unifying the separate colonies, since the buttons existed prior to the United States of America and visually displayed the symbol of a single, united political entity.

The large quantity of food remains and the large fragments of food bone contrast with the meager evi-

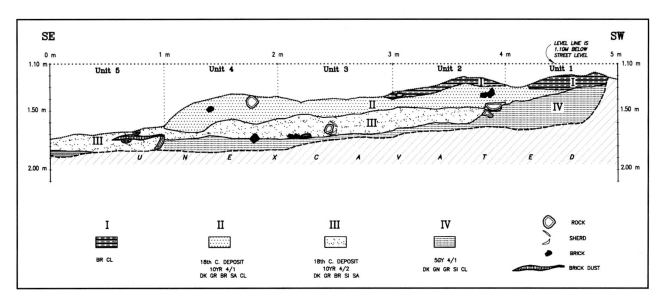

Figure 4.3. Section drawing of the south wall of the excavation. Surface of the excavation is 1.2 meter below the street level in the southwest corner.

Table 4.1. Type and Number of Ceramic Sherds Recovered from the Two Strata Excavated at the British Guard House

Ceramic Type	Stratum II	Stratum III	Total
Lead-glazed buff earthenware	27	25	52
Lead-glazed red earthenware	10	12	22
Tin-glazed buff earthenware	31	13	44
White salt-glazed stoneware	57	54	111
Creamware	48	89	137
Pearlware	4	8[a]	12
Porcelain	36	37	73
Gray salt-glazed stoneware	20	22	42
Other[b]	18	10	28

[a] Pearlware sherds from Strata II and III crossmend in a single blue hand-painted pearlware bowl.

[b] A sherd of agateware, 10 sherds of black-glazed redware, and 17 sherds of brown and buff salt-glazed stoneware are combined in this category.

Figure 4.4. Hand-painted, polychrome creamware bowl, 7 inches in diameter, from the British guard house.

Figure 4.5. Blue hand-painted, 6-inch-diameter pearlware bowl from the British guard house.

dence reported from campsites, where small fragments of calcined bone are more common. Cow, chicken, pig, horse, beaver, sturgeon, and deer remains have been identified in this collection. Large pieces of mandibles and horn cores still attached to skull fragments indicate that soldiers butchered animals in front of the guard house and discarded the waste in the center of the street (Figure 4.7), after the

Figure 4.6. Revolutionary War period *USA* button, 7/8-inch diameter, from the British guard house.

Figure 4.7. Cow horn core and skull fragment from the British guard house.

horn was removed for use as raw material.

The domestic nature of the soldiers' occupation may be observed further in the multiple evidence of cottage production. Wampum in several stages of production, leather fragments from shoe making or repair, scraps of iron and brass, a number of straight pins, and even the raw material for basket making, a coiled strip of birch bark, were present. The most direct evidence of the soldiers' domestic life at this location may be the remains of a small puppy apparently buried in front of the guard house.

The comparison of the collection made in 1972 from the interior of the guard house with that from the 1998 excavation of the drainage trench in front of the structure demonstrated a basic similarity. There are military items in both collections, although the quantity is small. Over 70 percent of the pipe-stem bore diameters from both collections were 4/64 and 5/64 inch, which are associated with dates from 1720 to 1800, clearly representing a mid-eighteenth-century occupation (Deetz 1977). Tobacco pipes from both the interior and exterior of the guard house were marked with the initials of the pipe maker Robert Tippets. This mark has been recorded at many eighteenth-century military sites in New York State, such as Fort Hunter, Fort Ticonderoga, and Fort William Henry (Moody and Fisher 1989).

The ceramic collection from the 1972 excavations in the interior of the guard house is primarily tin-glazed buff earthenware, lead-glazed buff earthenware, and white salt-glazed stoneware. The exterior collection contains sherds of these ceramic types, in addition to sherds of later-manufactured creamware and pearlware. The similarity of the two collections reflects a single occupation, while the longer time frame of the exterior collection is viewed as a result of the later flooring of the building, which left only the very earliest occupation trash present within the guard house. Additional support for this interpretation is present in the mean ceramic dates for the two collections. The interior collection produced a mean ceramic date of 1754, which is slightly earlier than the mean ceramic date of 1763 for the exterior collection. Both of these dates are the result of a ceramic collection that was manufactured in the early decades of the third quarter of the eighteenth century.

The archaeological collection represents material items discarded from the occupation of the guard house, the material evidence of the soldiers' daily life in the center of the city. This trash was located only in the vicinity of the guard house in the center of State Street and does not reflect general urban waste discarded across the entire street as observed at other locations in Albany. The material relates to the military occupation of the guard house during and after the French and Indian War, with the additional evidence of continued use by military occupants during the Revolutionary War. The objects found outside the guard house are very similar to those found within the guard house during the earlier 1972 investigation.

Summary

The English colonial contest against the French in the eighteenth century resulted in continued English occupation of the Dutch community at Albany. The town was fortified for protection from the French and for control of the hostile Dutch colonists. This led to the construction of a guard house within the center of the town that enabled the British military to watch over the hostile inhabitants.

Archaeological evidence from this guard house reflects well-supplied garrison soldiers and their continued presence after the French were defeated. The soldiers in the city had access to a wide variety of material culture. They engaged in the local economy through cottage production and/or repair of wampum, shoes, and baskets. The occupation by the military after the treaty of 1763 points to the increased tension between the colony and the British, resulting in the continuing need for a police force within the town.

Just before the beginning of the American Revolution, the British abandoned Albany, and the Continental Army took over this position. This demonstrated a new political order in the city. In contrast, the trash discarded by the new occupants of the guard house reflected the continued acquisition and use of English consumer goods during the revolution.

Acknowledgments

The excavations at the British guard house were conducted under an interagency agreement between the New York State Education Department (SED) and the New York State Department of Transportation (DOT). I would like to thank these agencies for their efforts in this project. Particularly important to the completion of this research were Peter Howard and Tom Giammattei of DOT and John Hart and Clifford Seigfried at SED. The cooperation and aid of the contractor, Herb Bohl, and his crew working on the Pearl Street Reconstruction Project were appreciated. Paul Huey, Lois Feister, and Joe McEvoy shared their field notes, artifact inventory, references, and observations on this site.

Staff at the New York State Museum who contributed to this project in the field and lab include Nancy Davis, Scott Cardinal, Aaron Gore, George Bailey, Joel Ross, Ben Kahn, Pat Fortunato, Mike Twist, Tracey Thomas, Rebecca Erwin, Amber Raggie, Hillary Pielet, and Tiffany Streeter. Lihua Shi completed the drawings included here.

References Cited

Anon. n.d. *Plan of the City of Albany, 1756 and 1757.* The Crown Collection, Series I, Vol. 2, No. 39. New York State Library, Albany.

Carola, C. 1999. Doodle a Ditty with History. *Albany Times Union,* July 4, p. D-7.

Colden, C. 1853. Colden's Letter to Secretary Conway, New York, February 22, 1766. In *Documents Relating to the Colonial History of the State of New York,* Vol. 7, edited by E.B. O'Callaghan and B. Fernow, p. 812. Weed, Parsons and Co., Albany.

Deetz, J. 1977. *In Small Things Forgotten: The Archeology of Early American Life.* Anchor Books, Doubleday, Garden City, N.Y.

Grant, A. 1903. *Memoirs of an American Lady.* Dodd, Mead and Company, New York.

Hackett, D.G. 1991. *The Rude Hand of Innovation: Religion and Social Order in Albany, New York 1652–1836.* Oxford University Press, New York.

Huey, P.R. 1988. *Aspects of Continuity and Change in Colonial Dutch Material Culture at Fort Orange 1624–1664.* Doctoral dissertation, University of Pennsylvania, Philadelphia. University Microfilms, Ann Arbor, Mich.

Johnson, W. 1996. Journal of Warren Johnson, 1760–1761. In *Mohawk Country, Early Narratives About a Native People,* edited by D.R. Snow, C.T. Gehring, and W.A. Starna, pp. 250–273. Syracuse University Press, Syracuse, N.Y.

Kenney, A. 1969. *The Gansevoorts of Albany: Dutch Patricians in the Upper Hudson Valley.* Syracuse University Press, Syracuse, N.Y.

McAnear, B. 1947. The Albany Stamp Act Riots. *The William and Mary Quarterly* 4(4):486–498.

Merwick, D. 1981. Becoming English: Anglo-Dutch Conflict in the 1670s in Albany, New York. *New York History* 62:389–414.

———. 1990. *Possessing Albany, 1630–1710: The Dutch and English Experiences.* Cambridge University Press, New York.

Moody, K., and Fisher, C.L. 1989. Archaeological Evidence of the Colonial Occupation at Schoharie Crossing State Historic Site, Montgomery County, New York. *The Bulletin: Journal of the New York State Archaeological Association* 99:1–13.

Morgan, E.S., and Morgan, H.M. 1995. *The Stamp Act Crisis: Prologue to Revolution.* University of North Carolina Press, Chapel Hill.

Murray, S. 1999. *America's Song: The Story of "Yankee Doodle."* Images from the Past, Bennington, Vt.

CHAPTER 5

Out of the Ashes of Craft, the Fires of Consumerism: A 1797 Deposit in Downtown Albany

Matthew Kirk

August 4, 1797: It was a warm night, and a gentle breeze pushed across the Hudson River from the southeast. An ember of flame caught the wind and floated into a bale of hay in the stable of Widow A. Bradt on Montgomery Street, in what is today downtown Albany. Soon the summer heat was magnified by a tremendous fire that swept over three city blocks, consuming 216 structures including homes, businesses, stables, and warehouses. No one was killed in the blaze, but nearly 1,000 people were left homeless (*Albany Centinel* 1797).

As part of the data retrieval plan for the Picotte–New York Department of Environmental Conservation (DEC) site excavations, located in downtown Albany, structural remains from the 1797 fire were actively sought (Figures 1.1 and 5.1). Evidence from the fire was an important component of our excavations for two main reasons. First, a burn level could aid in interpreting and dating stratigraphic levels, and second, it was possible that significant deposits dating from the fire could be found in situ.

To positively identify structural remains from the 1797 fire, two criteria had to be met. First, the structure had to show obvious signs of fire, including burned wood and artifacts. Second, the structure would have to be oriented along the pre-1797 street alignment (Figure 5.1). Following the fire, several streets in the vicinity of the project area were realigned to their present locations. Most significant to this discussion is Watervliet Street that ran at an odd angle in relation to other streets and subsequently became the modern-day route of Broadway, previously Market Street (Figure 5.2).

Through a bit of luck, a good research design, and hard work, three pre-1797 structures were positively identified. This discussion focuses on the best-preserved ones, at what later became 611–613 Broadway.

Excavations by Hartgen Archeological Associates, Inc., in 1998 uncovered an area approximately 14 feet by 15+ feet of the bottom floor of a house. The remains of the house consisted of field stone foundation walls, brick and mortar exterior walls, and wood flooring and interior walls. The floor boards and associated sleepers were highly charred but were so well preserved that individual wide board planks could easily be identified (Figure 5.3). Following the fire the shell of the building was demolished in situ and the charred debris used to fill the lot, leaving a mass of brick, mortar, and ash directly above the foundation.

Maps, deeds, and other historic accounts concur that the property complete with "dwelling house, storehouse, and stable" was owned and occupied by John Bogart (*Albany Centinel* 1797). Following the fire, he retained ownership for at least a year. By 1800 General Philip Schuyler purchased the property, likely as a speculator in the real estate market.

Excavation of the house uncovered the remains of one interior wall and a possible fireplace base. Within one of the interior walls of the structure was a small pit feature (Figure 5.4). Inside the pit was a small, rope-tied barrel. The barrel staves and ropes had disintegrated, but impressions from the ropes were clearly visible in the clay of the pit. The function of

People, Places, and Material Things: Historical Archaeology of Albany, New York edited by Charles L. Fisher, New York State Museum Bulletin 499, © 2003 by the University of the State of New York, New York State Education Department, Albany, New York.

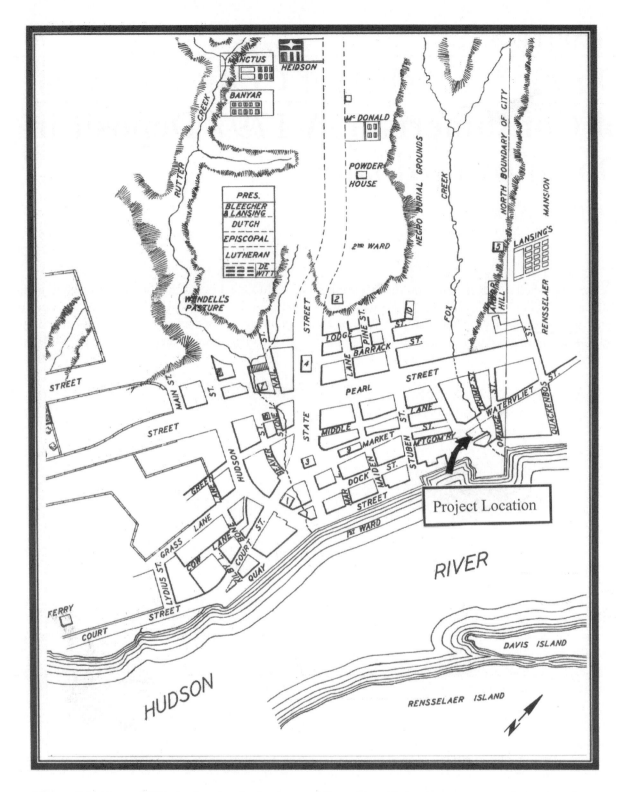

Figure 5.1. Picotte–DEC site location in downtown Albany, New York, shown on a rendering based on Simeon DeWitt's 1794 *Map of the City of Albany*, with the old Watervliet Street alignment.

this pit remains a mystery. Barrels are often used as privies, but this one lacked the night soil typical of privies. It may have been used for food storage or a hiding place for valuables. Artifacts recovered from the barrel pit include: a knife with a bone handle, heavy iron chain links, an axe head, a well hook, var-

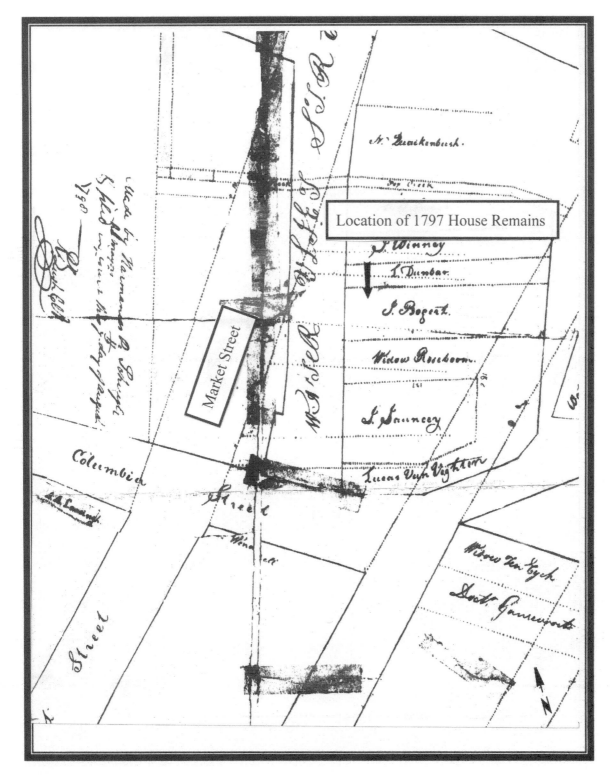

Location of 1797 House Remains

Market Street

Figure 5.2. Ca. 1798 *Map of the City of Albany* (Albany County Hall of Records). Area of 1797 fire shown with both the old Watervliet Street and the new Market Street (later renamed Broadway) alignment.

ious ceramic sherds, and a badly crushed pocket watch, among various other broken and whole items. Approximately 50 feet northeast of the house was

a wood-lined privy (Figure 5.5). Like the house structure, the privy also showed signs of burning, and it too was oriented along the old Watervliet Street

Figure 5.3. View south of the 1797 house-remains. At the far end is a fireplace base. The interior wall is to the right, and the partially excavated floorboards and associated sleepers are in the center. The trench from which the field stone exterior wall was robbed is in the immediate foreground.

Figure 5.4. The excavated pit feature within the western portion of the interior wall.

Figure 5.5. Interior view of excavated wooden privy with a clay-lined bottom. Note the charred wood at the top of the privy walls.

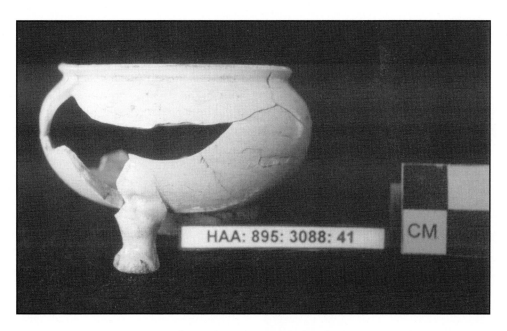

Figure 5.6. Creamware saltcellar with anthropomorphic foot, recovered from the debris level immediately above the burned floorboards.

alignment. The privy contained various ceramics, the majority of which was creamware, as well as numerous bottles and faunal remains. A mean ceramic date of 1794 was calculated from 277 diagnostic ceramic sherds that were recovered (Rosenswig 1999).

The assemblage from the house provides us with

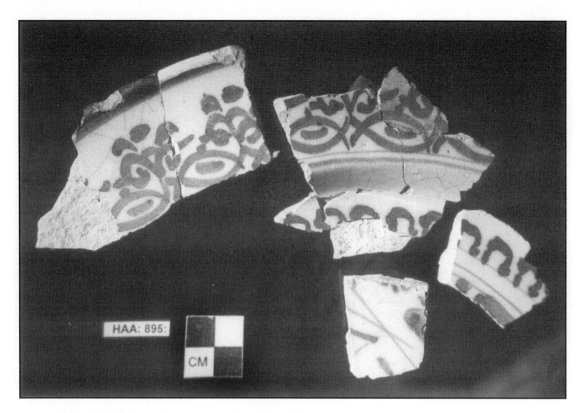

Figure 5.7. Tin-glazed enamel plate with Sepharitic letter decorations.

an excellent opportunity to study the consumption patterns of its residents. Most of the artifacts recovered from the house were found in the demolition

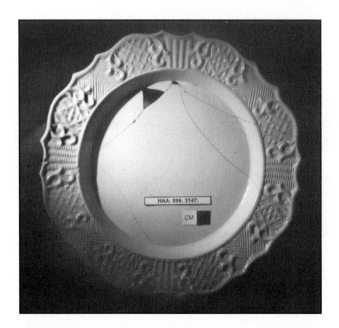

Figure 5.8. Dot, diaper, and basket-weave patterned white salt-glazed stoneware plate, recovered from the pit feature within the house.

layers directly above the burned floorboards and from the small pit feature inside the house. The assemblage displays evidence of burning and represents the contents of the Bogart household when the fire consumed the structure in August 1797. A small number of items were recovered from beneath the floorboards and appear to have been intentionally placed there prior to the fire.

An assortment of ceramic goods was evidenced in the Bogart home including French faience, slip-decorated earthenwares, English delft, tin-glazed earthenware, Chinese export porcelain, white salt-glazed stonewares, clouded wares, creamwares, cauliflowerwares, Jackfield, Staffordshire, Westerwald, Astbury engine-turned redware, and various types of pearlwares, including underglaze blue and brown, transfer print, annular, and polychrome decorations. The ceramic types evidence the household's wide range of tastes, as well as the ability to acquire these goods.

The forms of ceramic goods are nearly as diverse as the types. They include more utilitarian items, such as large bowls, a platter, and plates, as well as tableware with various-sized bowls, plates, saucers, and cups, tea servers, and a saltcellar (Figure 5.6).

Nearly all of these ceramics were produced in fac-

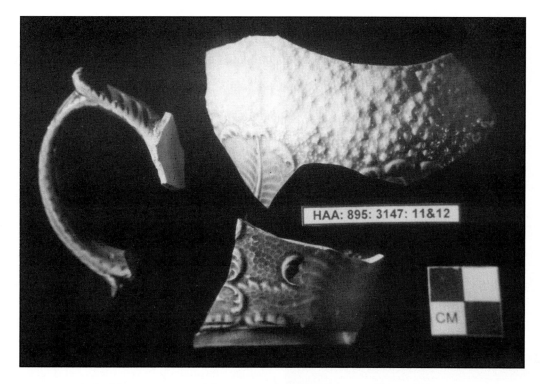

Figure 5.9. Whieldon-ware or "cauliflower-ware" tea server, recovered from the pit feature within the house.

tory settings, mostly in England. What is of particular interest is the way they illustrate the nature of the change in production through time. Many of the items were handcrafted and hand-decorated including the tin-glazed earthenware plates (Figure 5.7) and tiles, finely painted Chinese porcelain, and numerous varieties of slip-decorated earthernware. These goods represent the largest proportions of the ceramic assemblage.

A smaller (and chronologically later) portion of the ceramic assemblage contains mass-produced ceramic vessels. Created through the use of molds, these goods include white salt-glazed stoneware plates with dot, diaper, and basket patterns (Figure 5.8) and a cauliflower-ware tea server (Figure 5.9), among many others. Engine-turned pottery wheels increased production and accelerated the process of decoration in creating ceramics such as Astbury redware.

Mass-produced ceramics were decorated by a variety of means, some by hand and some by other means. Overall there is far less hand decoration on the ceramics, and sherds with hand decoration are limited to sponge painting, annular patterns, and the like with the exception of some hand-decorated pearlwares. Although limited in numbers, several sherds are decorated with an underglaze transfer print, which further accelerated the production process and reduced its cost. In sum, ceramics become lower in quality and easier to produce through time, making these items cheaper and more readily available to Albany households.

In addition to the ceramic goods, many other household items were found within the structure. Glass vessels in the form of wine and case bottles were among the most common. Craftsmen typically free-blew these items, such as the American chestnut bottle found in the demolition layers. A variety of vessel glass stemware fragments was also recovered, including a molded, green tinted wineglass with a diamond relief pattern. Also recovered were fragments of a pharmaceutical bottle embossed with the letters "ROB TURLI 1754". The bottle is likely Robert Turlington's Balsam of Life, an elixir imported from England and available in the United States between 1744 and the mid-nineteenth century (Ketchum 1975). The 1754 version was produced in an effort to stop counterfeit bottle production (Noël Hume 1969).

Like ceramics, glass evidences a change in production style from free-blown to dip-mold and hinge-mold bottles, of which the Robert Turlington medi-

Figure 5.10. Copper alloy, cross pendant, recovered from beneath the burned floorboards.

cine bottle was one of the earliest examples. There were only a few glasshouses in the United States at the end of the eighteenth century, one of which was the Albany Glasshouse in Guilderland (Huey 1980). In this assemblage from the Bogart house, the majority of glass was imported from Europe, more specifically England. European glasshouses specialized in mold-blown and cut glass that flooded the American market.

A large variety of artifacts gives evidence of daily household activities at the Bogart house, including a spigot key for a tap, two tine forks, knifes, an axe blade, a chisel, a wood plane, a horseshoe, lead shot of various calibers, and copper thimbles. It is not possible to describe here the method of manufacture for each item listed, but in general they were likely produced and obtained directly from local craftsmen.

Personal items from this site include apparel and shoe buckles (one heavily filigreed), Revolutionary War buttons with the inscription "USA", numerous other buttons of bone, metal, and glass, a copper alloy cross pendant (Figure 5.10), a variety of jewelry including a drop earring, lice combs, hair brushes, coins, and the pocket watch. With the exception of the coins, artisans and crafters produced most of these articles. Mass production had not yet begun for many of these types of goods. But, like ceramics and glass production, a shift from traditional handcraft to more mechanized production was imminent.

One unexpected object found in the assemblage is

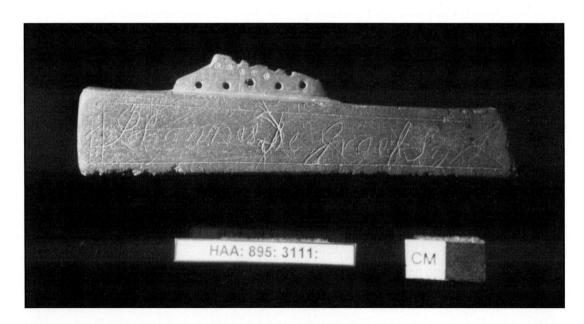

Figure 5.11. Red calumet pipe fragment engraved "Johannes De Graef Syn" (*syn* meaning "his" in Dutch). Found intentionally placed under the burned floorboards.

a calumet pipe worked from catlinite-like stone (Figure 5.11). This, along with the cross pendant and other items, was intentionally placed under the floorboards of the house. The partially broken pipe measures approximately 11.4 cm long 2 cm wide and 2 cm thick, with the bowl now missing. "Johannes De Graef Syn" is engraved on the sides of the soft stone pipe, meaning Johannes De Graef "his" in Dutch, likely meaning "his pipe." These pipes are typically associated with Native Americans, and some have been excavated from Seneca villages in western New York State that were occupied during the late seventeenth and early eighteenth centuries. Likely the pipe would have been used to engender relations between Native American traders and possibly the owner of the pipe Johannes De Graef.

In many ways the pipe symbolizes the transition of the entire assemblage from the colonial to federalist period of Albany's history. During the seventeenth and early eighteenth centuries, the economy of Albany was predicated on the ability of Native Americans to obtain fur. By 1797 the Revolutionary War and new westward expansion had broken down the colonial economy once reliant on Native American groups. By the end of the eighteenth century, Albany merchants shifted focus from furs to agricultural and mercantile trade with Europe and other emerging American markets.

The Bogart house assemblage contains a significant quantity and variety of everyday household goods, the majority of which were handmade, produced by craftsmen and artisans. Examples of these include the hand-painted ceramics, hand-blown glass, the pocket watch, jewelry, hand-forged nails, and shoe buckles. The assemblage also contains goods that were just beginning to be mass produced, including white salt-glazed stoneware with dot, diaper, and basket patterns, cauliflower-ware, Astbury, and even coin currency and medicine bottles all manufactured in significant quantities through the use of molds and dies.

The artifacts from the pre-1797 household deposit suggest a certain level of wealth and access to consumer goods. The household was not constrained in its selection of goods, particularly ceramics, which served more than a utilitarian function as evidenced by the recovery of cauliflower-ware. A vessel of this type would not be well suited for the daily usage of eating, drinking, and cleaning due in part to its unwieldy shape, thin fragile body, and lack of functional elements. Cauliflower-ware is an aesthetic form reflecting the wealth and status of the Bogarts.

John Bogart and his family were not excessively wealthy by the standards of the day. More likely they were part of a growing middle class. By the end of the eighteenth century, Albany was a major port city that provided easy access to New York City, the entire eastern seaboard, and even Europe and Asia via the Hudson River and the Atlantic Ocean. Tons of consumer goods moved in and out of the city on a daily basis, thus affording its residents the opportunity to purchase a variety of items at relatively low costs. The port city not only provided opportunity for the middle class, but also was a catalyst in creating new middle-class citizens. Members of this burgeoning new social order in Albany now could obtain higher-status goods, such as cauliflower-ware, costume jewelry, and timepieces that were once reserved for the elite.

Throughout the nineteenth century, mass production of goods and new transportation routes into interior portions of America increased. The evolution of the canal, and later the railroad systems, brought not only consumer goods to the American interior but the opportunity of advancement into the middle class. A new economic age was emerging where mass production and industrialization was fueled by the mass consumption of goods, particularly at the household level.

The 1797 Bogart household actively sought and consumed material goods at an impressive rate, as evidenced by the quantity and variety of recovered artifacts. This assemblage of household materials provides us with an opportunity to study the consumer habits of middle class Albanians at the very genesis of a new social and economic order. Craft-produced items typically associated with the colonial period are still present within the assemblage, but consumption patterns are shifting toward mass-produced items, lower in quality yet more abundant and lower in price.

Just as the last embers of eighteenth-century colonialism were smoldering, the new fires of nineteenth-century consumerism were about to ignite. Herein lies the potential and value of this pre-1797 household assemblage, which reflects middle-class household consumption patterns on the eve of industrialization.

References Cited

Albany Centinel. 1797. Dreadful Conflagration, August 8. American Antiquarian Society, Worchester, Mass.

City of Albany. 1798. *Map of the City of Albany.* Albany County Hall of Records, Albany, N.Y.

Dewitt, S. 1794. *Map of the City of Albany.* New York State Library, Albany.

Huey, P.R. 1980. The Albany Glassworks from 1790 to 1800: A Study of American Industry During the Federal Period. *Journal of Glass Studies* 22:36–52.

Ketchum, W.C. 1975. *A Treasury of American Bottles.* Bobbs Merrill, New York.

Noël Hume, I. 1969. *A Guide to Artifacts of Colonial America.* Vintage Books, New York.

Rosenswig, R.M. 1999. Nineteenth Century Urbanism and Public Health: The Evidence of Twelve Privies in Albany, New York. *Northeast Anthropology* 58:27–45.

CHAPTER 6

Skeletal Analysis of the Human Remains from the Lutheran Church Lot, 1670–1816

Shawn M. Phillips

Introduction

Skeletal remains from the historic Lutheran Church lot in Albany were discovered and excavated by the New York State Museum's Cultural Resource Survey staff through an agreement with the New York State Department of Transportation during the reconstruction of Pearl Street in 1998 (Figures 1.1 and 6.1). Five individuals were identified, three individuals within separate wooden coffins and two individuals

Figure 6.1. Photograph of New York State Museum archaeologists excavating Burial 1 under shelter by artificial light.

People, Places, and Material Things: Historical Archaeology of Albany, New York edited by Charles L. Fisher, New York State Museum Bulletin 499, © 2003 by the University of the State of New York, New York State Education Department, Albany, New York.

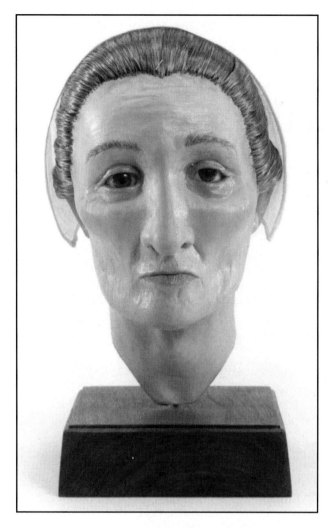

Figure 6.2. Facial reconstruction created upon the cast of the adult female skull from Burial 1. Gay Malin, New York State Museum.

with a Lutheran ceremony. Prior to reburial, plaster casts were made of selected bones from each individual for future study. The cast of the female's skull was the basis of a facial reconstruction, which was carried out by Gay Malin of the New York State Museum (Figure 6.2).

The initial background research identified the current intersection of Pearl Street, Norton Street, and Howard Street as the location of the Lutheran Church and cemetery dating from the 1670s to 1816 (Fisher 1997). Although documentary sources indicated that the graves were removed from this location prior to the street enlargement in the 1790s, archaeological investigations were recommended to search for evidence of the seventeenth-century church and the church house constructed here in 1742. In the course of this field study, human remains were discovered and excavated.

The three individual burials were adults (Table 6.1) interred before the middle of the eighteenth century, based upon the artifacts found in the grave shafts. The burial records were insufficient to identify the names of these individuals and reveal why they were left behind when the cemetery was relocated. The three individuals were within coffins with their heads placed at the west in the grave and their feet on the east end. Their location beneath the west side of Pearl Street resulted in disturbances from utility lines constructed throughout the twentieth century.

Skeletal Analysis of Burial 1

Burial 1 was approximately 95 percent complete and was well preserved. The skull and mandible were present, and all the postcranial elements were represented. Throughout the entire skeleton, the external bone surfaces were weathered in only a few locations. Thus the condition of the remains was optimal for most macroscopic observations. Moreover, the skeletal remains exhibited minimal postmortem damage.

represented by a single bone each recovered from grave-shaft fill. These remains were examined at the New York State Museum following recording standards presented in Buikstra and Ubelaker (1994) and subsequently reburied in the Albany Rural Cemetery

Table 6.1. Summary of Burials

	Sex	Age (yr)	Ancestry	Stature
Burial 1	Female	40–45	European	5 ft, 1 in
Burial 2	Male	25–30	European	5 ft, 10 in
Burial 3	Male	40–45	European	5 ft, 6 in

Of the five individuals recovered, Burial 1 was in the best condition.

Dental Health

The dental health of Burial 1 was particularly poor. Examination of the visible tooth sockets (19) showed that 12 of the teeth (63 percent) were lost before death. We can tell the teeth were lost before death because the alveolar bone, the bone structure that anchors the teeth, was quite resorbed. The teeth that were present were in poor condition. Eighty-six percent (6) of the remaining 7 teeth evidenced disease in that they displayed some destruction of the enamel or dentine. Also two abscesses were present on the inner surface of the maxillary alveolar bone. The combination of high percentages of tooth loss, dental disease, and the presence of the alveolar abscesses indicate this individual suffered a great deal from oral infections that would have been detrimental to her quality of life.

Diet

Diet can be difficult to assess from skeletal remains. The presence of dental calculus observed on the maxillary molars indicates a basic diet composed of starchy, gruel-type foods. In addition, the remaining teeth were marked with linear enamel hypoplasias (LEH). LEH are enamel densifications that occur when growth and development are arrested due to severe bouts of stress (Aufderheide and Rodriquez-Matin 1998; Hillson 1996). In most cases the stress is associated with acute infection, lack of adequate nutrition, or a combination of both. The presence of LEH on Burial 1's dentition indicates some form of severe stress was experienced and survived during late infancy or early childhood, the period when the permanent dentition develops. Finally, the right and the left tibiae were slightly symmetrically bowed. Tibial bowing is normally associated with rickets, a nutritional deficiency that affects normal growth and development. Rickets is caused by a deficiency in vitamin D, which is required to properly metabolize calcium (Aufderheide and Rodriquez-Matin 1998; Roberts and Manchester 1995). If there is a deficiency in vitamin D, long bones will not "harden" normally as they develop, because calcium is not available, and they will bend under the stresses of body weight and gravity, resulting in bowed long bones.

Paleopathologies

Burial 1 exhibited a variety of general and specific skeletal lesions. None of the lesions was directly linked to a cause of death. However, most lesions can provide information about the epidemiological environment in which the person lived. Paleopathological data can shed light on cultural, economic, and behavioral patterns that are not available in any other form in the historical or archaeological record. Dental health and paleopathologies indicative of diet were discussed above, so those categories will not be repeated here.

The skeletal remains of Burial 1 had four separate areas affected by some form of infection. First, Burial 1 had some of the lesions that are suggestive of a trepanematosis infection. For example, the skull exhibited a series of approximately 18 diseased pits on the outer table of the right and left parietals, symmetrically positioned around the posterior aspect of the sagittal suture. The diseased pits, defined both by appearance and positioning, were caries sicca. Caries sicca are diagnostic markers of trepanemal infection, which is caused by a microorganism known as *treponema* (Aufderheide and Rodriquez-Matin 1998). Among Europeans in North America, trepanemal infection was most commonly spread venereally and is known as syphilis. Though caries sicca are diagnostic of trepanemal infection, other markers such as the resorption of the nasal aperture and symmetrical infections of the long bones were not present. Thus the diagnosis of a trepanemal infection must remain tentative. Through the process of differential diagnosis, other possible infections have been determined to be less likely to be the cause of the lesions than trepanematosis. The second lesion was more clearly identified. An active infection was present at the time of death in the maxillary sinus cavity. The reactive new bone present in the cavity is diagnostic of sinusitis (Roberts and Manchester 1995). The third infection identified was on the visceral aspect of the midribs, where there was reactive, new bone and vascular impressions buttressed by sclerotic formations that thickened the ribs. These rib lesions represent an upper respiratory infection that was related to the sinusitis infection. Finally, the fourth lesion was periostitis on the left tibia and fibula. Periosteal reactions are nonspecific infections that can arise from trauma external to the body or a systemic infection (Aufderheide and Rodriquez-Matin 1998).

In addition to infections, Burial 1 also had a pattern of lesions suggestive of a metabolic disease. The intermediate foot phalanges of Burial 1 had a thin, "waisted" appearance that deviated from normal variation. Also, the second right and left cuneiforms had large diseased lesions that exhibited a "burst-bubble" appearance that suggests gout (Baker, personal communication 1998). Gout is a metabolic disease that is characterized by increased serum levels of urate and the deposition of urate crystals into the joints (Aufderheide and Rodriquez-Matin 1998). Although no other disease fits the diagnostic pattern present except gout, there are some variations from the typical pattern that prevent a firm diagnosis. Gout predominantly affects males or older individuals, and in nearly all cases the first metatarsals are affected. Because gout is the most parisimonious diagnosis, it is possible that the epidemiological pattern for gout was different in historical populations. Perhaps the etiology of gout can be further investigated to better understand the discontinuities seen with this individual and the typical, contemporary clinical sufferer of gout.

Finally, the joints of Burial 1 tended to be free of the advanced stages of degenerative joint disease. Only the glenoid fossa of the temporal bones and the mandibular condyles exhibited advanced osteoarthritis (OA). OA of this joint is referred to as temporal-mandibular joint disease (TMJ). It is possible that this woman was engaged in an activity or labor that put proportionally more stress on the joint in comparison to other joints. Another possibility is that her advanced tooth loss resulted in extension of the mandible to compensate when eating.

Skeletal Analysis of Burial 2

Burial 2 was approximately 90 percent complete and was well preserved. The most salient problems with completeness and preservation resulted from postmortem damage associated with construction activities that predate the 1998 project. The cortical bone of the skeletal elements that were present was in excellent condition for the purposes of macroscopic analysis. Of the five individuals recovered, Burial 2 was as well preserved as Burial 1 with the exception of the absence of an intact skull.

Dental Health

The dental health of this young adult male was notably poor. Examination of the visible tooth sockets (16) showed that seven of the teeth (44 percent) were lost before death. Of the nine teeth present, one tooth was carious (11 percent), one tooth had an abscess in the alveolar bone, and there were two abscesses in the alveolar bone associated with lost teeth. Although the dental health of Burial 2 did not appear to be as poor as Burial 1, it should be noted that Burial 2 was 15 to 20 years younger than Burial 1.

Diet

There were few data available to make assessments of dietary status. LEH was observed on the teeth of Burial 2. Given the conflicting factors that LEH are markers of growth arrest and this individual was tall, one may conclude that an adequate diet was available during or after the stress that caused the LEH. Presumably, proper nutrition enabled him to survive the early life stress and recover with no lingering biological consequences. The dental health of Burial 2 suggests a diet high in carbohydrates. This assertion is based on the assumption that the high degree of tooth loss resulted from dental caries (Hillson 1996). It is possible, however, that the tooth loss was caused by trauma, extraction, or some other infectious process that is no longer detectable.

Paleopathologies

Aside from the dental pathologies mentioned above, Burial 2 exhibited three separate infectious lesions. The most diagnostic lesions were on the lower thoracic vertebrae, T-11 and T-12. The two vertebrae were compressed and created an angle in the spine, kyphosis, with new bone formation connecting the two. The new bone was an indication that some healing occurred after the compression of the two vertebrae. Also there were diagnostic pits on the anterior aspects of vertebrae T-10 to L-1. This constellation of lesions is consistent with an advanced case of tuberculosis (TB) (Aufderheide and Rodriquez-Matin 1998). It is likely that the TB infection either caused or contributed to the individual's death. Second, like Burial 1, the visceral aspect of the midribs had reactive bone with vascular impressions and sclerotic buildup. Again, this pattern of lesions on the ribs can be linked with an upper respiratory infection and therefore can be symptomatic of the TB infection. Finally, the right and left tibiae had well-healed periosteal infections, where reactive bone was present on the cortical bone. Because the lesions are symmetrical, it is most likely that they resulted from a systemic infection. It is not likely, however, that the periosteal lesions on the tibiae were directly associated with the TB infection, because that is not part of the typical TB pattern.

There were two areas of the skeleton that exhibited evidence of well-healed trauma. Three left midribs exhibited healed fracture calluses around the midshaft. Also there were two fully fused vertebrae, C-6 and C-7. Vertebral fusion of this type is most likely the result of trauma to the neck. It is possible that the trauma to the ribs and cervical vertebrae occurred at the same time, but there is no way to prove this relationship. It is certain that the trauma occurred long before death, because the fractures healed.

Another significant feature of Burial 2 was that the skeletal muscular markers were overdeveloped and the long bones were quite robust. This suggests that the individual engaged in some form of heavy, routine exertion during life. Also the lower thoracic and first lumbar vertebrae had Schmorl's node depressions, which are caused by heavy lifting. Under the strain of extreme exertion, the intervertebral disks can herniate and rupture into the nearby vertebral body, resulting in a Schmorl's node (Aufderheide and Rodriquez-Matin 1998).

Skeletal Analysis of Burial 3

Burial 3 was approximately 75 to 80 percent complete. The burial was truncated by early twentieth-century utility installations at both ends of the coffin. The disturbance resulted in loss of the cranial elements, upper cervical vertebrae, and both feet. The preservation of the remaining postcranial elements varies from good to poor. The long bones and os coxa were in good condition, but all had some degree of postmortem damage. The ribs and vertebrae were in an advanced weathered state.

Dental Health

Only one isolated tooth, a permanent upper central incisor, was recovered with Burial 3. The incisor was carious. Aside from the loose incisor, a fragment of the mandible was present with one visible molar socket; the molar was lost postmortem. Thus of the known teeth, none was lost before death, but 100 percent was carious. Little can be determined regarding dental health of Burial 3 given the limited data available.

Diet

The one tooth exhibited LEH. Once more, this indicates some form of acute stress that interrupted growth was present during infancy or childhood.

Paleopathologies

Burial 3 had the same visceral rib lesions as those present on Burials 1 and 2. Again, this is indicative of an upper respiratory infection. No other infectious lesion was visible on the remains.

The left radius was fractured on the distal end. The distal articular surface was remodeled due to the fracture, and the left lunate exhibited OA and eburnation as a result of the fracture and a misaligned articulation with the radius. Eburnation is often associated with OA when cartilage is destroyed and bone is exposed. This type of fracture is referred to as Colles' fracture (Ortner and Putschar 1981). The fracture may have been caused by a fall, although it is possible that it could have been related to a combat injury. In either case, it was well healed at the time of death.

The missing aspects of the skeleton and the poor preservation limit the description and analysis. Fortunately, the remains were intact enough for sex, age, and stature determinations (Table 6.1). No clear data is available to confirm ancestry. The one incisor recovered was not shovel shaped, a characteristic of Native Americans although it appears in individuals from other populations (Ubelaker 1989). The individuals represented in Burial 1 and 2 appear to have been of European ancestry. It is likely that Burial 3 was of European descent as well, due to the association among these burials of proximity and similar burial practices.

Commingled Remains

A humerus of a juvenile was commingled with Burial 1. This commingling problem most likely occurred during earlier construction activities that intruded upon both burials. There were no obvious lesions or premortem trauma visible on the humerus.

Two cranial fragments of an infant were commingled with Burial 3. A similar process that commingled the juvenile with Burial 1 also transpired between Burial 3 and the infant remains. There was no indication that more than one individual was interred in a coffin.

Discussion

The skeletal remains associated with the Lutheran Church lot date to the colonial period of northeastern North America, specifically between 1680 and the mid-eighteenth century. The remains demonstrate life experiences that included chronic infections, trauma, nutritional diseases, poor dental health, and acute infections during childhood and adulthood. These stresses notwithstanding, the stature of the individuals does not appear to have been stunted, and they survived many health insults that occurred during their lives. Because the sample size is small and few comparative data are available, few general conclusions can be drawn concerning the unique epidemiological environment of colonial Albany. It is possible to note, however, that the diseases present in the skeletal sample still persist in this century, although most of the illnesses are treatable with modern medicine.

We note the following patterns:

1. All three adults had LEH on their dentition.

2. All three adults had a high percentage of dental caries.

3. Of the two adults who had visible tooth sockets, both had several abscesses and antemortem tooth loss that exceeded 40 percent.

4. All three adults had reactive bone on the visceral aspect of their ribs.

5. None of the adults seemed to have suffered from growth stunting.

These consistencies suggest an environment that was conducive to the spread of infectious diseases. Because the individuals appear to have thrived in this environment and reached heights similar to contemporary Americans, it is likely that adequate nutrition aided the adaptive process that was necessary to survive an environment thick with infectious agents. Even though the individual represented in Burial 2 died at a fairly young age, most likely due to complications associated with TB, he seems to have been an active and strong individual prior to the TB infection, based on long bone robusticity.

Finally, there were some notable differences between the males and the female. Although the female suffered several disease processes, more than the males, her skeletal remains do not exhibit traumatic fractures. Both males had bones with well-healed trauma (ribs, cervical vertebrae, wrist). Also OA is more advanced on the males' skeletal remains in comparison to the female's remains. The difference in trauma and OA may be indicative of highly prescribed gender roles that dictated the social activities and behaviors of males and females during this period of history.

References Cited

Aufderheide, A.C., and Rodriquez-Matin, C. 1998. *Cambridge Encyclopedia of Human Paleopathology.* Cambridge University Press, Cambridge.

Buikstra, J., and Ubelaker, D. (editors). 1994. *Standards for Data Collection of Human Skeletal Remains.* Arkansas Archaeological Survey Research Series, No. 44.

Fisher, C.L. 1997. Archaeological Background Study: PIN 1753.58.121, Pearl Street from McCarty Avenue to Livingston Avenue, City of Albany, New York. Cultural Resource Survey Report, Anthropological Survey, New York State Museum, Albany.

Hillson, S. 1996. *Dental Anthropology.* Cambridge University Press, Cambridge.

Ortner, D.V., and Putschar, W.G.J. 1981. *Identification of Pathological Conditions in Human Skeletal Remains.* Smithsonian Contributions to Anthropology No. 28. Smithsonian Institution Press, Washington, D.C.

Roberts, C., and Manchester, K. 1995. *The Archaeology of Disease.* Cornell University Press, Ithaca, N.Y.

Ubelaker, D. 1989. *Human Skeletal Remains* (2nd ed.). Smithsonian Institution, Taraxacum, Washington, D.C.

CHAPTER 7

Trace Elements and Stable Isotope Analysis of the Human Remains from the Lutheran Church Lot

Charles L. Fisher

Introduction

The diet of the colonial Albany's inhabitants may be derived from historic references, archaeological remains of plant and animal foods, and direct measurements from the physical remains of people. The combination of these three methods provides the most comprehensive picture of the colonial diet. The primary methods of direct investigation of food consumption are trace element and stable isotope analysis (Keegan 1989).

Stable Isotope Analysis

The established relationships between the chemical composition of human bone and the types of food consumed enable the direct study of diet from the analysis of human bone (Ubelaker 1989:141). Stable isotope analysis

> is based on the comparison of values measured in human bone collagen with those measured for items identified as having been consumed, and because isotopic compositions can only be used to distinguish certain food groups rather than individual food items, it is important to remember that this technique is not an independent method of diet reconstruction. (Keegan 1989:224)

Stable isotope ratio analysis was performed on bone samples from each of the three adults excavated from the Lutheran Church lot (Figure 1.1). This analysis was performed by Geochron Laboratories in Cambridge, Massachusetts. They reported their results to the New York State Museum on May 20, 1999, as delta carbon-13 and delta nitrogen-15 values. The values were determined using the notation presented in Katzenberg (2000:313).

Chemical and physical changes may occur in human bone after burial, as a result of the specific soil environment. Because collagen stable isotope values have been found to resist alterations and strontium and stable isotope values in apatite have been found to vary, the latter were not considered here (Katzenberg 1992:109). A small sample is not considered a problem in this analysis "because variation is so small [less than 1 percent] within a group of animals eating the same diet" (Katzenberg 1992:111).

An important application of this technique by archaeologists has been to delineate the introduction of corn agriculture into the Eastern Woodlands. Plants are classified as C3 and C4 plants, based on the way they metabolize carbon dioxide during photosynthesis. Maize, along with sorghum, millet, and sugar cane, is among the C4 plant group.

> One process produces a compound with three carbon atoms (C3 plants) and the other a compound with four carbon atoms (C4 plants). These photosynthetic pathways equate with different proportions of the stable carbon isotopes, carbon-12 and carbon-13. Since carbon in bone collagen comes from foods consumed, the isotopic ratios reflect the proportions of C3 and C4 plants ingested. (Ubelaker 1989:141)

In a well-known example provided by Ubelaker (1989:141), a series of prehistoric skeleton populations from the Eastern Woodlands showed fairly constant, very low, carbon-13 values until approximately A.D. 500. The rapid increase in carbon-13 values after this date reflects increased C4 plants (maize) in the diet. By the late Prehistoric Period, C4 plants make up approximately 70 percent of the diet.

This technique was used to evaluate the role of corn in the diet of the individuals from the Lutheran Church lot in Albany. Janowitz, referring to contemporary documentary sources such as Van de Donck and De Vries, states that maize was "an important part of Dutch-American foodways" by the mid-seventeenth century. Although wheat and rye were grown in New Netherland,

> maize was both bought from the Indians and taken from them as taxes . . . Its cultivation by Europeans was common by mid-century . . . maize had the advantage of growing in all sorts of soils and could be cultivated with a simple broad hoe rather than a plow . . . It also had a higher yield than other grains. (1993:12–13)

Cornmeal was eaten in a porridge, similar to the way the Dutch used European grains. These dishes were

> important components of the Dutch diets, especially among the middle and lower economic groups. In the mid-18th century, the Swedish naturalist Pehr Kalm . . . observed that sappan [cornmeal porridge] was a universal dish among Dutch-Americans in Albany and New York City. (Janowitz 1993:13)

Direct evidence of the consumption of this dish was observed in the skeletal analysis of the individuals from the Lutheran Church lot. Dental calculus was found on the maxillary molars of Burial 1, an adult female. This is "indicative of a basic diet composed of starchy, gruel-type foods" (Phillips 1998).

Janowitz concluded that the documentary evidence indicates that the Dutch in New Netherland maintained a diet that was essentially European, with the addition of some available foods. "Common foods were grain products, meat, and fish. Domestic and wild animals were eaten as well as fish and domestic and wild birds. Maize was the most important adopted food" (1993:14).

The delta carbon-13 values, in parts per thousand, for the three adults from the Lutheran Church lot were as follows: -19.0 for Burial 1, -16.0 for Burial 2, and -18.1 for Burial 3. Burial 2 evidenced the greatest

consumption of C4 plants. Burials 1 and 3 appear to have consumed fewer plants of the C4 class (Ubelaker 1989:141).

The distribution of

> values for C3 and C4 plants is bimodal with virtually no overlap between them. C3 plants include temperate grasses, all trees and shrubs, all fruits and nuts, and cultivated roots and tubers; C4 plants are predominately tropical grasses (e.g. corn, sugarcane, sorghum, some amaranths, and some chenopods) and other pioneering weeds. (Keegan 1989:227)

The value range for C3 plants is -20 to -35, whereas that for C4 plants is -9 to -14 (Katzenberg 2000:314). When the difference is considered between the delta carbon-13 in the diet and the value found in the bones, which is about 5 parts per thousand greater in bone (Katzenberg 2000: 314), the adults from the Lutheran Church lot are associated with the consumption of C4 plants, such as maize.

Nitrogen isotopes were evaluated for additional evidence of diet. Delta nitrogen-15 values have been found greater among human populations with marine-based diets than among those with terrestrial diets (Ubelaker 1989:142). The values for the individuals from the Lutheran Church lot varied between 9.6 and 10.8, suggestive of a mixed diet rather than one centered on either terrestrial or marine foods. Nitrogen isotope values between 9 and 10 and delta carbon-13 values between -15 and -20 may represent a diet focused on mixed feeder herbivores, both grazers and browsers (Keegan 1989:227). If this is correct, the individuals from the church lot depended largely upon wild and domestic animals.

Trace Elements

Analysis of trace elements was performed by Inductively Coupled Plasma on bone samples from each adult individual recovered from the Lutheran Church lot. EMSL Analytical, Inc., of Westmont, New Jersey, conducted this analysis. Their report was received in April 1999 (Table 7.1).

Trace element analysis is based upon the idea that

> Foods of animal origin have inherently higher concentrations of certain elements, such as zinc and copper, than those derived from plants. Conversely, other elements including strontium, . . . and calcium are usually found in higher

Table 7.1. Summary of Trace Element Analysis

Element (in ppm)	Burial 1	Burial 2	Burial 3
Arsenic	< 49.9	< 49.9	< 49.9
Copper	66.6	102.0	25.4
Lead	42.7	147.0	36.7
Mercury	.24	.90	<.10
Strontium	268.0	513.0	681.0
Zinc	145.0	1660.0	235.0

quantities in plant resources. (Sandford 1992:83)

Variation in the chemical content of the soil and water environment of the burials may result in substantial contributions to the quantities of trace elements in human bone. As a result, the trace element comparisons among the three individuals found in the Lutheran Church lot may be more meaningful than comparisons to other skeletal populations, because they were in the same postmortem environment. At the same time, there is evidence that some trace element quantities in human bone are altered very little by their surroundings. "Zinc and strontium have been widely regarded by past researchers as less susceptible to diagenesis" (Sandford 1992:87).

Strontium

Strontium is a useful indicator of the quantity of plant consumption, in part due to its relative stability. Diets consisting primarily of plants will result in greater strontium quantities in human bone. The lowest levels of strontium may be expected among groups with high proportions of meat in their diets (Aufderheide 1989:243; Ubelaker 1989:142).

All three of the individuals studied have strontium levels higher than those reported usually for modern adults. The strontium content of Burial 1 is 268 parts per million, that of Burial 2 is 513 parts per million, and the amount in Burial 3 is 681. "Common adult skeletal strontium concentrations are in the range of 150 to 250 ppm (ash)" (Aufderheide 1989:243). This implies that the amount of meat in their diet was less than the stable isotope information suggests, and the amount of plant material greater. The consumption of

shellfish, however, has been noted to greatly increase the strontium content, creating the erroneous appearance of a vegetarian diet (Aufderheide 1989). Both clam and oyster shells are prevalent in archaeological contexts at the Lutheran Church lot and seventeenth- and eighteenth-century contexts in Albany in general. Oysters were mentioned as food in historical accounts, such as Danckaerts' journal of 1679–1680 (Janowitz 1993:14). Oysters and other shellfish are frequently depicted as foods in Dutch art of the seventeenth century. Most likely, the consumption of shellfish rather than an absence of meat in their diet created higher levels of strontium in these individuals. Other trace element amounts, such as that of zinc and copper, support this conclusion.

The strontium content among the three individuals from colonial Albany may reflect some differences in the type of vegetables they consumed. The higher strontium levels in Burials 3 and 2 may reflect consumption of more root crops than leafy vegetables, as evident in Burial 1 (Ubelaker 1989:142).

Zinc

The normal bone content of zinc is about 200 parts per million in modern adults (Aufderheide 1989:247). Zinc is present in many foods, but particularly concentrated in meats, seafoods, and some crustaceans.

Of all the study elements, zinc emerged as the most promising dietary discrimination, demonstrating significantly higher levels in the hunting and gathering population and appearing to have been less subject to post mortem alteration. (Sandford 1992:90)

Burial 1 had slightly below the normal content of zinc, with 145 parts per million, and Burial 3's value of 235 parts per million was slightly above the normal content. Problems resulting from zinc deficiency include growth retardation, infections, and sexual immaturity (Aufderheide 1989, Table 1). At present, however, there is no information concerning the level of zinc in human bones of individuals suffering from zinc deficiency. Although bone from Burial 1 had a low zinc content and suffered from several infections, we do not know if this was a result of zinc deficiency. The exceptionally high zinc content in Burial 2 (1660 ppm) may be the result of far greater quantities of meat and shellfish consumption by this person than the other two individuals.

Lead

Studies of prehistoric skeletons from North America generally indicate an absence of lead. This is in contrast to modern adult Americans, who average about 40 parts per million of lead in bones. Two of the burials from the Lutheran Church lot (1 and 3) had lead amounts of 42.7 and 36.7 parts per million, within the range of modern individuals. Burial 2, however, had a lead quantity of 147 parts per million, well above the usual amount in modern individuals.

Some researchers have suggested that different lead content in human bones from colonial cemeteries is a result of status differences. For example,

> mean skeletal lead content of the wealthy owner's family members on an A.D. 1700 plantation was found to be 185 ppm (ash), whereas that of their largely black slave labor group interred in a segregated cemetery was only 35 pps (ash). (Aufderheide 1989:252)

The social dimensions of lead use in the colonial period include pewter plates and tankards and lead-glazed ceramics by wealthy individuals. In contrast, unglazed earthenware and vegetable containers were used to a greater degree by the laboring poor.

> For tablewares, the poorest [Dutch] used red earthenwares, wood, or ate directly on the table; the slightly better off also used pewter, particularly as serving vessels. Middle-class households used delftwares—the generic term for tin-enameled refined earthenwares, which include earlier majolica and later faience . . . and pewter. The elite used pewter plates for the most part. (Janowitz 1993:8)

The average lead values from the colonial Albany's Lutherans suggest a continuity of social divisions in Dutch traditional foodways in New Netherland. The use of pewter by the wealthy members of society and the lack of pewter among the poor resulted in different lead values. A higher status lifestyle in regard to access to lead is evident in the individual represented in Burial 2 from the Lutheran Church lot.

A number of other sources of lead in the eighteenth century have been identified (Emsley 1987). Lead piping, lead storage tanks, canned food was contaminated by lead solder, lead paint, and lead acetate hair dye were all in use at this time. These items are usually associated with wealth and support the social differences in lead exposure. In addition, lead was used in medicines for treating tuberculosis (TB),

venereal disease, hemorrhages, and diarrhea (Emsley 1987:66). Because the individual represented by Burial 2 suffered from TB, it is possible that medicine use contributed to the high lead content in this skeleton.

Copper

The usual bone content of copper is about 25 parts per million in modern adults (Aufderheide 1989). Two of the individuals from the Lutheran Church lot contained greater amounts than expected. Burial 1 had a copper content of 66.6 parts per million, and Burial 2 had a copper content of 102 parts per million. Burial 3 had an amount considered average, 25.4 parts per million. Although anemia is associated with copper deficiency, the result of excessive copper is unknown. The high amount of copper in Burial 2 may be a result of a large amount of shellfish, particularly oysters, in the diet of this individual (Medeiros and Percival 2003). This is consistent with the results of zinc, lead, and isotope ratios that indicate this individual was different from the other two studied.

Arsenic and Mercury

The presence of small amounts of dangerous elements, such as mercury and arsenic, do not appear to have affected these individuals during their lives. Mercury is usually found in human bone at the rate of 0.7 to 0.9 parts per million. Burials 1 and 3 had mercury levels well below the normal amounts, while Burial 2 was within the higher part of the normal range.

Summary

The use of stable isotope and trace element analysis has provided additional evidence of the diet of these individuals. The analysis reported here indicates a varied diet for these people: one that did not rely on a few specific foods. Specifically, the stable isotope analysis indicated a diet that included maize, as some historical sources report. Similarly, the nitrogen isotope ratios provided evidence that these individuals did not rely solely on either aquatic or terrestrial resources, but most likely used both.

The high strontium content of the bones of these individuals suggests that their meat consumption was low, which contrasts with the results of both the stable isotope and other trace element studies. It is more likely that the consumption of shellfish, which concentrates strontium, has complicated the interpretation of the strontium content in regard to meat consumption in these people. Oysters and other shellfish are abundant in seventeenth- and eighteenth-century archaeological deposits in Albany, indicating that these were a common food. The difference in strontium among these individuals, however, reveals an important difference in their diets. Apparently the two males, Burials 2 and 3, consumed a greater amount of root crops, and the female, Burial 1, ate a larger amount of leafy vegetables. This dietary difference may reflect sexual roles and status.

The zinc and copper content for these individuals indicates large amounts of meat and shellfish consumption in the diet of Burial 2, and lesser amounts in the other two. Burial 1 may have suffered from zinc deficiency, although this is not certain. She suffered infections that could have resulted from her low level of bone zinc, but the minimum level of bone zinc necessary to avoid physical problems is currently unknown.

In addition to the dietary information obtained from this analysis, evidence of social differentiation among these individuals was acquired. The bones of the 25- to 30-year-old male (Burial 2) varied considerably in zinc, copper, and lead bone content from the other two individuals. Most likely, these differences reflect the higher social status of this individual.

The lead content of colonial people has been the subject of study because of the use of lead-glazed ceramics and pewter plates and drinking vessels in the past. Aufderheide et al. (1981) found the lead content of a colonial Virginia planter's family cemetery was much greater than that of the laborers and slaves from the same plantation. This higher lead content of the planter's family was attributed to the greater use of pewter and lead-glazed ceramics by the plantation owners. The laborers and slaves had lower lead content as a result of their restricted access to pewter and lead-glazed ceramics.

Janowitz (1993) has suggested a similar situation for the Dutch of New Netherland. Pewter plates were associated with the social elite and were frequently depicted in the still life paintings of the seventeenth century. In contrast, the poor used earthenware and wooden plates, reducing their exposure to lead.

Another potential source of lead was medicines used for treating tuberculosis (TB), venereal disease, hemorrhages, and diarrhea (Emsley 1987:66). Burial 2 had TB; the lead content of this individual's bones may be at least in part a result of treatment efforts.

In addition to the higher lead content, the bone from Burial 2 had a higher copper content and a zinc content more than seven times that of the other two individuals. This may be a result of his greater access to meat and shellfish. The stature of Burial 2 was estimated to have been about 5 feet, 10 inches, which made him the largest of the three individuals. The older male, Burial 3, was estimated to have been about 5 feet, 6 inches tall.

The association of higher bone lead, zinc, and copper and greater stature in Burial 2 suggests an individual with higher status. This individual had greater access to meat and shellfish, as well as to pewter, lead-glazed tableware, and medicines.

Differences in the diets of the males and female were observed as a result of this study. The female represented by Burial 1 had the lowest zinc bone content and the lowest strontium bone content. This indicates that she ate less meat and shellfish but more leafy vegetables than the males, who also consumed more root vegetables.

References Cited

Aufderheide, A.C. 1989. Chemical Analysis of Skeletal Remains. In *Reconstruction of Life from the Skeleton*, edited by M.Y. Içcon and K.A.R. Kennedy, pp. 237–257. Wiley-Liss, John Wiley & Sons, New York.

———, Neiman, F.D., Wittmers, L.E., Jr., and Rapp, G. 1981. Lead in Bone II: Skeletal-Lead Content as an Indicator of Lifetime Lead Ingestion and the Social Correlates in an Archaeological Population. *American Journal of Physical Anthropology* 55:285–291.

Emsley, J. 1987. When the Empire Struck Lead. *New Scientist* 25:64–67.

Janowitz, M.F. 1993. Indian Corn and Dutch Pots: Seventeenth-Century Foodways in New Amsterdam/New York. *Historical Archaeology* 27(2):6–24.

Katzenberg, M.A. 1992. Advances in Stable Isotope Analysis of Prehistoric Bones. In *Skeletal Biology of Past Peoples: Research Methods*, edited by S.R. Saunders and M.A. Katzenberg, pp. 105–119. Wiley-Liss, John Wiley & Sons, New York.

———. 2000. Stable Isotope Analysis: A Tool for Studying Past Diet, Demography, and Life History. In *Biological Anthropology of the Human Skeleton*, edited by M.A. Katzenberg and S.R. Saunders, pp. 305–327. Wiley-Liss, John Wiley & Sons, New York.

Keegan, W.F. 1989. Stable Isotope Analysis of Prehistoric Diet. In *Reconstruction of Life from the Skeleton*, edited by M.Y. Içcon and K.A.R. Kennedy, pp. 223–236, Wiley-Liss, John Wiley & Sons, New York.

Medeiros, D.M., and Percival, S.S. 2003. *Nutrients: Copper*. American Society for Nutritional Sciences. Available at: http://www.nutrition.org.

Phillips, S.M. 1998, November. Skeletal Analysis Report for the Pearl St. Human Remains. On file at the New York State Museum, Albany.

Sandford, M.K. 1992. A Reconsideration of Trace Element Analysis in Prehistoric Bone. In *Skeletal Biology of Past Peoples: Research Methods*, edited by S.R. Saunders and M.A. Katzenberg, pp. 79–103. Wiley-Liss, John Wiley & Sons, New York.

Ubelaker, D.H. 1989. *Human Skeletal Remains* (2nd ed.). Smithsonian Institution, Taraxacum, Washington, D.C.

Section 3

Places

CHAPTER 8

The Cultural Landscape at the Site of the Lutheran Church Lot and Burial Ground

Nancy L. Davis

Introduction

The New York State Museum Cultural Resource Survey Program was given the opportunity to study the environment of colonial Albany during an archaeological investigation for the New York State Department of Transportation in 1998. During a reconstruction of Pearl Street in downtown Albany, data recovery excavations took place at the corner of South Pearl Street and Howard Street in the location of several proposed utility installations.

Prior investigations near that location identified historic deposits in association with the backyards of early houses along State Street. Historic maps and other documentation indicated that this street corner was the location of the property of the Lutheran Church during the seventeenth and eighteenth centuries, and a burial ground was established there at that time (Figure 1.1).

During the excavations in the spring and summer of 1998, several important features were discovered at the site: three coffin burials and the wooden floor remains of a mid-eighteenth-century structure on the south corner of Howard and Pearl Streets, and on the north side of Howard Street, the lower portion of a wooden barrel privy and another refuse pit dating from the middle through late eighteenth century (Figure 8.1). The first burial was female and the other two were males (Chapter 6, this volume).

These were encountered approximately 2 meters below the current street pavement while investigating a large utility trench. Several meters away from Burial 1, wooden planks were found 1.8 meters below the current sidewalk surface at the site.

As part of the excavations, soil samples were collected from the east wall profile near Burial 1 to recover pollen data that would reflect soil matrix formation processes and provide an indication of the historical ground cover and land-use practices at the church site. A column of contiguous samples was collected by archaeologists every 2 cm from the undisturbed matrices of the profile (Figure 8.2). Eight of these samples, spaced to examine all major strata, were selected for analysis, which was conducted by Gerald Kelso.

Along with the preserved wood fragments from the coffins, samples of some of the many wood chips and fragments found in the occupation layers in the burial excavation were taken and analyzed to determine tree species. This work was completed by Susan E. Anagnost of State University of New York, College of Environmental Science and Forestry in Syracuse.

Finally, soil samples were taken from the intact remains of the wooden barrel privy and from the trash pit found several feet away. These were processed by flotation, and the collected seeds were identified by Nancy Sidell.

The information from these archaeological sources in and near the Lutheran Church lot, combined with maps and historical accounts from the time period, can help form a picture of the landscape at different times in this part of the colonial city of Albany.

Pollen

The pollen grains in each sample were counted and graphed. Many pollen types were identified for

People, Places, and Material Things: Historical Archaeology of Albany, New York edited by Charles L. Fisher, New York State Museum Bulletin 499, © 2003 by the University of the State of *New York*, New York State Education Department, Albany, New York. All rights reserved

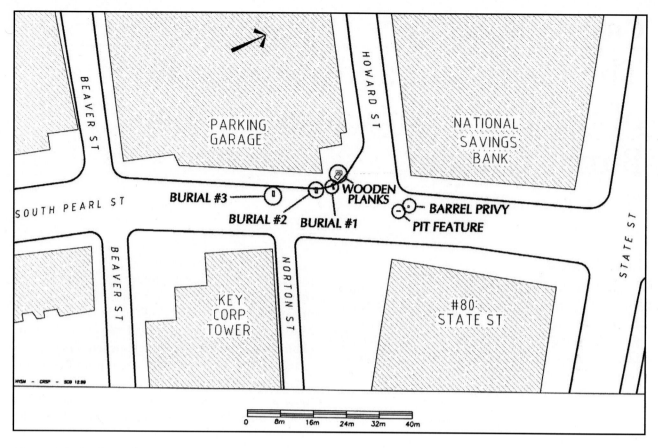

Figure 8.1. South Pearl Street and the location of the archaeological features found during the investigation.

each stratum and categorized into two main groups: tree and herb (Figure 8.3). Table 8.1 lists the Latin and vernacular names of plants shown in the graph and discussed in the text. The herb pollen is most indicative of plants growing in the immediate site location at any given time, because the herb plants are usually insect pollinated. They produce much less pollen than wind-pollinated plants, and they disperse it much more narrowly. The pollen that is not carried away by insects is deposited with fallen flowers very close to the place where the parent plants were growing. In contrast, trees typically produce a lot more pollen than herbaceous plants. The pollen is dispersed by wind and tends to be carried a considerable distance from the parent trees. At the Lutheran Church lot, more than half of the total pollen concentration in each stratum of the profile is from tree pollen (Figure 8.4). The tree pollen remains consistently high despite the expected deforestation characteristic of the colonial period in other places. This indicates that the tree pollen found at the church lot is from outside the city and that there was no dense tree

cover on the lot during the sequence analyzed.

Pine and oak dominate the types of tree pollen observed in the spectrum. Of the pine pollen observable, very little of it is white pine (Figure 8.5). The majority is an indeterminate species of pine in all layers of the spectrum. This is not surprising given the proximity of the Pitch Pine–Scrub Oak barrens located to the west of Albany. This area is known as the Pine Bush and is a unique environment established in the wind-blown sands deposited by glacial Lake Albany ca. 20,000 years ago (Dineen, Huey, and Reilly 1975).

The Pine Bush is significant to the colonial settlement, because it occupied the region immediately to the west of the city and it was the location of the primary trade route west from Albany on the Hudson River. It was also a vital source of wood for the inhabitants of the city. The predominant tree species in the Pine Bush is pitch pine, sometimes called yellow pine, and is considered a hard southern pine, though its range extends north of Albany. As several of the wood fragments sampled from the eighteenth-century

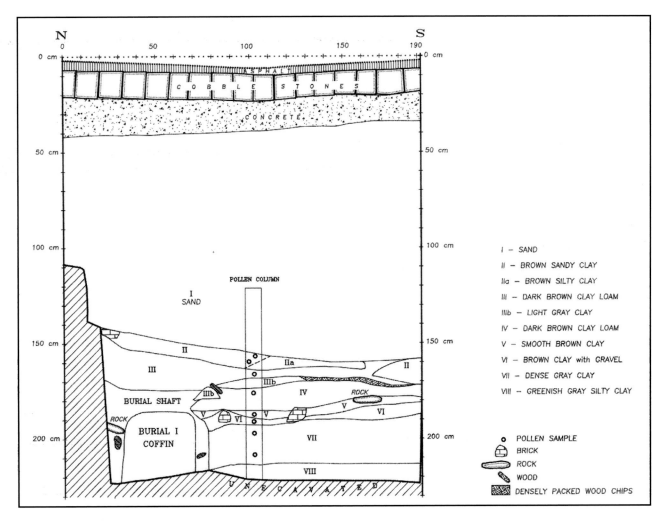

Figure 8.2. Profile of the east wall of Burial 1 excavation, showing the location of the pollen column.

layers of the Howard Street excavation were identified as a species of hard southern pine, it seems probable that the wood was pitch pine from the local Pine Bush.

Eight distinct soil strata were excavated near Burial 1, and four separate time periods were identified by the presence of index artifacts found in each stratum (Figure 8.6). The earliest cultural deposit in the profile, dating to the late seventeenth century, was the ground surface prior to the burials. At this time the church was located just inside the stockade wall of the town and adjacent to the back lots of houses facing State Street. The Rutten Kill creek flowed into the stockade part of the city from the west and bordered the Lutheran Church lot on the south and east, then turned to flow east down the hill into the Hudson River. According to a petition of 1672, the Lutherans were responsible for maintaining the bridge over the

Rutten Kill and a public path across their lot, with a gate for horses and cattle. The church, the Rutten Kill, and the bridge are depicted on the 1698 map of Albany by Wolfgang Römer (Figure 8.7).

Two pollen samples were studied from Stratum VII. The lower sample indicated a natural herbal environment dominated by a large quantity of aster-type pollen. This pollen is probably from species of sunflowers and goldenrod, which favor previously, but not actively, disturbed soils in open areas. This suggests that the Lutheran Church lot was clear and open. The pollen samples also show honewort and black snake root plants, members of the carrot family, which prefer shade and moisture as in a wooded area. This combination may indicate a forest edge situation that could be accounted for by the steep bank or ravine created by the Rutten Kill where moisture-loving trees and shrubs would grow.

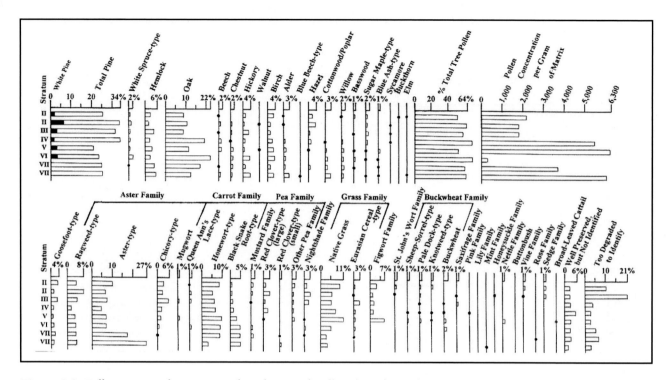

Figure 8.3. Pollen types and percentages based on total pollen sums for each major soil stratum of the Burial 1 east wall profile (Kelso 1999). "•" is equal to a single pollen grain.

The pollen record in the upper part of the layer shows several nonnative plants that were introduced into the area. These are chicory-type pollen, which is likely from dandelions, and also Eurasian cereal-type pollen. The cereal would have been wheat, barley, oats, or rye. The presence of these in the upper part of the stratum indicates initial Euroamerican activity in the area. Cronon (1983) points out that grazing animals, such as cattle, horses, and sheep, were the chief agents in bringing many "weeds," as we know them, to America. His examples of weeds introduced in this manner are dandelions, chickweeds, bloodworts, mulleins, mallows, nightshades, plantains, and stinging nettles. Since we know from documentation that there was a path and gate for livestock through the Lutheran Church yard, it is likely that weeds and the cereal pollen were deposited with the manure of free-ranging livestock that used the path. Anne Grant visited Albany in the middle of the eighteenth century and noticed that "each family had a cow, fed in a common pasture at the end of the town. In the evening they returned all together, of their own accord, along the wide and grassy street, to be milked at their master's doors" (1903:76).

The period generally from the late seventeenth to the middle of the eighteenth century (1680–1740/50) is represented by Strata IV, V, and VI of the Howard Street profile. During this time period there was a considerable amount of activity on the lot. It was used for burials starting in the late seventeenth century, with interments continuing into the first half of the eighteenth century. The original church building deteriorated and was taken down ca. 1736 (Heins 1976). Phillip Livingston used part of the lot for 6 years, building a small stable and hauling timber there. By arrangement with the Lutheran Church, he built a new parish house on the lot at the corner of Howard Street and Pearl Street by 1742. It was constructed over a stone cellar and was rented to Johannes Evertse who resided there and built a cookhouse, shed, and fence by 1745 (Hart and Hart-Runeman 1976). That some of these soil layers are very thin and have relatively few artifacts reflects the rapid change in activities on the site. Based on the presence of white salt-glazed stoneware fragments found in the shaft fill, Burial 1 was interred about the time the parish house was built in the 1740s.

The pollen analysis of soil Strata IV, V, and VI is interesting, because the pollen concentration of the clay and gravel of Stratum VI is very low, relative to those

Table 8.1. Latin and vernacular names of plants discussed in the text.

ARBOREAL PLANTS

Taxonomic Name	Common Name	Taxonomic Name	Common Name
Acer saccarum	sugar maple	Pinus	pine
Alnus	alder	Pinus strobus	white pine
Batula	birch	Platanus	sycamore
Carya	hickory	Populus	cottonwood/poplar
Castanea	chestnut	Quercus	oak
Corylus	hazel	Rhamnus	buckthorn
Fraxinus quadrangulata	blue ash	Salix	willow
Juglans	walnut	Tilia	basswood
Ostrya/Carpinus	blue beech type	Tsuga	hemlock
Picea glauca	white spruce	Ulmus	elm

HERBACEOUS PLANTS

Taxonomic Name	Common Name	Taxonomic Name	Common Name
Agropyron	wheatgrass	Fabaceae	pea family
Ambrosia	ragweed	Fagopyrum	buckwheat
Amaranthus	amaranth	Guttiferae	St. John's wort family
Andropogon	beardgrass	Helianthus	sunflower
Apiaceae	carrot family	Hordeum	barley
Artimisia	mugwort	Lamiaceae	mint family
Asteraceae	aster family	Liguliflorae	chicory-type
Avena	oats	Liliaceae	lily family
Brassaicaeae	mustard family	Poaceae	grass family
Caprifoliaceae	honeysuckle family	Polygonaceae	buckwheat family
Caryophyllaceae	pink family	Polygonum-type	knotweed-type
Chenopodiaceae/Amaranthus	goosefoot-type	Pyrolaceae	rose family
Chicorium	chicory	Rumex acetosella/acetosa	sheep sorrel-type
Cephalanthus	buttonbush	Rumex mexicanus	pale dock
Cryptotaenia	honewort	Sanicula	black snake root
Cyperaceae	sedge family	Saxifragaceae	saxifrage family
Daucus carota	Queen Anne's Lace	Scrophulariaceae	figwart family
Echinochloa	cockspurgrass	Secale	rye
Elymus	wild rye	Solanaceae	nightshade family
Eurasian cereal	cultivated European grains	Taraxicum	dandylion
		Trifolium	red clover

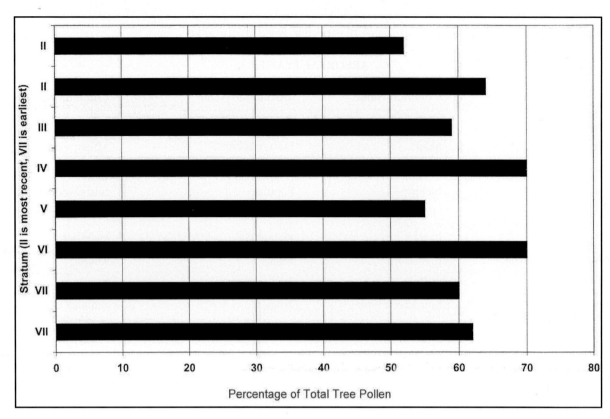

Figure 8.4. Bar chart of the percentage of total tree pollen found in each stratum of the Burial 1 east wall profile.

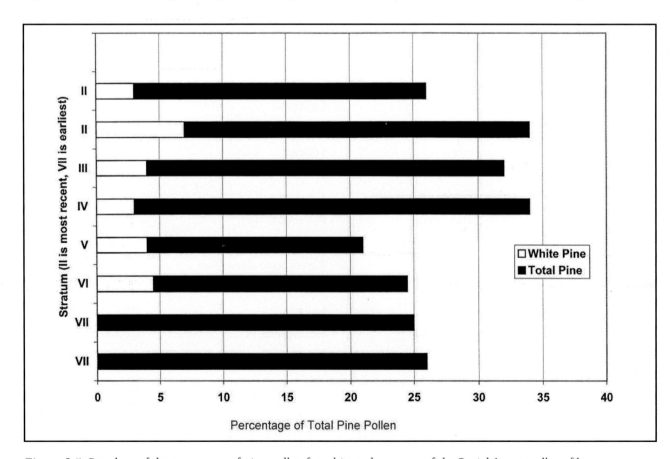

Figure 8.5. Bar chart of the percentage of pine pollen found in each stratum of the Burial 1 east wall profile.

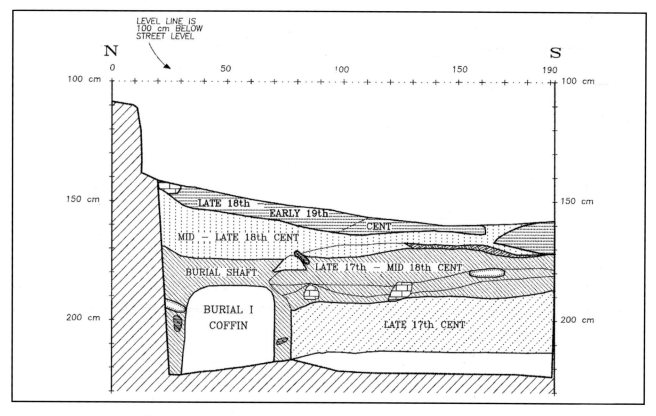

Figure 8.6. East wall profile showing time periods assigned to the soil strata as determined by index artifacts present.

of the layers above and below. The presence of gravel in this stratum, and no other stratum in the profile, led to the determination that the soil was exotic to this location. It may have originated from a deep, natural context and was then redeposited on the surface, possibly when digging a deep burial shaft nearby or from a construction or landscaping episode at that time. The low pollen count indicates that it had not been exposed for a very long time before other soils were deposited on top of it. However, the pollen types in Stratum VI are still generally consistent with those of the other samples in the lower half of the profile. This indicates that this soil had been affected by the local pollen rain after being deposited in the churchyard (Kelso 1999).

The pollen spectra in Strata VI and V also indicate an expansion in the native grasses and the chicory-type pollen, along with the initial appearance of European red clover, and other plants of the pea family, sheep sorrel, pale dock, knotweed, and buckwheat. The Eurasian cereal pollen also persisted and increased somewhat through this time period. Peter Kalm visited Albany in 1749 and observed wheat,

rye, and oats growing in cultivated fields. He saw many haystacks with movable roofs known as hay barracks. He also commented that "the Dutch and Germans who lived there sowed peas in great abundance and shipped them to New York in great quantities" (1937:335).

A dense concentration of small wood chips found in Stratum IV was identified as "hard pine" which is likely pitch pine from the Pine Bush. By historical accounts, this would have been the time period when the inhabitants of the city were under military threat and, for security, had troops garrisoned in blockhouses in and near the stockade. The city taxed the inhabitants in firewood and stockade posts and gave permission to cut wood from the Pine Bush for this purpose (Huey 1975:7).

Stratum III, corresponding to the occupation of the parish house from the mid through late eighteenth century, was marked by a large quantity of domestic artifacts and also contained a considerable number of wood fragments and chips. The dark brown clay loam soil, probably a former topsoil, postdates the digging of the Burial 1 grave shaft and lies directly above it. A

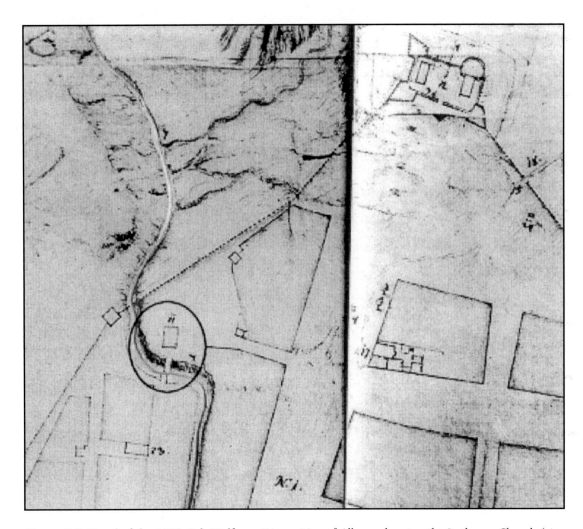

Figure 8.7. Detail of the 1698 Col. Wolfgang Römer Map of Albany showing the Lutheran Church (circled) and the Rutten Kill bridge.

thin layer of wood chips, identified as white oak and eastern white pine, marked the base of this topsoil and could have been a work surface or a path in a yard. The heavy clay soil in this part of Albany is extremely difficult to dig and becomes a slimy mess when it gets wet. This may explain the shallowness of Burial 1 relative to the occupation layer of the parish house and the need for a mulch of wood chips for a yard surface.

It is interesting that Burial 1 was not only very close to the surface in the later half of the eighteenth century, but also very close to the new parish house: only 3 meters (10 ft) away. It suggests a very different view of death from our modern view, which is to remove death from our daily lives, in part, by burying our dead in remote cemeteries, out of sight.

Seeds

The wooden barrel privy and the trash pit feature were 17 meters up the street from the church lot located in what may have been the back lot of the Schuyler house. Based on the artifacts found, these features date from the later half of the eighteenth century. Both features yielded seeds of many kinds of edible plants, mainly fruit. These are listed in Table 8.2. The cherry and plum pits are considerably larger than wild varieties that grew in the Northeast, which suggests that they were from horticulturally improved varieties (Sidell 1999). The blueberries and huckleberries may likely have come from the wild bushes that grew to the west of the city in the Pine Bush. The wild grapes are a species commonly known as fox grapes that grow all over the Northeast and were cul-

Table 8.2. Latin and vernacular names of seeds discussed in the text.

Taxonomic Name	Common Name	Taxonomic Name	Common Name
Citrullus vulgaris	watermelon	Prunus spp.	cherry (improved variety)
Chenopodium cf. album	lambsquarters	Prunus cf. nigra	plum
Crataegus spp.	hawthorn	Rubus spp.	raspberry, dewberry
Cucurbita spp.	squash		
Fragaria spp.	strawberry	Sambucus spp.	elderberry
Gaylussacia baccata	huckleberry	Sambucus canadensis	elderberry
cf. Liliaceae	lily family	Trifolium spp.	clover
Malus spp.	apple	Vaccinium spp.	blueberry
Morus rubra	red mulberry	Vitis larusca	fox grape
Phytolacca americana	pokeweed		

tivated into popular strains such as the Concord, Champion, and Chautauqua, among others. Peter Kalm (1937) noted that the woods and river banks around Albany abounded with grapevines in 1749. He also noted that apples, which are not native to North America, were growing in orchards in Albany.

Other plant seeds found include lambsquarters, pokeweed, clover, and hawthorn. Lambsquarters is in the goosefoot family and, though edible, is a common native weed growing in disturbed soil. Goosefoot-type pollen appeared consistently throughout the pollen spectrum of the church lot site, so it is not surprising to find seeds from the plant in a pit feature on the site.

The late eighteenth and early nineteenth century is represented by Stratum II which corresponds to the period when the city widened the section of Pearl Street south of State Street. In 1786 the Common Council paid someone to remove burials from the Lutheran Church cemetery for the purpose of the street widening (Wolcott 1998). By 1794 the Lutherans were using the large cemetery to the west of the city indicated on the DeWitt map of Albany of that date. The stockade was gone, and the city no longer needed military protection. The street widening would have involved straightening the street alignment on the church property to cross the Rutten Kill by filling and channeling it. Construction of this nature, along with normal human and animal traffic, would have been very disruptive to the soil. This is

evident in the pollen profile as well. In Stratum II pollen concentrations are low, and this is accompanied by markedly higher counts of grains that were too degraded to identify. This phenomenon is often accounted for by disturbances that churn up the soil, thereby aerating it, which in turn can degrade pollen that falls there. The lower pollen counts in Stratum II may also be explained by an increase in the rate of soil accumulation on the site. The street widening and burial removal in the late eighteenth century may account for both of these factors.

We also see in Stratum II evidence of sedge pollen, a grass-like herb of wet habitats such as wet fields, ditches, marshes, and stream banks (Niering and Olmstead 1979). Sedge is also known to grow in muddy areas on construction sites where water is allowed to stand. Sedge pollen was not present in any of the earlier strata despite the proximity of the creek, so the appearance of it in the late eighteenth century again points to the disturbed nature of the street at that time period. Peter Kalm (1937) stated that the streets in Albany were very dirty, because people left their cattle in them during the summer nights. Warren Johnson, who passed through Albany in 1760, noted the lack of stone paved streets, and thought the "streets of Albany the dirtiest [he] ever saw" (1996:269).

In the early nineteenth century, the Lutheran Church traded the lot to the city and moved to a new location. A city market was established at the corner of Pearl and Howard Streets, and, as the city expanded, Pearl Street became a main north-south thoroughfare. The street was leveled, paved over, and eventually lined with modern high-rise buildings.

Summary

The seventeenth-century environment of the Lutheran Church lot was primarily open, with meadow plants like asters, sunflowers, and goldenrods, while the nearby Rutten Kill ravine would have been moist and wooded, providing an ideal place for the more shade loving herbs that were also found there. By the third quarter of the seventeenth century, plants introduced from Europe were present in the church lot, possibly introduced by domestic animals using the gate and path through the area. The stockaded part of the city would not have been densely forested.

The rapid change in activities on the site in the first half of the eighteenth century, which led up to and included the construction of the church house in 1742, is evident in the exotic soil and low pollen count of Stratum VI. This time period saw the expansion of some of the European-introduced cereal pollen along with European red clover and other plants.

By the late eighteenth and early nineteenth century, sedge plants were growing in the parish house lot indicating there were probably spots with standing water around the yard created by burial removal, street construction, and human and animal traffic on an unpaved street.

With the wood and plant evidence examined from the archaeological excavations at the Lutheran Church lot on Pearl Street, we can see how humans have influenced their environment throughout Albany's colonial history. It has provided us with a glimpse of the landscape, not only inside the city, with its phases of construction and development, but also with its link to the area outside the city—its pastures, cultivated fields, even the Pine Bush as a local natural resource for wood and food. Today the landscape of Pearl Street is very different from the picture we have been able to glimpse with the aid of the archaeological investigations conducted there.

Acknowledgments

I would like respectfully to acknowledge and thank Gerald K. Kelso for doing the pollen analysis, upon which most of this paper was based. I would also like to thank Nancy Asch Sidell for doing the seed identification on short notice, and Susan E. Anagnost for doing the wood identification.

Sylvie Browne and Scott Cardinal assisted with the graphics. Joe Sopko and Steve Tesser gave insightful comments on early drafts of the paper. I thank them all. I especially thank Charles Fisher for his ideas, encouragement, support, and for recognizing my interest in the plant-related aspects of the project in the first place.

References Cited

Anagnost, S.E. 1999. Report of Wood Fragment Analysis from Features Found at Howard and Norton Streets, Pearl Street Reconstruction Project, Albany, New York. Letter to Charles Fisher, January 5. On file at the New York State Museum, Albany.

DeWitt, S. 1794. *A Plan of the City of Albany*. Reprinted 1968 by Historic Urban Plans, Ithaca, N.Y. From the original in the Library of Congress, Washington, D.C.

Dineen, R.J., Huey, P., and Reilly, E.M., Jr. 1975. *Geology and Land Uses in the Pine Bush, Albany County, New York*. Circular 47. New York State Museum and Science Service, Albany.

Cronon, W. 1983. *Changes in the Land, Indians, Colonists, and the Ecology of New England*. Hill and Wang, New York.

Grant, A. 1903. *Memoirs of an American Lady*. Dodd, Mead and Company, New York.

Hart, S., and Hart-Runeman, S. (translators). 1976. *The Albany Protocol, Wilhelm Christoph Berkenmeyer's Chronicle of Lutheran Affairs in New York Colony, 1731–1750*. Bound by New York State Library, Albany.

Heins, H.H. 1976. *The Swan of Albany: A History of the Oldest Congregation in the Lutheran Church in America*. Published in observance of the bicentennial of the United States of America by the First Lutheran Church, Albany.

Huey, P.R. 1975. History of the Pine Bush from 1624 to 1815, Albany County, New York. In *Geology and Land Uses in the Pine Bush, Albany County, New York*, edited by R.J. Dineen, pp. 7–8. New York State Museum and Science Service Circular 47, Albany.

Johnson, W. 1996. Journal of Warren Johnson [1760–1761]. In *Mohawk Country, Early Narratives About a Native People*, edited by D.R. Snow, C.T. Gehring, and W.A. Starna, pp. 250–273. Syracuse University Press, Syracuse, N.Y.

Kalm, P. 1964 [1937]. *Peter Kalm's Travels in North America. The English Version of 1770.* Revised from the original Swedish of 1748–1750 and edited by A.B. Benson. Dover Publications, New York.

Kelso, G.K. 1999. Report of Pollen Analysis of Soil Profiles at Howard Street and Norton Street, Pearl Street Reconstruction Project, Albany, New York. Report on file at the New York State Museum, Albany.

Niering, W.A., and Olmstead, N.C. 1979. *The Audubon Society Field Guide to North American Wildflowers.* Alfred A. Knopf, New York.

Römer, Col. W.W. 1698. *Plan of the City of Albany.* New York State Archives, Cultural Education Center, Albany.

Sidell, N.A. 1999. Report of Seed Analysis from the Privy and Pit Features Found at Howard Street, Pearl Street Reconstruction Project, Albany, New York. Notes on file at the New York State Museum, Albany.

Wolcott, J. 1998. Memorandum to Charles Fisher on the Dutch Lutheran Church of Beverwyck, and Early Albany, July. On file at the New York State Museum, Albany.

CHAPTER 9

The Garden That Didn't Die: Archaeological Explorations West of the Visitors' Center, Schuyler Mansion State Historic Site, Albany, New York

Lois M. Feister

Introduction

One way in which the eighteenth-century elite typically distinguished themselves from others was by the creation of a formal garden, an "improvement" to the landscape that demonstrated the owner's wealth and awareness of the latest in design and science. Archaeological excavations at Schuyler Mansion State Historic Site in Albany, New York, revealed evidence of two gardens established by the elite Schuyler family during the eighteenth century (Figure 1.1). In addition, the archaeology demonstrated that the garden continued to exist in somewhat different form throughout the nineteenth century, until 1915.

Historic Background

Philip Schuyler (1733–1804) was a descendant of some of Albany's earliest settlers. By 1764, he had built a Georgian-style brick house for his family on a bluff south of the city overlooking the Hudson River (Figure 9.1). With the outbreak of the American Revolution, Schuyler was a delegate to the Continental Congress and a major general in command of the northern department. The Schuyler house in Albany became the center of his military activities. George Washington, Benjamin Franklin, and Benedict Arnold were among his guests in addition to Alexander Hamilton, who married Schuyler's daughter Elizabeth at the mansion in 1780. After the war, Schuyler was an ardent federalist, acted as an Indian commissioner for Congress, and served in both the New York and United States senates.

Following his death in 1804, the estate's many acres were sold, and the house became a private residence for several different families. In 1886 the St. Francis de Sales Asylum, a Roman Catholic orphanage, was established there. After the orphanage moved to another location, the State of New York purchased the property in 1912, restored the mansion, built a caretaker's house, and opened the historic site to the public.

Evidence for the Schuyler Mansion Garden

Archaeological excavations were conducted in 1986 and in 1994 in an area west of the Visitors' Center (caretaker's house) at Schuyler Mansion State Historic Site (Figure 9.2). The purpose of the project was to uncover evidence from the earth that could be combined with documents, maps, and photographs. Oral history was obtained also through an interview with a former inhabitant of the caretaker's house.

In 1969 Orin Bullock produced a study of the

People, Places, and Material Things: Historical Archaeology of Albany, New York edited by Charles L. Fisher, New York State Museum Bulletin 499, © 2003 by the University of the State of New York, New York State Education Department, Albany, New York. All rights reserved

Figure 9.1. Photograph of Schuyler Mansion, Albany. New York State Office of Parks, Recreation and Historic Preservation.

Schuyler Mansion property in which he overlaid several historic maps on a modern map of the site. By superimposing two of his maps, the relationship of the garden shown on DeWitt's 1794 map (Figure 9.3) to the modern-day Visitors' Center becomes clear. The west wall of the caretaker's house (Visitors' Center) was built in 1915 against the edge of the old garden. Two rows of rectangular garden beds extended westward under today's parking lot. To the south they met present Delaware Street. The south edge of the first row of beds would have been beyond the edge of the hillside that exists today. This hill was cut back after Schuyler's death, to create house lots along Delaware Street, thus destroying the southern half of the garden. Excavations, interviews, and a study of maps

made it possible to trace the changes that have occurred in this area through two and a half centuries.

The excavations established that this area was a garden as early as 1760, and that it remained a garden until the building of the caretaker's house in 1915. Although the first known graphic representation of planting beds at the mansion dates from 1794, documentary references indicate that a garden was present earlier. In October 1777 Richard Varick wrote, "Mrs. Schuyler's Poultry & gardens have suffered" (Lehman 1986:10). The layout of the garden was described about 1790 as "with here and there parterres, some of which are nicely lawned" (Gibbons and Stott 1977:34). Simeon DeWitt's 1794 map shows a formal pattern of rectangular beds divided by pathways, thus

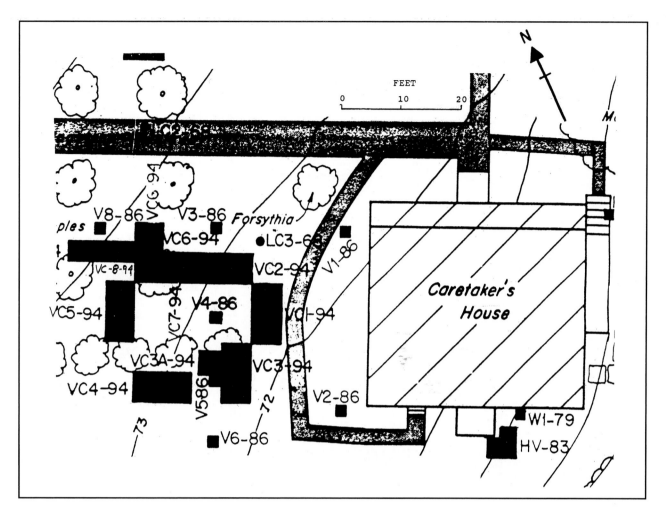

Figure 9.2. Plan of the archaeological test units excavated in 1986 and 1994.

confirming the 1790 description. The reference to Mrs. Schuyler might indicate she was the person primarily responsible for directing the plan and upkeep of the gardens, especially because her husband was often away on public service. "The mistress of a family frequently was the chief source of gardening enthusiasm in the eighteenth century" (Rogers 1984:149; see also Weber 1996).

Parterre is defined in Webster's dictionary as "a flower garden, plot, level ground" (1806:217). The *American Heritage Dictionary* defines the word as "a flower garden whose beds form a pattern" (1994:605). By placing paths across a garden so as to create rectangular flower beds between the walkways a parterre pattern could be formed.

Details of the Excavation Work

Archaeological testing to the west of the Visitors' Center began in 1986 when eight 2-foot by 2-foot test units were excavated (V186–V886 on Figure 9.2) in an effort to determine if archaeological deposits remained in the area. These excavations suggested that intact deposits dating to the eighteenth century were present, and it was recommended that any development there be preceded by more extensive archaeological work (Feister 1986).

Therefore, when plans were proposed for a new addition on the west side of the Visitors' Center, six 10-foot by 5-foot trenches were laid out across the area of impact. Also in 1994, another 5-foot by 5-foot unit (No. 7), a 3-foot by 3-foot unit (No. 3A), and a 12-foot by 3-foot trench (No. 8) were excavated to

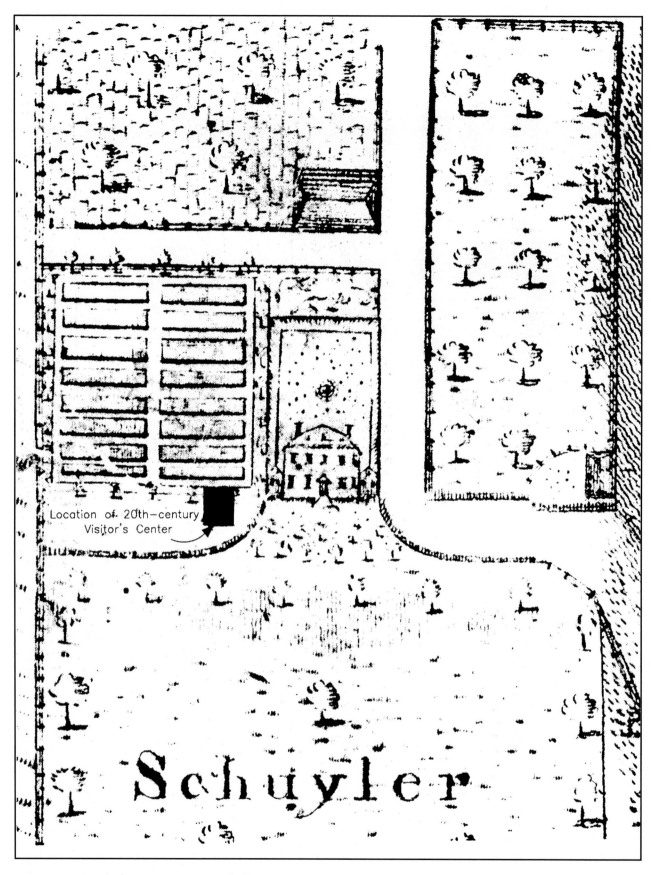

Figure 9.3. Detail of 1794 DeWitt Map of Albany (Gibbons and Scott 1977:34). The house faces east. Location of twentieth-century Visitors' Center to the south of the house is shown in black.

explore and sample discoveries made in the first six trenches. The trenches were laid out so that continuous profiles could be obtained both north to south and east to west across the area.

Units were hand excavated to and below the subsoil horizon, and artifacts were collected by stratigraphic association. The four sides of each excavation unit were profiled; plan views were drawn of all features. Features were sectioned and those profiles drawn. Artifacts were processed in the archaeological laboratory at Peebles Island, and number codes were applied that referred to the stratigraphic sequences and association. Metal objects were selected for conservation. All artifacts have been placed in acid-free boxes and are stored by catalog number at the Peebles Island office and repository of the Bureau of Historic Sites. The records have been archived there in fireproof cabinets.

Schuyler's Garden Prior to the American Revolution

The archaeological work for the proposed Visitors' Center addition concentrated on the eastern end of the original garden. Thus the conclusions below reflect conditions and features found in about 25 percent of the total garden area.

The earliest garden remains identified in the archaeological excavations were those of the Schuyler garden before the American Revolution. Soil layers and features dating from ca. 1760 to ca. 1780 were found in several trenches excavated in 1994 and in two units excavated in 1986.

The archaeological evidence indicates that the prewar garden was smaller than what is shown on the earliestknown documentary image, the 1794 DeWitt map. This early garden did not extend as far south as the one depicted on that map. Instead, the southern limit of the prewar garden was about even with the south wall of the present-day Visitors' Center. Test units excavated farther south contained evidence of a garden dating after the American Revolution, but from before Philip Schuyler's death. Thus the garden was expanded south during peacetime and before the Schuyler family left the property.

Unexpectedly, the excavations show that the Schuylers' early garden featured subterranean, or deep-trenched, flower beds (Figure 9.4). These were

Figure 9.4. View of a specialty garden, ca. 1768 (Diderot 1959:Plate 10).

found in Trenches 3, 3A, 4, 6, and 7. To the casual observer in the eighteenth century, the garden appeared as a flat surface. It consisted of a series of square or rectangular boxes excavated into the dense subsoil clay. The clay was removed and replaced with loamy, fertile soil. Ridges of the subsoil clay were left around some of the clay subterranean beds for edging. The beds were about 30 inches long. The depths of the loam inside ranged from as shallow as 5 inches to a more common depth of 12 inches. The artifacts within the loam included fragments of brick of the same size as those used to build the mansion, eighteenth-century lime mortar, hand-wrought nails, charcoal, a few fragments of food bone, eighteenth-century glazed redware, window glass, a white clay tobacco pipe stem, oyster shell, eighteenth-century wine bottle fragments, and charred wood. These same types of artifacts have been found above the clay subsoil elsewhere in the general vicinity of the mansion. The evidence suggests that when the house and its outbuildings were constructed, the entire top of the bluff was cleared of soil to the dense clay. At that time debris from the building of the house was spread across the site as this stockpiled loam was returned. Because the area for the new garden already had been graded down to subsoil, digging subterranean beds and filling them with loam might have been an efficient way to establish the first garden.

At Bacon's Castle, located in Surry County, Virginia, excavations in the late seventeenth- to early-eighteenth-century garden revealed subterranean flower beds. Here they formed the borders and the north edge of the garden. These may have been starter beds (Luccketti 1988:16). The area subject to the 1994 archaeological excavations at Schuyler Mansion was at the extreme east end of the Schuyler garden. The subterranean beds found there thus may also have been starter beds established at the edge of the garden as they were at Bacon's Castle.

Subterranean planting beds also were found at Carter's Grove in Virginia. "Excavation of one of the planting beds also showed that as much as two feet of subsoil had been originally excavated and replaced with humus" (Kelso 1984:161). Similar beds were found in the backyard of the Peyton Randolph house in Williamsburg, Virginia (Brown and Samford 1990:108–109). These subterranean beds ranged in size from 20 feet to 32 feet long by 4 feet to 12 feet wide, cut 0.75 foot and 1.5 feet into the subsoil clay. Seed remains obtained from the loam fill indicated that they may have been asparagus beds.

Lying between the subterranean beds at Schuyler Mansion were flat layers of garden soil resting directly on subsoil. These may have been planting areas, also, as a few early planting holes were found. One of these was circular, 16 inches in diameter, and had a taproot 3 feet deep. The presence of this type of stain with a deep taproot suggests that a small bush once was planted there in the original Schuyler garden. Another planting hole dating to the early garden was found along the south wall of Trench 5. It was oval, basin-shaped at the bottom, and had a taproot stain that continued down. The soil in the feature was about 6 inches deep, but the feature measured 20 inches by 24 inches. The only artifact found was a brick fragment.

Larger numbers of artifacts were found in these flat areas between the subterranean beds, suggesting they were traffic areas. The finds included construction materials such as more of the early red brick fragments, corroded nails, lime mortar, and window glass. Food related items were few, as one might expect in a garden, but included some food bone, a single piece of a glazed redware plate, six fragments of gray salt-glazed stoneware crock, a piece of Chinese porcelain with hand-painted blue design, and six fragments of glass containers (wine bottles, medicine bottles, and a wineglass fragment of lead glass). There were also a few personal items: two fragments of white clay tobacco pipes and a single copper-alloy straight pin with a wire-wound head, the type in use in the eighteenth century. These few artifacts were part of a general scatter of trash across the garden rather than representative of concentrated areas of activity. All are types commonly in use before ca. 1780, thus dating these strata to before the end of the American Revolution.

No direct evidence of walkways was found associated with this prewar garden. Gravel present on the surface of Stratum VI in Trench 4, however, suggests the presence of now-obliterated pathways.

Evidence of fencing was found. Postholes, dark stains in the ground that sometimes still contained remains of posts, provided evidence of such features. Postholes that dated to the earliest garden were reused at later dates. Some of the early posts were very large with diameters of more than 1 foot. Others had diameters of about 6 inches. Small posts, those with diameters of about 4 inches, probably were plant supports rather than fencing.

Archaeological work at Carter's Grove in Virginia revealed postholes, which once held cedar posts varying from 6 inches to 1 foot in diameter (Kelso 1984:160). Thus the sizes of the posts at Schuyler Mansion may be quite typical of eighteenth-century fencing. As Kelso wrote,

> not a fence in the modern sense, the wooden palings of the colonial period often appear to have been similar to fort stockades, 10-foot-high solid barriers quite capable of keeping the largest and most athletic animals . . . and the smallest and more elusive creatures . . . out of the cultivated areas. Certainly the large postholes found at Carter's Grove are indicative of such massive height, and contemporary records consistently show that such imposing garden barriers were the norm in England and America. (1984:162)

One other posthole was found in the soil layers representing the early Schuyler garden. It was located inside the second subterranean bed in Trench 4. The posthole was 8 inches across (the pointed post would have been smaller) and only 10 inches deep. Its size and location inside a planting bed suggests that the post was a support for a plant rather than a fence post.

The number of postholes with fill dating to the period of Schuyler's early garden would not by themselves form a fence. Other posts for which there is archaeological evidence dating to after ca. 1780 replaced earlier, rotted ones. The prewar posts and soil were removed and new posts and fresh soil placed in the same holes. This new soil included postwar artifacts. The holes themselves, however, were dug earlier and are discussed below.

The Schuyler Garden, ca. 1780–ca. 1804

The war having been won, landowners like the Schuylers turned their attention once more to domestic affairs. One development on their property was the expansion of the garden.

Much more archaeological evidence for this larger garden was found. Remnants of it appeared in all trenches except Trench 3, where layers dating to the late eighteenth century had been greatly disturbed by nineteenthcentury activities.

The postwar garden was changed and expanded by the addition of fill, fresh loam placed over the top of the old subterranean beds. The garden was extended farther south. Test units excavated close to the

edge of what today is a steep bank demonstrate that the postwar garden extended farther in that direction than the previous one had. In fact, scaling the size of the garden from the DeWitt map (1794) shows that the garden by that time extended all the way to what is now Delaware Street. The use of subterranean beds had been abandoned.

An eighteenth-century gravel pathway that ran north to south across the excavated area was found in Trenches 6, 8, 5, and 4. The same route had been used twice, once in the eighteenth century and again in the middle of the nineteenth century, when new gravel was added that widened and lengthened the old path. The original pathway was about 8 feet wide. It was constructed of shale gravel mixed with a dark yellow-brown clay loam. It was about 5 inches thick and quite hard packed, at least in comparison to the nineteenth-century gravel path directly above. The compactness of the feature is confirmed by the lack of artifacts in the gravel fill. Artifacts dropped here remained on the surface of the walkway instead of sinking in. Most artifacts left lying on the surface then were swept away or removed to keep the garden area tidy.

Archaeological evidence indicates gravel was used by the Schuylers to form an apron emanating outward from at least three sides of the house (Feister 1995b:60, 69–70). It also was commonly used in gardens in the eighteenth century "both for paths and for larger expanses. Besides its cheapness, gravel had the advantage that it could be raked over when the top surface had become discolored" (Cruickshank and Burton 1990:197–199).

The largest artifact found in the eighteenth-century gravel path was an iron file. Eight inches long with a prong extension for a handle, the piece was discovered protruding from the surface of the path excavated in Trench 4. Along with the iron file were a few fragments of oyster shell, two food bone fragments, some red brick, a single white clay pipe stem, and charcoal. No artifacts were found in the pathway fill in Trenches 5 and 8. In Trench 6 the walkway had become so disturbed that it was not possible to separate the eighteenth-century path from the nineteenth-century one above. However, several artifacts found in the combined fill were from the eighteenth century: a fragment of yellow-glazed buff earthenware, some hand-painted pearlwares and porcelains, a brick fragment that matched the brick of the Schuyler Mansion, and a hand-wrought nail. These probably were part of the earlier walkway before it was renewed and mixed in with the upper gravel. Even so, these few finds demonstrate that not many artifacts penetrated the hard surface of the pathway while it was in use between ca. 1780 and ca. 1850, when the new one was laid.

The path also was slightly domed in the middle, so as to shed water. In Trenches 4 and 6 there was evidence that the edges of the gravel paths were cut down into the soil around them so that the gravel would stay in place. J. Glenn Little, during archaeological excavations conducted on the Schuyler Mansion property in 1968, discovered a similar feature closer to the house. This gravel and clay soil pathway was only about 3 feet wide and was located near the site of Schuyler's office (Feister 1995b:68). The pathway also was cut down into the eighteenth-century ground surface along its edges. This apparently was the preferred method for path construction.

The flower bed surfaces found in the postwar garden were flat beds with slightly mounded surfaces. They averaged about 8 inches thick.

Several postholes and even the remains of wooden posts were discovered. Table 9.1 summarizes the sizes of these various posts and their dates. The posts were from 5 inches to 8 inches in diameter, but often they were found inside much larger postholes. This indicates the hole originally was dug for larger-sized posts. Five- to 8-inch-diameter posts are substantial

pieces of wood, but the posthole sizes suggest that the earlier posts were closer to a foot across. Plotting of eighteenth-century posthole locations clearly demonstrates that they originally surrounded the smaller, earlier garden (Figures 9.5, 9.6a, and 9.6b). Smaller posts, such as Catalog Number 842, may have functioned as a secondary support for the fence around the enlarged garden or as a support for a large plant.

Artifacts found both in the postmold itself and in the fill layers in the posthole included eighteenth-century materials such as creamware, pearlware, gray salt-glazed stoneware, hand-wrought nails, and more general artifacts such as food bone, brick, and lime mortar.

Planting holes for the postwar garden also were found. In Trench 2, a 4-inch-deep, 20-inch-wide planting hole with an undulating bottom contained a taproot in its center, probably left from the planting that once grew there. The root continued down for about 4 inches below the base of the feature. Found in the fill soil was a fragment of food bone, creamware, brick, and a single piece of transfer-printed pearlware. The printed pearlware probably was introduced into the fill during later cultivation activities.

Another feature in Trench 3 was probably part of one of the rectangular planting beds. Only a remnant of it remained, but there was enough to determine

Table 9.1. Posthole and Post Remains Uncovered During Excavations for the Schuyler Mansion Visitors' Center Addition Project

Location	Posthole Diameter	Post Diameter	Posthole Depth	Post Depth	Date	Cat. No.
TR 67	12	NA	24	NA	< 1780	801
TR 7	20	?	24	24	< 1780	799
TR 4	8–9	NA	10	NA	< 1780	843
TR 1	10	6	32	30	1780–1804	763
TR 1	7	5	18	17	1780–1804	842
TR 2	9	6	28+	24+	1780–1804	769
TR 6	12	8	20	13	1780–1804	753
TR 3	12	NA	5	NA	1780–1804	788
TR 1	8	5	15	15	> 1850	839
TR 3A	6	4	28	23	> 1850	811
TR 3	6	NA	6	NA	> 1850	785

Note: Measurements of diameters and depths are in inches.

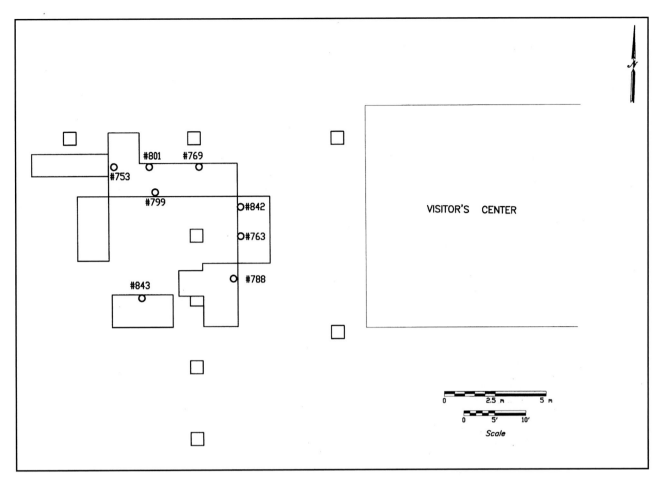

Figure 9.5. Plan of the postholes found during the 1994 excavations. Their outline suggests that Schuyler's early garden may have been almost square. The south and west sides of the fencing plan would fall into unexcavated areas.

that it turned a right angle and was about 8 inches deep. Found in the soil were late eighteenth- and early nineteenth-century artifacts. A layer that contained coal surrounded this remnant—also probably a section of one of the early beds that became mixed through later cultivation.

Undisturbed areas that dated to the postwar garden were flat loamy areas. Numerous artifacts were found in the soils. They were part of the scatter of material spread through the garden while it was in use and probably represent some trash deposits from the mansion.

A few of the artifacts found here deserve further mention. One is a copper-alloy button, completely intact except for a slightly bent eye on the reverse. The flat front is plain; the eye on the back was soldered in place. Almost 1 inch in diameter, it was a type in use after ca. 1750 (Noël Hume 1970:91). Its size identifies it as a coat button or one used on the waistband

of knee breeches. The iron file, already described as protruding from the eighteenth-century gravel path, was missing its handle. It is 8 inches long, a little over 1/2 inch wide near the tip, and 3/4 inch wide across the blade section. The prong that fit into the missing handle is 3/16 inch wide. Examples of tools from the eighteenth century are relatively rare in archaeological contexts. There were also 13 fragments of a delft tile, some of them little more than glaze chips. The tile decoration is in a mulberry (purple) color with the typical double-circle center common to Friesland biblical tiles. The corner design is a purple carnation. Similar tiles have been found elsewhere on the Schuyler property (Feister 1995b:56, 67, 69, 82, 87, 90). Finally, two gunflints were found. These are in addition to a pistol flint found in 1986 in V6. The two found in 1994 are larger specimens. Each is about an inch across, made of gray European flint. Neither had been used.

Figure 9.6a. Photograph of posthole and post remains (Catalog No. 753) in Trench 6.

The Garden, ca. 1804–ca. 1850

Schuyler's garden continued in use after his death, although it probably did not receive the same degree of care. Trench 8 and Trench 2 excavated on the north side of the study area and Trench 3 excavated on the southeast side each contained soil strata dating after ca. 1804 but before ca. 1850. Soil layers dating to this period were defined as those having no coal but containing artifacts such as transfer-printed pearlwares and whitewares. Few such strata were identified because most were disturbed by later nineteenth-century garden work. Although the property underwent several changes in ownership, the archaeological evidence suggests that the garden continued to be used by the occupants of the mansion just as before.

A planting hole was identified from this time period, intrusive from a layer dating to the first half of the nineteenth century into strata dating to the Schuyler gardens. The fill in the planting hole contained creamware, pearlwares, early nineteenth-century window glass, and a corroded nail. The feature was about 10 inches in diameter and about 2 inches deep but with a root stain going down another 10 inches into subsoil. The width and shallowness of the planting hole suggests a small bush that developed a good-sized taproot.

The two soil layers associated with the early nineteenth-century garden were 8 inches and 16 inches

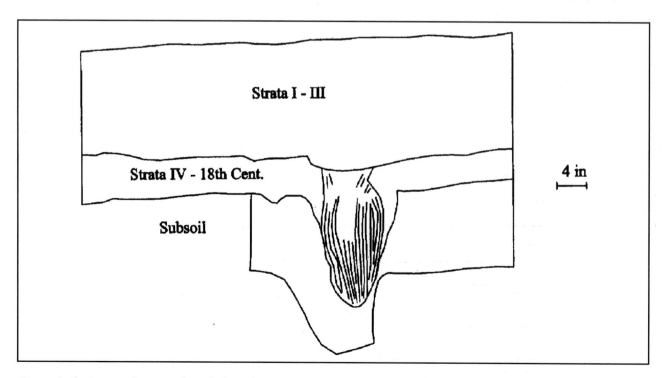

Figure 9.6b. Section drawing of posthole and post remains (Catalog No. 753) in Trench 6.

thick. A mixture of eighteenth-century artifacts and those dating to the early years of the nineteenth century were found. Also, for the first time, redware flowerpot fragments appeared.

The Garden After 1850

Massive changes to the garden area after ca. 1850 suggest that much work was needed to bring the area back into useful production. New loams were spread over the area (although apparently not required as much on the very north edge). Some posts that existed in the Schuyler garden were pulled and the postholes covered with the new soil. New posts apparently replaced others. Various prominent local families owned the property. One widow, Caroline Carmichael McIntosh, married former-President Millard Fillmore in the house in 1858 (Gibbons and Stott 1977:50).

That the new owners succeeded with the garden is shown by the rapture of an 1872 visitor who wrote,

> turning the lefthand corner of the old mansion … the garden stretches out broadly and queenly. And such a garden of beauty is not of frequent occurrence even in the picturesque suburbs of Albany. Weeding paths, groves of fruit-trees, beds of flowers, arbors of grapes, and a profusion of vegetable treasures, take possession of the eye. (Street 1872:506)

The presence of many toys (doll parts and teawares), as well as white glass buttons, is evocative of the orphan children who occupied the mansion by 1886 and played in the garden. An 1895 description of the property mentions that the house was "sadly changed" but that "the whole of the plateau . . . is still the garden, where some attempt has been made to keep up the flower beds surrounded by their box borders" (Reynolds 1895:424). Things were different by ca. 1905. A photograph taken sometime after that date shows the east end of the garden still in existence and still laid out in formal fashion, but the rest of the grounds were either grassed or occupied by structures.

Four posthole features, two rock borders, and four sections of gravel paths were found associated with the post1850 garden. The rest of the area evidently consisted of planting beds.

Postholes and post remains were found in Trenches 1, 3, 3A, and 7 and in V4 excavated in 1986. The posthole discovered in Trench 1 first was noted in a stratum dating from after 1850. The post, originally a clothesline support, was square and had been inserted into the hole upside down because near its base, an iron hook was found still attached. The identical hook was shown and described in the *Illustrated Catalogue of American Hardware* published in 1865 by the Russell and Erwin Manufacturing Company of New Britain, Connecticut, as "Clothes Line Hooks, No. 1" (Nelson 1980:87). The excavated iron hook is about 3.75 inches long and was screwed to a base almost 2 inches square. Traces of a silver color still cling to some areas, evidence of white metal or tin plating. The posthole had a 6-inch diameter; the post a 5-inch diameter and was almost 2 feet in length. Found in the posthole fills were eighteenth-century artifacts, such as hand-wrought nails, delft, and creamware, as well as later materials, such as flowerpot fragments, clear window glass, and coal.

A posthole in Trench 3A contained no artifacts other than post remains. The post appears to have been somewhat pointed; about 17 inches of it was left intact, although fragments of it were found as deep as 24 inches below the top of the posthole. The top of another posthole, found in Trench 3, was in a soil layer containing coal but which originally was probably part of the postwar garden. It was a square hole about 6 inches in diameter, and it did not penetrate into subsoil. It may have been a support for a plant. Its location between the clay ridges bordering the earliest garden suggests it may have been used earlier than the artifacts in the soil layer suggest. Only a single piece of red flowerpot was found in the posthole fill.

Feature E, also found in Trench 3, was a square stain 12 inches wide on each side. It contained only charcoal and was found at the top of subsoil. The posthole described above was in one corner of it. This suggests that the square stain represents an earlier, larger post, part of which was reused for the later smaller plant support post. Feature E, then, is interpreted as an earlier Schuyler garden post. The hole was about a foot in diameter, but only about 5 inches of its depth was left.

Trench 7 contained another posthole with much of the post remaining. Located against the south wall of the trench and thus bisected by it, the post dated to the early garden. The posthole was about 20 inches in diameter; the post fragments appeared to taper to a point, and perhaps to a length of as much as 2 feet. In profile, a taproot is shown at the base of the posthole.

The stone border was found in Trenches 3 and 4, forming one continuous, although somewhat disturbed, line running east to west. The border definitely dated from after ca. 1850, and probably to the orphanage period. The border was made of reddish sandstone and was only one layer of stone deep.

New garden paths were laid after ca. 1850. These were placed directly over the older gravel paths, indicating the original pattern of the Schuyler garden was still intact. These new paths were not as hard packed as the underlying ones and were about 8 feet wide, perhaps as wide as 12 feet in Trench 5. The gravel was about 6 inches thick. It also was domed for easier drainage. In Trench 4 it extended farther east than the earlier path, indicating the sizes of the beds there probably had changed. Artifacts were found in the gravel fill: coal, shell, creamware, pearlware, whiteware, window glass, brick, and white clay pipe fragments, again representing a scatter of small trash items across the landscape.

Features associated with this post1850 garden were few. Most of the area consisted of flat groundlevel planting beds or perhaps grassed areas. No evidence of the box borders mentioned in the 1895 description was found.

There were many artifacts ranging in type from coal to doll parts to earlier materials. There were many redware flower pot fragments, white glass buttons, a jack knife, an iron table knife with a wooden handle, eighteenth-century straight pins, a clay marble, and two marked clay pipe fragments. One of these marks is "WG", one letter molded on each side of a small spur heel. The WG mark was common in the Revolutionary War era (Calver and Bolton 1950:281). Oswald also lists the mark, as incised on the backs of pipe bowls and common to ca. 1760 through 1780. Oswald suggests the mark belongs to William Goulding (Gould), a pipemaker in London between 1733 and 1762. He also suggests that spur marks date to between 1730 and 1770, as opposed to bowl marks, which are later (Oswald 1975:80, 137). The second marked clay tobacco pipe dates to ca. 1850 and is almost a complete piece. Manufactured in the "apple" style (i.e., with a rounded bowl), the molded letters "M & T & S" appear on one side of the bit of stem still attached. Faint ribbing can be seen on the side of the bowl. These types of nineteenth-century pipes often were a form of advertising, and the letters may stand for the name of a business rather than a maker.

Many more artifacts were found mixed in the garden soils dating after ca. 1850 than in those from earlier layers. Dumping trash in the garden apparently

became more common by the middle of the nineteenth century. Later, trash removal to large city dumps became the norm.

The Twentieth-Century Garden

Twentieth-century strata were identified by the presence of round nails (common after 1890) and then by plastic. The construction of the caretaker's house (now the Visitors' Center) by 1915 signaled the end of the garden. The unusually deep cellar dug under the cottage produced vast amounts of backdirt that may have been spread across what was left of the garden, effectively burying its features. The landscape probably was planted with grass and became a yard area for the caretaker and his wife. Janet Aumic, who lived in the cottage with her grandparents, Andrew and Jesse McMath from 1930 to 1944, was interviewed by the author and Paul Huey in May 1998 about her life there. She confirmed that the landscape around the cottage was grassy lawn with a vegetable garden on the hillside behind.

Gardens of the Elite in the Eighteenth Century

During the first half of the eighteenth century, there arrived in America from London and other European metropolitan centers "what can be called a patrician culture . . . new notions about [how] the character of houses and gardens shaped the colony's landscape." People "often took their bearings from material things—from houses and fields, from yards and table settings" (Hudgins 1990:59). The elite sought to increase the distance between themselves and their more common neighbors (Leone and Shackel 1990:164; Upton 1990:84; Weber et al. 1990:150), and when they developed landscapes around their mansions, they made these distinctions even clearer. The gentry relied on the symbolic power of material things to "legitimize their social and political positions. Reading the symbolic value of signs on the cultural landscape was a much-practiced skill" (Hudgins 1990:68).

Placing a house high on a bluff overlooking the surrounding countryside was one way an elite family made a statement about its status (Miller et al. 1990:262; Weber et al. 1990:150; Yentsch 1989). Also typical was the inclusion of a large formal garden, which, in addition to the house and its numerous outbuildings, "improved" the landscape in ways not possible for those of lesser means.

In the eighteenth century, geometrically planned, terraced gardens were powerful statements of wealth and the right to own it. Gardens were displays of financial resources, but more importantly they were displays of knowledge; a garden implied familiarity with literature, classics, and art, as well as the "natural sciences" of geometry, botany, husbandry, hydraulics, surveying, and architecture. Gardens, as controlled domains of nature, were therefore powerful media for men, and occasionally women, of the colonial elite to communicate and negotiate their social identity. (Kryder-Reid 1994:131–132)

While the mansion was being built, Philip Schuyler visited England where he purchased the latest furnishings for his new home and undoubtedly observed the latest in landscape fashion, returning with a desire to emulate what he saw, as far as was practical in the New World.

Of 51 elite estates of the eighteenth century located in the northern part of the United States, 45 had gardens specifically shown on maps or described by visitors (Feister 1995a:56–58). These landscape features obviously were considered important. Most "garden archaeology" in the United States, however, has been done in the south at sites such as Monticello, Bacon's Castle, Carter's Grove, Mount Vernon, and Williamsburg. A large project also was conducted at Morven, an elite site in New Jersey, which has resulted in several short articles written for publication (e.g., Metheny et al. 1996; Miller et al. 1990; Yentsch et al. 1987). Another project was conducted at Father George Rapp's nineteenth-century garden in Economy, Pennsylvania, a feature found to be "as important and informative an object of Harmony Society material culture as the buildings, items of furniture, and manuscripts" (De Cunzo et al. 1996:113). The archaeological project to discover and study the layout and size of the gardens at Schuyler Mansion was one of the first such studies in New York State.

Any area where there were stretches of open land, clumps of trees, and inspiring vistas was considered "garden" in the eighteenth century. Thus the "garden" area of Schuyler Mansion encompassed the entire property. When eighteenth-century sources defined gardens as places to walk for contemplation and relaxation, they were referring to areas beyond the formal layout of walkways and planting beds. Great amounts of money and time were spent on European estates to create artificial landscapes that would impress visitors. Professionals such as Capability Brown carefully laid out areas that offered unexpected surprises to strollers: features such as statues, fountains, and false ruins as well as benches, summer houses, and pavilions for resting. Although pavilions and benches were used,

> no one in America tried to create a landscape calculated to awe anyone else. The Natural Bridge did [that] for visiting foreigners in search of that sort of sensation. American gardens were for domestic enjoyment, with collections of shrubs and flowers. Trees were kept for shade or bloom or beauty. (Leighton 1976:362)

For the Schuyler family, a trip to Cohoes Falls would provide a sensational experience; at home, they could enjoy their lofty views of the Hudson River, their large brick house with its many dependencies, and the formal layout of their neat pathways and planting beds stretching away to the south.

Gardens in North America typically involved a walkway that centered on a house doorway. From there, behind the house or at one side, with terracing, would be formal flowerbeds "in oblongs or squares, with a wide path, which led down through a small orchard to the vegetable and fruits gardens" (Leighton 1976:364). Terraces had "almost universal popularity" (Cummings 1983:130). Rozbicki noted that "sloping terraces had become an almost mandatory design ingredient" (1999:855). One example offered by Cummings is a description from 1776 by Elihu Ashley, who noted that Timothy Ruggles had land that "descends to the south, and he designs to make three squares one about four feet above the other, which will make a most agreable Graduation" (Cummings 1983:131). The Schuyler Mansion gardens descended to the south and may have been terraced.

Walkways in American gardens ranged from "trodden earth paths" to "gravel, stone, and brick" (Favretti and Favretti 1978:15). The main walkways were from 4 feet to 15 feet wide (Favretti and Favretti 1977:34). A book on gardening from 1791 defines a walk around a garden as 6 feet wide filled with gravel or sand (Fallowfield 1791:8). Gardens often were enclosed with a fence, hedge, or wall, unless the enclosure interfered with a view. At Monticello, Jefferson placed his terraced garden south of his house with a retaining wall that was more than 1,000 feet long. A paling fence 4,000 feet in length surrounded the area (Joyce 1986:45). The archaeological work at Schuyler

Mansion revealed gravel pathways 8 feet wide; the gardens were enclosed with a wooden fence, the earliest one probably being the paling type.

Summary

Archaeological and documentary evidence shows that formal gardens were present at the Schuyler Mansion and that the garden contained elements mentioned in all of the above descriptions.

The small planting garden established by the Schuyler family expanded and contracted over the years, but it survived until ca. 1915. Features such as planting beds, gravel paths, planting holes, and post-holes remained as archaeological evidence, and the story of the garden's changes was established using stratigraphic analysis and the dating of excavated artifacts.

The early garden contained some subterranean planting beds, consistent with those at other eighteenth-century historic sites. A palisade-type fence, judging by the size and depth of the postholes (and sometimes parts of posts), surrounded the planting area. This also was consistent with eighteenth-century garden practices elsewhere in North America.

After the American Revolution, a much larger garden was laid out, one that today would have extended south to Delaware Street and west across the property. It probably was gently sloping or was terraced, a common eighteenth-century practice. Now the planting beds were at ground surface, and new loam was brought in for the expansion.

The planting gardens may have suffered some neglect after Schuyler's death in 1804, and the south end was removed for the establishment of building lots along Delaware Street. Eventually, however, by the middle of the nineteenth century, as the property of prominent families, the garden once again was restored, as evidenced by references to its beauty as late as 1872. New soil was applied and new gravel placed over the top of old gravel paths, renewing and widening them.

By the early years of the twentieth century, the garden once again had shrunk to almost its original size, but its formal layout was maintained, as shown by a photograph dating to the orphanage period. Children played along its paths, and vegetables were grown for use on the table. The garden became a symbol of both historical continuity and practicality (see Kryder-Reid 1994 and 1996 for discussion of another elite estate that became the property of a religious order).

With the construction of the site manager's house in 1915, the garden was covered over with fill, probably much of it from the digging of a deep cellar hole under the new building. Fresh topsoil was brought in, and the area became a lawn.

Conclusions

Thus archaeological excavations in the area west of the Visitors' Center at Schuyler Mansion State Historic Site revealed the entire sequence of development of a landscape feature important to the history of this part of the property. Fortunately most of the garden area had been filled over with new soils when extensive changes were planned, thus burying earlier garden remains.

Archaeological excavations of early garden areas are a worthwhile enterprise that is becoming more common as an interest in studying historic landscapes develops. The arrival in America during the first half of the eighteenth century of what Hudgins calls "a patrician culture" led to the development of landscape designs intended to reflect the distancing of the elite from their more common neighbors. By placing their house high on a bluff overlooking the surrounding countryside, building several support structures and establishing a large formal garden, the Schuyler family displayed both their wealth and their knowledge of the classics and the natural sciences. The use of gravel paths, formal beds, fencing, and probably terracing on a sloping southern exposure demonstrates that the Schuylers were aware of the acceptable form for a pleasure garden. Thus they joined the other colonial elite in using these methods to display and justify their place in society.

Acknowledgments

The author wishes to express appreciation to the talented field crew that worked with her to make this analysis possible: Scott Alessio, Elizabeth Burt, Charles Fisher, Charles Florance, and Joe McEvoy. Special thanks go to Paul Huey who commented on draft versions of this text and on the larger field report that preceded this. Finally, the interest of Saratoga-Capital staff Cheryl Gold, Schuyler Mansion staff Sue Haswell, Glenn Griffith, and Jeff Bennett, and Peebles Island supervisor Jim Gold is gratefully acknowledged.

References Cited

American Heritage Dictionary. (3rd ed.). 1994. Bantam Doubleday Dell, New York.

Brown, M.R., and Samford, P.M. 1990. Recent Evidence of Eighteenth-Century Gardening in Williamsburg, Virginia. In *Earth Patterns: Essays in Landscape Archaeology,* edited by W.M. Kelso and R. Most, pp. 103–122. University Press of Virginia, Charlottesville.

Bullock, O.M., Jr. 1969. *The Pastures: The Home of General Philip Schuyler, Albany, New York: A Master Plan Study for the Development of This Historic Site of National Importance for the New York State Historic Trust.* Baltimore.

Calver, W.L., and Bolton, R.P. 1950. *History Written with Pick and Shovel.* The New-York Historical Society, New York.

Cruickshank, D., and Burton, N. 1990. *Life in the Georgian City.* Viking, Penguin Group, London.

Cummings, A.L. 1983. Eighteenth-Century New England Garden Design: The Pictorial Evidence. In *British and American Gardens,* edited by R.P. Maccubbin and P. Martin, pp. 130–135. College of William and Mary and Colonial Williamsburg Foundation, Williamsburg, Va.

De Cunzo, L.A., O'Malley, T., Lewis, M.J., Thomas, G.E., and Wilmanns-Wells, C. 1996. Father Rapp's Garden at Economy: Harmony Society Culture in Microcosm. In *Landscape Archaeology,* edited by R. Yamin and K.B. Metheny, pp. 91–117. University of Tennessee Press, Knoxville.

Diderot, D. 1959. *A Diderot Pictorial Encyclopedia of Trades and Industry,* edited by C. Coulston Gillespie, Vol. 1. Dover Publications, New York.

Fallowfield, J. 1791. *The Husbandman and Tradesman's Gardening Calendar with Directions to Manage the Kitchen, Fruit, and Flower Garden.* Walkers's Office, Preston, Great Britain.

Favretti, R.J., and Favretti, J.P. 1977. *For Every House a Garden: A Guide for Reproducing Period Gardens.* The Pequot Press, Chester, Conn.

_____. 1978. *Landscapes and Gardens for Historic Buildings: A Handbook for Reproducing and Creating Authentic Landscape Settings.* American Association for State and Local History, Nashville, Tenn.

Feister, L.M. 1986. Archeology for Visitors' Center Addition, Schuyler Mansion. Memorandum to Cheryl Gold, May 22. Archeology Unit files, Bureau of Historic Sites, New York State Office of Parks, Recreation and Historic Preservation, Peebles Island, Waterford.

_____. 1995a. *Johnson Hall Outbuildings, Landscape History, and Forgotten Features: Documentary and Archeological Research Conducted Between 1945 and 1991, Johnstown, Fulton County, New York.* Archeology Unit, Bureau of Historic Sites, New York State Office of Parks, Recreation and Historic Preservation, Peebles Island, Waterford.

_____. 1995b. *A Synthesis of Archeology at Schuyler Mansion State Historic Sites, Albany, New York Prior to the 1994 Visitor Center Addition Project.* Archeology Unit, Bureau of Historic Sites, New York State Office of Parks, Recreation, and Historic reservation, Peebles Island, Waterford.

Gibbons, K.L., and Stott, P.H. 1977. *Schuyler Mansion: A Historic Structure Report.* New York State Parks and Recreation, Albany.

Hudgins, C.L. 1990. Robert "King" Carter and the Landscape of Tidewater Virginia in the Eighteenth Century. In *Earth Patterns: Essays in Landscape Archaeology,* edited by W.M. Kelso and R. Most, pp. 59–70. University Press of Virginia, Charlottesville.

Joyce, E.J. 1986. Thomas Jefferson, Gardener. *Rodde's Organic Gardening,* 33(3):42–53.

Kelso, W.M. 1984. Landscape Archaeology: A Key to Virginia's Cultivated Past. In *British and American Gardens in the Eighteenth Century,* edited by R.P. Maccubbin and P. Martin, pp. 159–169. The Colonial Williamsburg Foundation, Williamsburg, Va.

Kryder-Reid, E. 1994. 'As Is the Gardener, So Is the Garden': The Archaeology of Landscape as Myth. In *Historical Archaeology of the Chesapeake,* edited by P.A. Shackel and B.J. Little, pp. 131–148. Smithsonian Institution Press, Washington, D.C.

_____. 1996. The Construction of Sanctity: Landscape and Ritual in a Religious Community. In *Landscape Archaeology,* edited by R. Yamin and K.B. Metheny, pp. 228–248. University of Tennessee Press, Knoxville.

Lehman, S.W. 1986. A Well-Cultivated Domain: A Documentary Study of Farming on the Schuyler Estate. Schuyler Mansion State Historic Site, February. Archeology Unit files, Bureau of Historic Sites, New York State Office of Parks, Recreation and Historic Preservation, Peebles Island, Waterford.

Leighton, A. 1976. *American Gardens in the Eighteenth Century: For Use or for Delight.* Houghton Mifflin, Boston.

Leone, M.P., and Shackel, P.A. 1990. Plane and Solid Geometry in Colonial Gardens in Annapolis, Md. In *Earth Patterns: Essays in Landscape Archaeology*, edited by W.M. Kelso and R. Most, pp. 153–168. University Press of Virginia, Charlottesville.

Luccketti, N.M. 1988. *Archaeological Excavations at Bacon's Castle Garden, Surry County, Virginia*. James River Institute for Archaeology, Jamestown Island, Va.

Metheny, K.B., Kratzer, J., Yentsch, A.E., and Goodwin, C.M. 1996. Method in Landscape Archaeology: Research Strategies in a Historic New Jersey Garden. In *Landscape Archaeology*, edited by R. Yamin and K.B. Metheny, pp. 6–31. University of Tennessee Press, Knoxville.

Miller, N.F., Yentsch, A., Piperno, D., and Paca, B. 1990. Two Centuries of Landscape Change at Morven, Princeton, New Jersey. In *Earth Patterns: Essays in Landscape Archaeology*, edited by W.M. Kelso and R. Most, pp. 257–276. University Press of Virginia, Charlottesville.

Nelson, L.H. (editor). 1980. *Illustrated Catalogue of American Hardware of the Russell and Erwin Manufacturing Company, an Unabridged Reprint of the 1865 Edition*. Association for Preservation Technology, Baltimore.

Noël Hume, I. 1970. *A Guide to Artifacts of Colonial America*. Alfred A. Knopf, New York.

Oswald, A. 1975. *Clay Pipes for the Archaeologist*. British Archaeological Reports 14. British Archaeological Reports, Oxford.

Reynolds, M.T. 1895. The Colonial Buildings of Rensselaerwick. *The Architectural Record* (April–June), 4(4):415–438.

Rogers, G.C. 1984. Gardens and Landscapes in Eighteenth-Century South Carolina. *British and American Gardens in the Eighteenth Century: Eighteen Illustrated Essays on Garden History*, edited by R.P. Maccubbin and P. Martin, pp. 148–158. The Colonial Williamsburg Foundation, Williamsburg, Va.

Rozbicki, M.J. 1999. Review of *Gardens and Gardening in the Chesapeake, 1700–1805* by B.W. Sarudy. *William and Mary Quarterly* 56(4):854–856.

Street, A.B. 1872. The Old Schuyler Mansion. *Appleton's Journal* 8 (November 9):506.

Upton, D. 1990. Imagining the Early Virginia Landscape. In *Earth Patterns: Essays in Landscape Archaeology*, edited by W.M. Kelso and R. Most, pp. 71–88. University Press of Virginia, Charlottesville.

Weber, C.A. 1996. The Greenhouse Effect: Gender-Related Traditions in Eighteenth-Century Gardening. *Landscape Archaeology*, edited by R. Yamin and K.B. Metheny, pp. 32–51. University of Tennessee Press, Knoxville.

Weber, C.A., Comer, E.A., Akerson, L.E., and Norman, G. 1990. Mount Clare: An Interdisciplinary Approach to the Restoration of a Georgian Landscape. In *Earth Patterns: Essays in Landscape Archaeology*, edited by W.M. Kelso and R. Most, pp. 135–152. University Press of Virginia, Charlottesville.

Webster, N. 1806. *A Compendious Dictionary of the English Language*. From Sidney's Press, for Hudson & Goodwin, Booksellers, Hartford, and Increase Cooke & Co., Booksellers, New Haven, Conn.

Yentsch, A.E. 1989. The Use of Land and Space on Lot 83, Annapolis, Maryland. *New Perspectives of Maryland Archaeology*, edited by R.J. Dent and B.J. Little. Special Publications of the Maryland Archaeological Society, Baltimore.

———, Miller, N.F., Paca, B., and Piperno, D. 1987. Archaeologically Defining the Earlier Garden Landscapes at Morven: Preliminary Results. *Northeast Historical Archaeology, Journal of the Council for Northeast Historical Archaeology* 16:1–19.

CHAPTER 10

From Refrigerator, to Oven, to Down the Drain: Nineteenth-Century Analogs of Twentieth-Century Household Conveniences in Old Albany

J.W. Bouchard

Introduction

This chapter describes the first-floor layout of a middle-class house at 27 Columbia Street that was the subject of archaeological investigations in 1998 at the site of the New York State Department of Environmental Conservation (DEC) office building at 625 Broadway in downtown Albany (Figure 10.1). The house was located at the southern boundary of the 2-acre site where its early to mid-nineteenth-century occupants made provision for everyday household tasks such as cooking, cold storage for food, supplying potable water, and getting rid of both used domestic water and storm-water runoff. Although historic research continues, I will begin with a short history of the development of the site and what is now known about the attorney-owner who was probably responsible for some of the nineteenth-century conveniences exhibited in this efficient house and who, along with his family, had the benefit.

Neighborhood History

Between 1650 and 1750, the site was one block north of the stockade line of the fortified community of Beverwyck (Figure 10.2). In this place was a small stream called Fox Creek that emerged from modern-day Sheridan Hollow and flowed into the Hudson River. Some of its first residents were late seventeenth-century Albany shoemakers and tanners. They located along Fox Creek where they remained until

the closing years of the eighteenth century. At the same time, the mouth of Fox Creek became a mooring spot for river sloops and other vessels where the creek channel formed a break in the Hudson River bank that allowed ships to approach close to shore. At the mooring, cargoes of lumber and grain to be shipped south toward New York were loaded, and manufactured goods imported from Holland and, later, England and elsewhere were off loaded. So successful was the mooring, by the third quarter of the eighteenth century, the largest of Albany's four public docks jutted more than a hundred feet into the river at the point where Fox Creek once issued into the Hudson (Figure 10.3).

Toward the end of the eighteenth century, the tanners were displaced by middle-class residents, traders, and merchants. In general, these Albanians divided into two groups. First, were the younger members of the fourth and fifth generation of Albany's first families, who had not inherited the bulk of the family wealth. Instead, they were forced to "work" for a living. The second group was ambitious Englishmen, Scots, and other immigrants who labored to break into the tight-knit social and economic order established and nourished by the Dutch over more than 150 years (Bielinski 1991, 1996). Most of the residences of both groups of Albanians faced west across Watervliet Street, the main thoroughfare leading north out of Albany. At the back of their lots along Montgomery Street were stables, privies, carriage

People, Places, and Material Things: Historical Archaeology of Albany, New York edited by Charles L. Fisher, New York State Museum Bulletin 499, © 2003 by the University of the State of New York, New York State Education Department, Albany, New York. All rights reserved

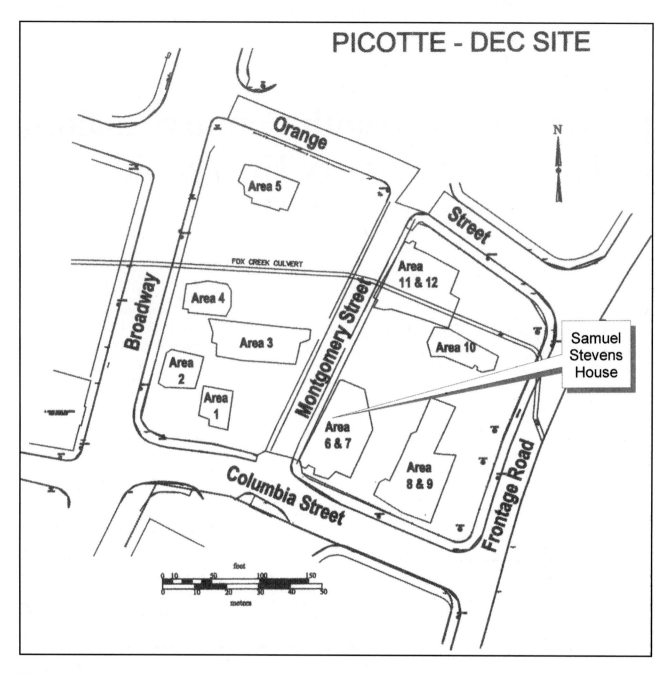

Figure 10.1. Project location and excavation areas at Picotte-DEC office building site, 597–643 Broadway, Albany.

houses, and other outbuildings. Warehouses stood on the land in the eastern part of the project, including the lot that would eventually become Samuel Stevens' home. Warehouses were erected here because the land was close to both the river and the North Dock.

The most important single event affecting how the neighborhood developed in the early nineteenth century occurred in 1797 when a devastating fire destroyed every dwelling, stable, outbuilding, and warehouse in the 2 acres covered by the Picotte-DEC project (Albany Centinel 1797). With the loss of all the buildings, the city government took advantage of the situation to encourage the landowners in the neighborhood to realign their lots and the adjacent streets to conform to the surrounding street pattern (Figure 10.4). Having done so, early nineteenth-century redevelopment along Broadway mostly reestablished the old land-use pattern. Middle-class land-

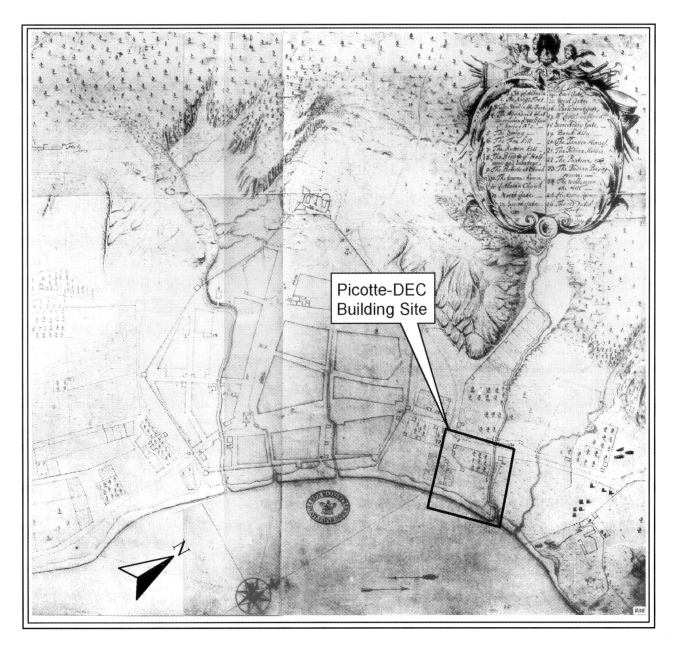

Figure 10.2. Albany in the late seventeenth century (Römer 1698).

owners on that street built new multifamily dwellings that often incorporated shops or professional offices on the first floors and comfortable residences on the second and third floors. On the other hand, many of the warehouses that had stood close to the North Dock in the eastern half of the project were replaced by residences and small businesses more modest in scale than those along Broadway. Nonetheless, the middle-class milieu of the neighborhood was reinforced when the Third Presbyterian Church was built about

1806 on Montgomery Street just behind the lot where, later, the Samuel Stevens house stood. Another bourgeois institution, the Albany Academy for Girls, was opened in 1814 in the lot just north of the church (J. Wolcott, personal communication 1997–1998).

In the first half of the nineteenth century, the Montgomery Street block was home to both working-class people and professionals. However, the balance shifted over time as the flight of the middle class was fostered by changes wrought by a transportation-ori-

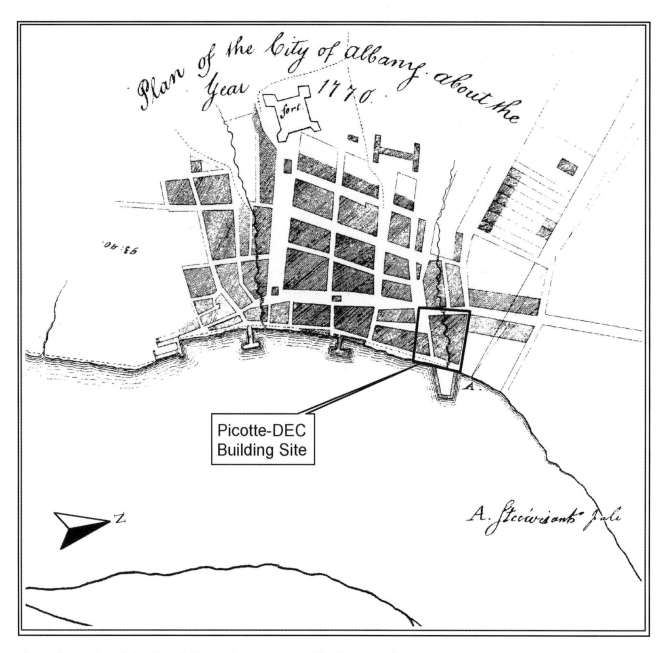

Figure 10.3. Plan of the City of Albany about the year 1770 (Yates 1770).

ented neighborhood focus. Lying close to the Hudson River waterfront, the neighborhood became host to the Albany Basin (Figure 10.5). The three-quarter-mile-long basin was an artificial harbor that grew out of Albany's position as a port city at the terminus of the Erie and Champlain Canals. The waters in the basin were current-free, a secure place to load and unload cargoes. More than 100 warehouses lined the pier on the east side of the basin; dozens more were built along Quay Street on the west side. Access to the warehouses on the pier was gained at three points: toward the south and north ends, and in the center. The drawbridge at the center connected the basin with the rest of the city along Columbia Street (Bradt and Carpenter 1828, 1843; Sidney 1850). In the 1830s and 1840s, heavy cart and wagon traffic lumbered along Columbia Street in front of Samuel Stevens' house, accompanied by the raucous clamor of crews from river sailing sloops, ocean-going ships, and mule-drawn canal boats.

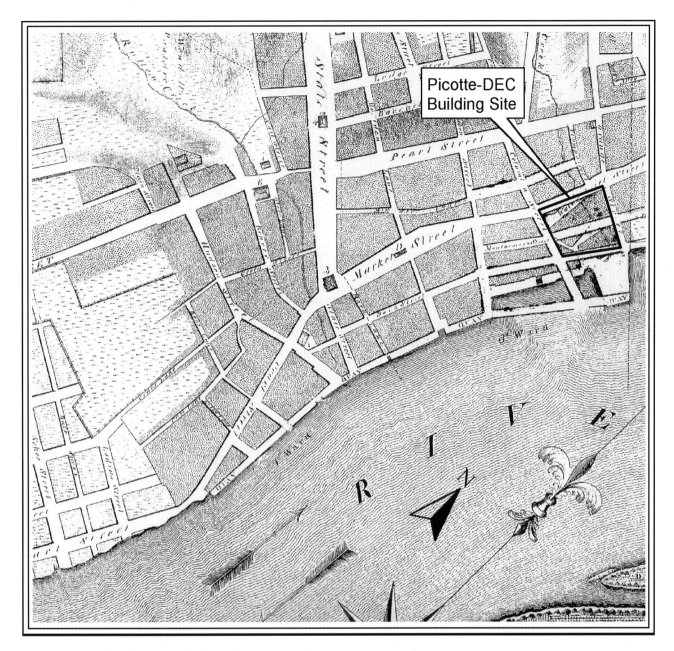

Figure 10.4. Map of the City of Albany (DeWitt 1794).

Although professionals migrated uptown in the second quarter of the nineteenth century, many of these community-minded citizens maintained a certain level of concern for the residents of the old neighborhood they were fleeing. As a measure of that concern, they turned the Third Presbyterian Church into a Seamen's Bethel or chapel. The chapel was meant to counteract the temptations targeted toward sailors in port cities everywhere (Munsell 1850:133, 134). The house of worship promoted sobriety, duty

to family (what today would be called family values), and Bible study, all ideals and pursuits in short supply along most harbor waterfronts.

By 1860 railroads were competing successfully with river and canal freight service, and with a nearly two-century-long history of commerce and transportation, Albany's waterfront continued the tradition by becoming a center for railroad freight as well. By the mid-1860s the entire eastern half of the Picotte-DEC project was taken over by the New York Central

Figure 10.5. Map of the City of Albany from original survey (Sidney 1850).

Rail Road (NYCRR) (Figure 10.6). All of the earlier buildings were demolished. The only structures on the block were wagon sheds, freight buildings, and ice houses that were part of the freight yard. The western half of the project along Broadway continued its evolution toward commerce, although a few work-

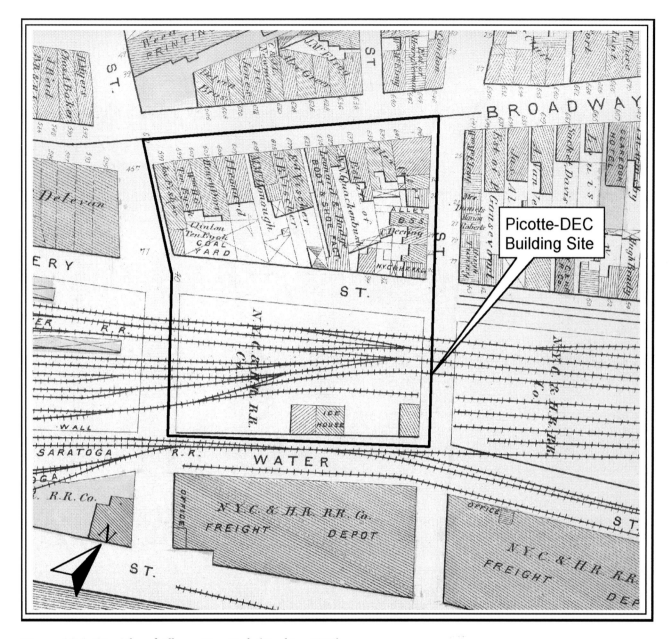

Figure 10.6. City Atlas of Albany, New York (Hopkins 1876).

ing-class residents and shopkeepers persisted (Hopkins 1876; Sanborn Map Company 1889).

By the turn of the twentieth century, the downtown freight yard was hemmed in by its neighbors. Unable to expand, the NYCRR moved the yard to West Albany, its present location. With the destruction by fire in 1894 of the block-long Delavan House hotel across Columbia Street from the Picotte-DEC site, the NYCRR saw the opportunity to establish a modern, elaborate, downtown rail passenger station. The NYCRR acquired the property, and Union Station opened in 1900. The rail passenger platform where the trains arrived and departed was on the east side of the building. It was a 20-foot-high structure that covered three city blocks, including the old freight yards where the Samuel Stevens house once stood. Both the freight yard and passenger platform were built with minimal ground disturbance. This benefited the archaeology by protecting most of the remains of the Samuel Stevens house as well as other important deposits and features (Gerber 1989).

Samuel Stevens

Samuel Stevens was an eminent Albany attorney of the middle decades of the nineteenth century. There were many sources of information including reminiscences about his career by contemporary attorneys and fellow members of the Albany bar, such as L.B. Porter (1886), Amasa Parker (1897), and John J. Hill (1884). Other details were obtained from Munsell's Annals (1855, 1858, 1859, 1869, 1871), an 1843 tax assessment map; Albany city directories (Child 1833; Hoffman 1839-40, 1840-41, 1841-42, 1842-43, 1843-44, 1846-47, 1847-48, 1848-1849, 1849-1850; Munsell 1855, 1856; Sampson Davenport & Co. 1870). There is also an interesting website that describes and interprets his grave marker and the cemetery plot in Rochester, New York, where he was interred when he died in 1854 (Orsini 2000).

Stevens was born in Washington County in 1794 (Orsini 2000) and by 1825 was serving the first of two terms as an assemblyman in the state legislature from the same county (Parker 1897:151). Stevens was a Clintonian Democrat in the 1820s, but eventually became a Whig (Porter 1886:140–141). He was defeated in a close Whig caucus vote as the party's candidate for attorney general in 1839. He was also nominated for lieutenant governor.

Stevens is listed in the city directories for fewer than 20 years, first appearing when still in his thirties and disappearing in middle age. There is no reference to him in directories predating 1834. In that year he is listed as an "attorney and counselor" with offices at 322 North Market Street and living at the City Hotel at 402 Market Street. Market Street today is known as Broadway, the street that bounds the west side of the Picotte-DEC project. Stevens shared his law office with young Peter Cagger who lived with his older brother and mother farther down Market Street. In 1833 Cagger is listed as a student at law, but in the late 1830s Stevens and Cagger shared a law practice at the 322 North Market Street office. The partnership was dissolved by the early 1840s. Samuel Stevens continued to practice law, this time in partnership with his younger brother, Cyrus. The law office moved several times, finally settling in at 480 Broadway. For his part, Peter Cagger set up his own practice at 57 State Street. Samuel and Cyrus Stevens are listed as attorneys until 1849–50 (Hoffman). In 1855 only Cyrus is listed (Munsell). Stevens' only other professional relationship was a law partnership with James Edwards in the 1820s (Porter 1886:143).

Samuel Stevens lived in the City Hotel from 1834 until 1836 or 1837, when he is first listed as residing at 27 Columbia Street. His name is associated with this address as late as 1850 (Figure 10.5). Living and working only one or two blocks away along Broadway, Stevens would undoubtedly have been familiar with the neighborhood surrounding Columbia Street. Indeed, his law practice must regularly have taken him along the same street as he strolled the waterfront or visited clients in their offices, stores, or at home. In any case, he continued to reside on Columbia Street for about half a decade, moving uptown about 1842 to 6 Academy Park one block below and one block north of the State Capitol, where he remained until he died in September 1854 (Figure 10.5). The changing ambience of the Columbia Street neighborhood may have provided the motive, but his successful law practice provided the means for the move.

In addition to a sketch of his career, the city directories and other sources also tell us something of Stevens' public life. A review of public and business institutions for the period during which Stevens' name appears in the city directories shows him as a member of the board of directors of the Albany Exchange Bank (Munsell 1869:296). He was also third vice president of the Albany Savings Bank in 1843 (Hoffman 1843-44) and second vice president in 1850 (Munsell 1869:339). He was one of the founders in 1838 of the Albany Medical College, helped prepare its articles of association, and served on the first board of trustees (Munsell 1867:220). In 1841 he advocated the building of a railroad bridge across the Hudson River at Albany just as the railroad from Boston was coming to completion (Munsell 1859:311). He was also an advocate for federal government protection of American industry (Munsell 1859:319).

Several references to his career and ability successfully to argue cases in court appear in sections on the Albany bar in histories of Albany by Porter (1886) and Parker (1897). Contemporary attorney John J. Hill also mentioned Stevens in his 1884 reminiscences (Hill 1884). Both Porter (1886:140) and Parker (1897:151) refer to him as "General" Stevens, a reference to his position as Adjutant General of the New York State Militia. Letters from Governor Hamilton Fish (1849) and John A. King (1849) relate to his mundane duties in that position.

One of the more interesting anecdotes of Stevens' early career was an appearance in 1832 before the Common Council where he advocated continuing the age-old practice in Albany of allowing hogs to run at-large in the city. Stevens was quoted as saying, "their running at large was eminently beneficial to the health of the city. If they were of advantage in other cities, they must be so here. Their free running was an old Dutch privilege, and we must be careful how we infringe it" (Munsell 1858:246). Stevens was unsuccessful employing this tactic, and the Common Council voted to fine the owners of free-running hogs.

Physically, Stevens was described as "short, thickset, tending to corpulence; his eyelids were always partly closed, as though they were affected by the light. He was of nervous temperament, active, energetic and restless," and "when at the Bar, his mouth was always occupied by a quid of tobacco, by no means infinitesimal in size" (Porter 1886:141). As concerns his end, Porter makes only a short mention in a discussion of another well-known Albany attorney and former law partner of Stevens, Peter Cagger:

> Mr. Cagger afterward associated himself with Mr. Samuel Stevens, and the firm name of Stevens & Cagger became speedily potential in legal circles. After a successful practice of some years, Mr. Stevens, a very able man and the peer of renowned lawyers in the legal arena, yielded to excessive labor. (Porter 1886:147)

According to the University of Rochester website that documents Stevens' grave site in Lot G72 at Mount Hope Cemetery in Rochester, New York, Stevens was an Episcopalian (Orsini 2000). In 1847 he gave $50 toward the construction of Trinity Church in Albany, a small Episcopal parish on Trinity Place one block west of South Pearl Street south of Madison Avenue (Hopkins 1876; Munsell 1871:348; Walworth et al. 1886:761). Stevens was prominent enough in the Albany establishment that his eulogy was delivered by William Seward, who as Secretary of State in 1867 was responsible for the Alaska Purchase.

Samuel Stevens apparently married twice. His first wife, Susan, died in 1839 (Munsell 1859:287). His second wife, Mary Smith, was from the well-to-do Smith family of Rochester. Stevens is buried in the Smith family plot at Mount Hope Cemetery. Stevens and Mary Smith had at least one son, also named Samuel, who is buried in the Smith plot. Young Samuel, who died in 1876, was born about 1846 when his father was 52 years of age.

As concerns Albany properties owned by Stevens, the Sidney map (1850), which was published four years prior to his death, shows that he owned at least three properties in the city. First, there was the house

at 27 Columbia Street where the archaeological study occurred. This building had a common wall with the residence to the east owned by James Kidd (Figure 10.7). That Kidd owned the east half of the building is of more than passing interest because Stevens and Kidd also owned a property two blocks to the northwest along North Pearl Street between Orange Street and Clinton Avenue (Figure 10.5). In the 1830s and early 1840s, Kidd was a carpet merchant who lived at 48 Columbia Street. He was also a director of the Mechanics' & Farmers' Bank (Hoffman 1839–40:160; 1840–41:145; 1842–43:118) and in the late 1840s he was county treasurer. By that date he lived at 101 Clinton Square, the building jointly owned by him and Stevens (Hoffman 1846–47:192). As mentioned previously, the third structure labeled with Stevens' name was the upscale 6 Academy Park address. This building survives today, although it was renovated early in the twentieth century by eminent Albany architect Marcus T. Reynolds. James Kidd's address is listed as 7 Elk Street (Academy Park) in the 1870 city directory, the residence immediately to the west of Stevens' 1854 address. Kidd outlived Stevens by at least 15 years, and his name appears at 7 Elk Street on the 1876 atlas (Hopkins 1876).

The Archaeology of the Samuel Stevens House

The Samuel Stevens house at the corner of Columbia Street and Montgomery Street was revealed through a combination of power equipment and hand excavation. The focus of the work was exposing the remains of the house buried beneath the 1860s railroad freight yard and partly destroyed by the concrete foundation on the west side of the early twentieth-century NYCRR passenger platform. The remains consisted of parts of three first-floor rooms, from south to north, the front or reception room that opened onto Columbia Street, the kitchen at the center, and the cold room on the north end (Figures 10.7 and 10.8). Backyard features included a small outbuilding at the rear of the lot and a water supply system consisting of a covered cistern and a buried lead pipe leading to the house. A description of the nineteenth-century domestic conveniences preserved in the house and backyard follows.

House Layout

The west (Montgomery Street) side of the front room, kitchen, and cold room had been truncated by

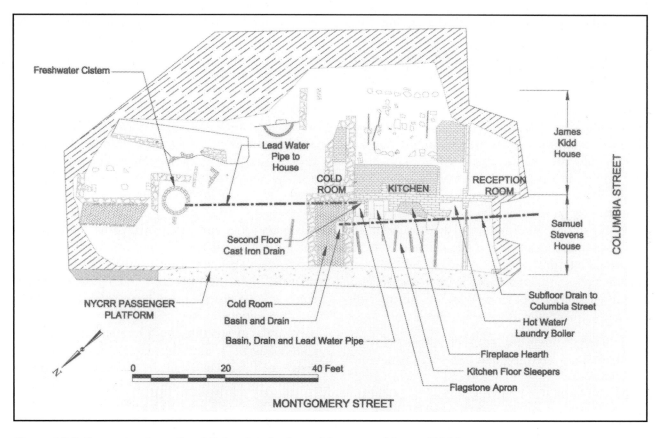

Figure 10.7. Excavation Areas 6 and 7 showing the Samuel Stevens and James Kidd houses.

the concrete footing for the NYCRR passenger platform (Figure 10.7). Nonetheless, the full dimensions of the house are estimated at a width of 24 feet (east-west) and a length of 48 feet (north-south). As a result of the need to maintain a passageway along the south side (front) of the building, only the northern half of the reception room of the house was excavated. Other than its walls, no details of the front room were exposed, although the neighboring residence of James Kidd, with which the Stevens house shared a common wall, had a large mortared brick fireplace in its reception room. Placing the front of the house about 6 feet from the edge of the street provides the reception room with dimensions of about 16 feet by 24 feet.

Kitchen Layout

With dimensions of 24 feet by 24 feet, the kitchen was the largest first-floor room (Figure 10.8). The only surviving doorway in this room was a 36-inch-wide opening leading to the reception room. There

was probably once a doorway connecting to the cold room to the north, but it was destroyed when the NYCRR passenger platform was built along Montgomery Street.

The only direct evidence of a heat source in the kitchen was a brick fireplace in the center of the east wall and a rectangular brick feature a few feet to the south. The fireplace had the proportions of a Rumford hearth, that is 1:3 (20 by 60 in), while the interior dimensions of the adjacent brick feature to the south that was probably the base for the hot water or laundry boiler were 21 inches by 28 inches. The fireplace opening was surrounded by an apron of flagstone to keep embers ejected from the hearth from burning the kitchen's wood floor. Although none of the planks of the kitchen floor remained, the planed logs, or sleepers, to which the planks were nailed survived. There were a half dozen sleepers; originally there were eight set on 30-inch centers. A few of the cut-iron nails used to secure the plank floor protruded from the tops of the sleepers.

One of the most interesting features in the kitchen

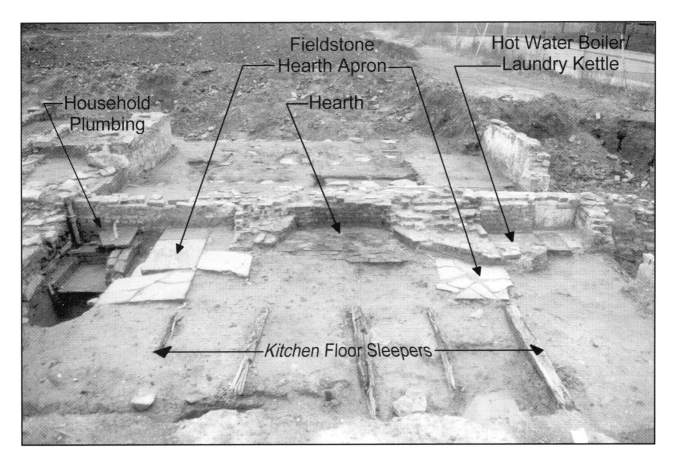

Figure 10.8. The Stevens house kitchen.

was the complex wastewater disposal system (Figure 10.9). The system was composed of a mortared brick and greywacke sandstone wastewater basin and inter-connecting drains. The basin measured 2 feet by 2.5 feet. The basin was only a few inches deep; an 18-inch-long, mortared brick, overflow drain on the west side of the basin connected to a separate north-south, mortared, brick drain that passed beneath both the kitchen and reception room floors before emptying onto Columbia Street.

Wastewater from what may have been a bathroom on the second or third floor of the house was disposed through a drain that ran down the interior of the northeast corner of the kitchen. The flow was carried through the interior of the house to the first floor by a cast-iron pipe that led into the northeast corner of the brick and sandstone basin described in the previous paragraph.

The kitchen was supplied by water drawn through a lead pipe leading from the backyard cistern. A hand pump undoubtedly raised the freshwater from the cistern. A second lead pipe directed wastewater into the drain basin, apparently from a sink above. As with the second-floor wastewater drain, domestic (cooking, laundry, and cleaning) wastewater passed out of the house through the drain beneath the kitchen and reception room floors.

Cold Room

The cold room was the smallest of the first-floor chambers (Figure 10.10). Enclosed by 2-feet-thick masonry walls and situated on the north side where it received the least exposure to the sun, the cold room was the best-insulated room in the house. The narrow dimension of the cold room was 5.5 feet to 6 feet. If built as wide as the house, it would have been about 24 feet long. A doorway undoubtedly connected the cold room to the kitchen, but it was destroyed in the closing years of the nineteenth century during the construction of the massive concrete foundation for the NYCRR passenger platform.

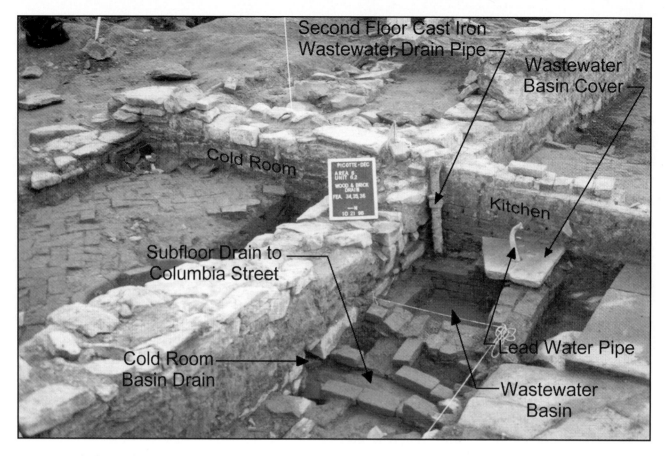

Figure 10.9. The Stevens house kitchen and second-floor drains and other wastewater features.

The cold room floor consisted of unmortared brick neatly laid in a herringbone pattern. The only feature on the floor was a red sandstone basin adjacent to the south wall. Its nominal dimensions were 36 inches by 24 inches. It was less than 6 inches deep and perforated by a 1-inch drain hole near the northeast corner. The drain hole led to a brick drain that passed beneath the east cold room foundation wall and attached to the subfloor kitchen drain (Figure 10.11). The basin may have been only a simple wash sink, but it also could have held a block of ice to cool the room.

Domestic Water Supply

A brick freshwater cistern with an exterior diameter of 5.5 feet and interior diameter of 4 feet was located about 25 feet north of the cold room and 36 feet north of the kitchen basin (Figures 10.7 and 10.12). The cistern wall was two rows of mortared brick wide; the interior was parged with water-proofing ce-

ment. What survived was 55 inches high. The cistern would have provided the Stevens household with 375 gallons of water. The cistern was set into the angle between adjacent walls of an outbuilding and was undoubtedly recharged by water running off the outbuilding roof. A 1-inch-diameter intake lead pipe passed through the cistern wall about 4 feet above the bottom (Figure 10.12). The pipe was planked for support and protection and led toward the house.

Discussion

The Samuel Stevens house is a fascinating example of how the nineteenth-century middle-class residents of Albany equipped their houses with conveniences that are generally associated with twentieth-century American domestic life. Just how sophisticated the domestic appliances may have been in the Stevens house is not fully apparent from the archaeology but is illustrated in Figure 10.13, an advertisement for kitchen and bath "suites" in the 1849 Albany city di-

Figure 10.10. The Stevens house cold room.

Figure 10.11. The Stevens house cold room and kitchen plumbing details.

Figure 10.12. The Stevens house freshwater cistern and lead water supply pipe.

rectory (Hoffman 1849–50).

The mid-nineteenth-century kitchen suite in Figure 10.13 consists of the following elements from left to right: a hot-water holding tank, coal or wood-fired laundry boiler, coal or wood-fired cooking range with two ovens, hot-water boiler, sink with running hot and cold water, and a cold-water pressure tank.

Although components of the kitchen suite may have been installed in the Stevens house kitchen, the archaeological evidence for particular elements is limited. As represented in the 1849 city directory advertisement, there is archaeological remains for the components that have masonry elements, namely, the laundry or water boiler and the kitchen sink, the latter indicated by the drain in the northeast corner of the kitchen. The other elements (hot-water holding tank, the cast-iron range, and cold-water pressure tank) were free-standing and had salvage value, which means that they were probably removed prior to demolition of the house in the 1860s. The obvious utility of the sink with hot and cold running water makes its presence a certainty, as does the range. That the house was equipped either with a wash boiler or

hot-water boiler is indicated by the brick feature to the right of the hearth in Figures 10.7 and 10.8.

When comparing Figure 10.13 to the Stevens house archaeological remains, it is clear that the Rumford fireplace was too small to have accommodated a range of the size shown in the advertisement. However, when the kitchen suite was retrofitted into their older house, the Stevenses could have chosen a smaller range or allowed the stove to extend into the kitchen.

The bathroom suite at the top of Figure 10.13 consists of the lavatory, commode, and combination bath and shower. The sink and bath-shower are furnished with hot and cold running water from the pressurized system in the kitchen on the first floor. No flushing device is apparent in the figure for the commode.

Situated on one of the upper floors of the house for which, of course, there are no archaeological remains, which elements of the bathroom suite were installed in the Stevens house remains a matter of conjecture. The sole evidence for a bathroom suite is the cast-iron drain in the northeast corner of the kitchen (Figure 10.9).

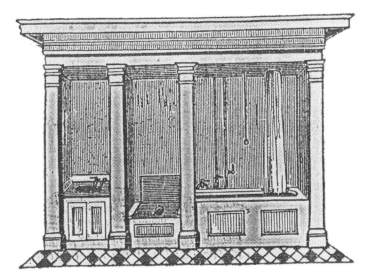

Figure 10.13. Ad for kitchen ranges and bathing apparatus (Hoffman 1849–50).

The archaeological evidence of the first floor of the Samuel Stevens house demonstrates that this prominent Albany lawyer was in the vanguard of domestic architecture before the middle of the nineteenth century. At a time when household plumbing was a rarity, the Stevens household was equipped with sophisticated domestic appliances and conveniences.

The kitchen conveniences in the Stevens house imply not only that this Albany attorney was interested in conveying modernity, but also that women had relatively high status in the household. Many of the appliances and conveniences were designed to ease the burden of household chores. Unfortunately, although the census data for the 1840s are useful for indicating the size and make-up of the Stevens household, they indicate neither kinship nor status. Thus details of household organization and relationships are unknown. Did attorney Stevens employ servants and how many? Were one or more of his parents or in-laws resident at 27 Columbia Street? Answers to these and other questions would help in interpreting the organization of the household, the division of work among its female members, and the role that servants might have played in accomplishing the increasing number of tasks that household work entailed.

These topics are covered in detail by scholars such as Hayden (1981), Katzman (1978), and Dudden (1983). Hayden in *The Grand Domestic Revolution: A History of Feminist Design for American Homes, Neighborhoods, and Cities* begins a discussion of the nineteenth-century feminist movement about 1870, a decade after the Stevens house and its occupants had passed from the Columbia Street scene. The Stevenses may have participated in the beginning stages of this movement by adopting aspects of the cult of domesticity but otherwise were ignorant of its precepts. Likewise, although detailing the relationships between largely women employers and household workers in the nineteenth century and into the twentieth century, Katzman and Dudden's works have limited applicability for understanding the Stevens house. On the other hand, Suellen Hoy's *Chasing Dirt* (1995) illuminates both the design and operation of the structure.

The expansion of American cities in the first half of the nineteenth century was largely precipitated by industrialization. Urban growth brought on a host of problems including large-scale outbreaks of communicable and fecal-borne diseases. Other difficulties faced by residents and city managers alike reflected a lack of urban infrastructure and related to the disposal of human, animal, and household waste: providing an ample and reliable supply of potable water; and removing wastewater from domestic, commercial, and industrial sites. The struggle in the United States to solve these problems brought on by urban growth, and the role of women and other activists in guiding public health policy is traced in *Chasing Dirt* (Hoy 1995). By describing women's contributions to advancements in public health during the nineteenth century, Hoy's book also contributes to placing Samuel Stevens' house in perspective and helps in assessing the important changes in waste management that were adopted citywide by the end of the nineteenth century and the beginning decades of the twentieth century.

Early on in *Chasing Dirt,* Hoy notes that

> Changes in cleanliness practices between the days of [John] Wesley and [Benjamin] Franklin and the expansive 1820s were so slow as to be invisible. But from then until the Civil War, the speed of change accelerated, and the idea and practice of cleanliness were carried along by the inexorable shift toward urbanism and industrialism. Neither of those two forces nor cleanliness, though, were more than partially in place by 1860 . . . City administrators and public health officials had begun holding "sanitary conventions" to seek solutions to common problems concerning sewerage, clean water, and the links between dirt and disease. (1995:6–7)

Hoy ties the gaining popularity of cleanliness among the middle class to the separation of home from work, especially for men, and the message of "respectability" that cleanliness sent to others. Drawn by a sense of domestic tranquility that was engendered by a clean house and pleasant surroundings, men returned home to a sheltering refuge from the workaday world.

That a clean home in Albany or any other urban setting was considered a refuge suggests that the city beyond the domestic doorstep was dirty. Hoy observes that "Each horse, for example, daily deposited an estimated twenty-two pounds of manure on the streets. Although hundreds of roaming pigs scavenged garbage thrown into fly-infested thoroughfares and kept them cleaner than they otherwise might have been, they too befouled the environment" (1995:12–13). Stevens' own 1832 defense of the right of the Albany poor to own free-roaming hogs serves to highlight the dichotomy between the domestic refuge at 27 Columbia Street and the dirty city that surrounded it.

The ability of mistresses who maintained homes (and presumably the servants retained by the growing middle class) to keep a house clean and neat was largely dependent upon the ease with which the means for cleaning could be obtained. For the most part, that meant access to a reliable supply of clean water.

> Since plumbing was largely non-existent, water for washing, cleaning, and cooking almost always had to be carried from one place to another. If a family had the wherewithal and the know-how to install a small force pump that would bring water through a lead pipe into the house, they were considered especially fortunate. (Hoy 1995:13)

The Stevens family's water system that supplied the house from the backyard cistern was a significant step in helping to maintain a clean home.

Even though there were significant moves afoot before midcentury to encourage household cleanliness, including washing of the "extremities" (hands, feet, and face), bathing the entire body was beyond the technical capability of most households at the time, because heating the amount of water needed to take a bath was so costly. In 1841 Catharine Beecher, sister of *Uncle Tom's Cabin* author Harriet Beecher Stowe and a crusader for American cleanliness in her own right, designed "an ideal cottage, where every room had a wood-burning fireplace, [but] only the kitchen had a sink" (Hoy 1995:21). It is significant, therefore, that the Stevens family's house far exceeded the recommendations of one prominent advocate of cleanliness.

The evolving ethos of middle-class cleanliness generated more work than could be reasonably done by one person. Because men's work increasingly took them away from home, the solution was to retain a domestic servant to do the work. Those middle-class families of modest means could afford only one and, depending upon how the mistress of the house viewed her own role, the servant's responsibilities might consist of virtually all of the housework, cleaning, cooking, laundry, and caring for the children. Wealthier households divided the tasks among nurses, maids, laundresses, gardeners, and others.

In the age before mechanical washing machines, laundry and ironing, especially, was onerous drudgery. As with other household tasks, some servants complained about how it wore them down (Katzman 1978:8–9, 20–21), but others (Katzman 1978:21) left domestic service to become washerwomen. Working at home, they had more time off than live-in servants. In any case, the combination of pumped water supply from the backyard cistern and the wash boiler or water heater in the Stevens house kitchen were significant improvements in making laundry work more efficient.

The trend toward supplying households with running water from onsite wells or cisterns in the first half of the nineteenth century, and increasingly from municipal water supplies thereafter, led to the problem of disposing of wastewater, both "gray" water from laundry, cooking, and other household chores and "brown" water laden with human waste. The need to remove wastewater from residential lots resulted in the development of, first onsite, then ad hoc offsite, and, finally, municipal wastewater management systems.

The Stevens house lot and other lots at the Picotte-DEC site illustrated the evolution of the disposal of waste and wastewater in one Albany block (Hartgen Archeological Associates, Inc. 2002). In the eighteenth century, the disposal of human and household waste was generally restricted to individual lots with offsite disposal becoming common after about 1840. Privies at Picotte-DEC dating from the eighteenth century encapsulated the waste in barrels set into the natural lake clay upon which Albany was built, or they surrounded a wooden box with a zone of sand between the privy proper and the impervious clay. Although popular, neither practice actually disposed of household or human waste. Privies were emptied periodically with the contents being transported to farm fields outside the city. There the "nightsoil" was spread on the fields to fertilize crops. Some of the harvest, sometimes produce, undoubtedly was brought to the city and sold in the downtown public street markets.

The second phase of waste management at three Picotte-DEC lots entailed connecting drains to privies that delivered the outflow to the Fox Creek culvert, the small covered stream that cut through the project from the west just before emptying into the Hudson River. Thus these 1830s privies, stone-lined and wood-lined boxes alike, were flushed from time to time, ostensibly by rainwater runoff from adjacent buildings.

The last stage of wastewater disposal is represented

by two somewhat different practices, one illustrated by the Stevens house, the other a few lots to the east at 19 Columbia Street. If both the kitchen and bathroom suites were installed at 27 Columbia Street, then the wastewater at the Stevens house included both gray and brown water. Meanwhile at 19 Columbia Street, a wooden privy was retrofitted with a clay tile drain that, like the brick drain at the Stevens house, led to Columbia Street. Because the Picotte-DEC archaeological investigation did not extend to Columbia Street, the destinations of the Stevens house and 19 Columbia Street drains is not known. Columbia Street apparently was not sewered until after 1860, and by that time both buildings should have been demolished for the NYCRR freight yard.

That the bathroom suite illustrated in Figure 10.13 lessened housekeeping labor is undeniable, but sanitary facilities of this sort made a much more important contribution to public health than to domestic convenience. Analysis of samples from 11 privies excavated at the Picotte-DEC office building site demonstrates that human parasites were endemic in Albany in the late eighteenth century, but decreased substantially through the nineteenth century (Reinhard 2000). The study revealed that giant intestinal roundworms, tapeworms, pinworms, head lice, and, possibly, protozoa were endemic among the city's residents. Reinhard reports that the highest concentrations recorded from any historic site to date were obtained from the Picotte-DEC samples. Reinhard concludes that "the city was heavily contaminated with infective eggs and that health problems from A. lumbricoides (giant round worm) were a critical problem" (Reinhard 2000:abstract). Because many human parasites are spread by exposure to human feces, from a public health standpoint the abandonment of individual privies in favor of offsite disposal would have contributed to an easing of the problem by lowering the probability of infection.

Conclusions

Excavations at the Samuel Stevens house at 27 Columbia Street in the southern part of the Picotte-DEC office building site revealed the remains of a mid-nineteenth-century downtown Albany home equipped with many analogs to modern household conveniences. Based upon the archaeological evidence, the kitchen was probably equipped with a cooking range that also would have heated the room, and had hot water or laundry facilities, and a sink, probably with running water. Although evidence for some other appliances and conveniences is wanting, there is intriguing evidence that the kitchen may also have had pressurized hot and cold running water and the upper floor may have had a sophisticated bathroom with commode.

What sparks interest in the Samuel Stevens house is the effort expended to make domestic life easier for the family women or household servants, people whose daily lives have until recently been largely neglected by both history and archaeology. Virtually all of the kitchen conveniences were designed to ease the labor of keeping house. This is especially the case with the domestic water supply and wastewater disposal, a system rare at the time, at least in this neighborhood. With respect to the cold room, at least one other house in the project had a storage room appended to its north side, but the Stevens house was the only one equipped with a system that might actually have kept perishables cold using ice.

The household conveniences at 27 Columbia Street reflect in part Samuel Stevens' position as a prominent member of the Albany bar. As an attorney, he was included in the long list of professionals who lived in the Broadway and Columbia Street neighborhood; his law practice was especially successful. Even so, he did not have the status of many of the city's "leading men" of the time such as Robert Townsend, Erastus Corning, and Stephen van Rensselaer. Stevens' subsequent uptown residence near the core of state government at 6 Academy Park was renovated in the early twentieth century. If similar conveniences were installed in that house, most of the evidence for them may have been removed.

The archaeological remains of the Stevens house also demonstrate that the women in the household were concerned with cleanliness, establishing a refuge from the work world, and adopting practices that improved public health. This movement gained popularity throughout America beginning in the second quarter of the nineteenth century and, fostered by the concern of women and other activists, culminated in citywide water and sewer systems, routine street cleaning, and municipally mandated trash removal and disposal, developments and practices that not only make urban life possible but also enjoyable for modern urban dwellers.

Acknowledgments

Archaeology at the Samuel Stevens house was conducted as part of compliance with the requirements of the New York State Historic Preservation Act of 1980 and was supported by the Picotte Companies, the owners of the Department of Environmental Conservation office building project on Broadway in downtown Albany. The archaeological work scope consisted of excavations at 12 of approximately 40 lots that encompassed the two-block project area. The archaeological study was completed by Hartgen Archeological Associates, Inc., of Troy, New York, in the summer and fall of 1998. Karen S. Hartgen, MA (RPA) was the principal investigator.

References Cited

Albany Centinel. 1797. Dreadful Conflagration, August 8. American Antiquarian Society, Worcester, Mass.

Bielinski, S. 1991. How a City Worked: Occupations in Colonial Albany. In *A Beautiful and Fruitful Place: Selected Rensselaerswijck Seminar Papers,* edited and indexed by N.A. McClure Zeller, pp. 119–136. New Netherland Publishing, New York State Library, Albany.

_____. 1996. *From Outpost to Entrepot: The Birth of Urban Albany, 1686–1776.* Colonial Albany Social History Project, New York State Museum, Albany.

Bradt, J., and Carpenter, G.W. 1828. *Map of the City of Albany.* G.W. Merchant, Albany, N.Y.

_____. 1843. *Map of the City of Albany.* George W. Merchant, Albany, N.Y.

Child, E.B. 1833. *Child's Albany Directory and City Register, for the Years 1833–4.* E.B. Child, Albany, N.Y.

DeWitt, S. 1794. *A Plan of the City of Albany.* Reprinted 1968 by Historic Urban Plans, Ithaca, N.Y. From the original in the Library of Congress, Washington, D.C.

Dudden, F.E. 1983. *Serving Women, Household Service in Nineteenth-Century America.* Wesleyan University Press, Middletown, Conn.

Fish, H. 1849. Letter dated 4 October 1849 to Samuel Stevens, Adjutant General of New York State, transmitting 51 military commissions signed by Fish. Manuscripts and Special Collections No. 5984, New York State Library, Albany.

Gerber, M. 1989. *Old Albany,* Vol. 5. Morris Gerber, 55 Sycamore Street, Albany, N.Y.

Hartgen Archeological Associates, Inc. 2002. On the Outside Looking In: Four Centuries of Change at 625 Broadway, Archeology at the DEC Headquarters, 625 Broadway, Albany, New York. On file at New York State Office of Parks, Recreation and Historic Preservation, Peebles Island, Waterford.

Hayden, D. 1981. *The Grand Domestic Revolution: A History of Feminist Designs for American Homes, Neighborhoods, and Cities.* MIT Press, Cambridge, Mass.

Hill, J.J. 1884. *Reminiscences of Albany by John J. Hill of Brooklyn.* John Medole & Son, New York.

Hoffman, L.G. 1839–40. *Hoffman's Albany Directory and City Register.* L.G. Hoffman, Albany, N.Y.

_____. 1840–41. *Hoffman's Albany Directory and City Register.* L.G. Hoffman, Albany, N.Y.

_____. 1841–42. *Hoffman's Albany Directory and City Register.* L.G. Hoffman, Albany, N.Y.

_____. 1842–43. *Hoffman's Albany Directory and City Register.* L.G. Hoffman, Albany, N.Y.

_____. 1843–44. *Hoffman's Albany Directory and City Register.* L.G. Hoffman, Albany, N.Y.

_____. 1846–47. *Hoffman's Albany Directory and City Register.* L.G. Hoffman, Albany, N.Y.

_____. 1847–48. *Hoffman's Albany Directory and City Register.* L.G. Hoffman, Albany, N.Y.

_____. 1848–49. *Hoffman's Albany Directory and City Register.* L.G. Hoffman, Albany, N.Y.

_____. 1849–50. *Hoffman's Albany Directory and City Register.* L.G. Hoffman, Albany, N.Y.

Hopkins, C.M. 1876. *City Atlas of Albany, New York.* Philadelphia.

Howell, G.R., and Tenney, J. 1886. *History of the County of Albany from 1609 to 1886.* W.W. Munsell & Co., New York.

Hoy, S. 1995. *Chasing Dirt: the American Pursuit of Cleanliness.* Oxford University Press, New York.

Katzman, D.M. 1978. *Seven Days a Week, Women and Domestic Service in Industrializing America.* Oxford University Press, New York.

King, J.A. 1849. Letter dated 2 July to Samuel Stevens, Adjutant General of New York State, calling his attention to Colonel Charles Hamilton. New York State Library, Manuscripts and Special Collections No. 21674, Albany.

Munsell, J. (editor). 1850. *The Albany Annual Register for 1850*. E.H. Pease & Co., Albany, N.Y.

_____. (editor). 1855. *Munsell's Albany Directory and City Register for 1855*. J. Munsell, Albany, N.Y.

_____. 1855. *The Annals of Albany*, Vol. 6. J. Munsell, Albany, N.Y.

_____. 1856. *Munsell's Albany Directory and City Register*. J. Munsell, Albany, N.Y.

_____. 1858. *The Annals of Albany*, Vol. 9. Munsell and Rowland, Albany, N.Y.

_____. 1859. *The Annals of Albany*, Vol. 10. Munsell and Rowland, Albany, N.Y.

_____. 1865. *Collections on the History of Albany from Its Discovery to the Present Time*. J. Munsell, Albany, N.Y.

_____. 1867. *Collections on the History of Albany from Its Discovery to the Present Time*, Vol. 2. J. Munsell, Albany, N.Y.

_____. 1869. *The Annals of Albany*, Vols. 1–4. (2nd ed.). J. Munsell, Albany, N.Y.

_____. 1871. *Collections on the History of Albany from Its Discovery to the Present Time*, Vol. 4. J. Munsell, Albany, N.Y.

Orsini, N. 2000. Speaking Stones. http://www. courses.rochester.edu/homerin/REL167/field_reports/stevens/stevens.html. Accessed September 7, 2000.

Parker, A.J. (editor). 1897. *Landmarks of Albany County, New York*. D. Mason & Co., Syracuse, N.Y.

Porter, L.B. 1886. The Bench and Bar. In *History of the County of Albany, N.Y. from 1609 to 1886* by Howell and Tenney. W.W. Munsell & Co., New York.

Reinhard, K. J. 2000. Archaeoparasitology of Features from the Picotte-DEC Site, Albany, New York. Prepared for Ms. Leslie E. Raymer, New South Associates, Stone Mountain, Ga.

Römer, Col.W.W. 1698. *Map of Albany*. New York State Archives, Albany.

Sampson, Davenport & Co. 1870. *The Albany Directory for the Year 1870*. Sampson, Davenport & Co., Albany, N.Y.

Sanborn Map Company (Sanborn-Perris Map Company). 1889. *Fire Insurance Maps of Albany, New York*. New York.

Sidney, J.C. 1850. *Map of the City of Albany from Original Survey*. M. Dripps, New York.

Yates, R. 1770. *Plan of the City of Albany About 1770*. New York State Archives, Albany.

Walworth, Rev. C.A., Dean, G.W., Battershall, W.W., Reese, J.L., Schwartz, D.L, Harrover, P.P., Gee, E.F., King, H.M., Schlesenger, M., Pratt, A.B., and McGowan, M. 1886. Religious Institutions: Adventists; Baptists; Catholic; Christian; Congregational; Episcopal; Evangelical; Hebrew; Liberal; Lutheran; Spiritualists, Unitarian; Universalist. In *History of the County of Albany, N.Y. from 1609 to 1886*. Howell and Tenney. W.W. Munsell & Co., New York.

Section 4

Material Things

CHAPTER 11

Making "Money" the Old-Fashioned Way: Eighteenth-Century Wampum Production in Albany

Elizabeth S. Peña

Wampum as "Money"

It is well known that shell beads and pendants were valuable items in protohistoric North America. In the seventeenth century, tubular clam or conch shell beads known as wampum, sewan, or sewant served as a medium of exchange between European colonists and Native Americans in northeastern North America. Archaeological and ethnohistorical studies have shown that, in the seventeenth century, coastal Algonquian groups made wampum to trade to Europeans for firearms and other items (Ceci 1977; Williams 1972). The Europeans used these wampum beads to obtain pelts from Native American hunters. Because of wampum's high value to many Native American groups, wampum strings and belts became important as a means of treaty agreement and ratification, or "wampum diplomacy." The exchange of wampum governed many transactions between Europeans and Native Americans. Wampum was a "primitive valuable" to Native Americans; that is, it circulated in noncommercial, ritual payments. In trade between Europeans and Native Americans, wampum was "primitive money"; that is, it maintained noncommercial uses while also functioning in the marketplace.

The importance of wampum within the European colonial community is less well known. In the seventeenth century, a severe specie shortage provided the impetus for the Dutch colonists of Beverwyck, or Albany, to use wampum beads as cash in local transactions. New Netherlanders' choice of wampum as a substitute for cash was not serendipitous; rather, it was the product of Dutch colonial experience. As early as the end of the sixteenth century, Dutch traders in West Africa were exposed to the use of shells as a medium of exchange. By the mid-seventeenth century, the Dutch East India Company imported cowrie shells from the Maldive Islands for use in the slave trade (Johnson 1970:23). Like the use of shell pendants and beads among native North Americans, West Africans used cowries for ornament and ritual.

Observing the Native Americans' high regard for shell beads and recalling experience with other shell currencies surely influenced the Dutch to consider adopting wampum as a medium of exchange in the fur trade. Although many colonial powers have tampered with native media of exchange, the phenomenon of a colonizer adopting a local "primitive valuable" for its own, culture-specific use is highly unusual, if not unique. In this case, Dutch colonists used wampum to fulfill the traditional criteria of money: It served as a medium of exchange; it had a common measure of value; it was a means of accumulating wealth; and it was a standard of deferred payment. Wampum was certified legal tender, and the colonial court records are filled with references to wampum exchange between colonists. People paid their debts in wampum, both strung (Van Laer 1974:35–36, No. 11a) and loose (Van Laer 1974:139–140, No. 53c); slaves bought their freedom with wampum (Van Laer 1974:82–83, No. 30b), and servants were paid with it (Van Laer 1974:86–87, No. 31c). Wampum often formed only part of a payment, as in a sale of cattle

People, Places, and Material Things: Historical Archaeology of Albany, New York edited by Charles L. Fisher, New York State Museum Bulletin 499, © 2003 by the University of the State of New York, New York State Education Department, Albany, New York. All rights reserved

for "two hundred and fifty guilders in good merchantable duffels at the current price and fifty guilders in loose sewan" (Van Laer 1974:182, No. 64c), the purchase of a plantation for "100 guilders in merchantable beavers and 310 guilders in good current sewan" (Van Laer 1974:423, No. 137b), and the substitution of one man for another in the military service of the Dutch West India Company for "the sum of seventy guilders in sewan and a pair of shoes" (Van Laer 1974:415–416, No. 135a).

In the mid-seventeenth century, wampum lost its legal status in New England, and poor-quality beads were dumped on the New York market; these beads were roughly made and often unpierced. New Netherlanders continued to use wampum even after 1664, when they came under English political control and officially became New Yorkers. Wampum remained legal tender in New York until the beginning of the eighteenth century. It is important to remember that, in general, the colonists in New Netherland were neither farmers nor pilgrims, but urban merchants and traders who had long been accustomed to cash transactions. New Netherland did receive some coins, mainly Spanish pieces-of-eight, from Dutch properties in the West Indies, but these coins had often been debased or clipped. By the mid-seventeenth century, New Netherlanders had become accustomed to using a wide variety of moneys, and wampum was sometimes listed in inventories as a type of money (Van Laer 1974:267–276, e.g., 87d[1]). By the early eighteenth century, when wampum was no longer legal tender and coinage seems to have become more plentiful, the use of wampum as cash seems to have abated; however, wampum remained useful in the fur trade, which had moved on to the frontier north and west of Albany, as well as in treaty negotiations.

The KeyCorp Site

When evidence of wampum production was unearthed at the KeyCorp site in downtown Albany, it seemed logical to assume that this material dated to the seventeenth century, when wampum was in local use as legal tender and when Beverwyck or Albany served as a fur-trade hub. The KeyCorp site, named for the bank tower that stands on the site today, was excavated by Hartgen Archeological Associates, Inc., in 1986 (Figure 1.1). In the colonial period, the KeyCorp site lay just south of the Rutten Kill, or Rat Creek, within the Beverwyck stockade. A house stood on the site as early as 1650, and in 1683, the property

was sold to the Dutch Reformed Church, which rebuilt the house for use as an almshouse. The property is listed in the Church's Act of Incorporation in 1720, but the history of the lot for the remainder of the eighteenth century is not well documented.

Because of the salvage nature of the KeyCorp project, analysis did not immediately follow excavation, and the presence of seventeenth-century trading materials such as glass beads notionally was linked to wampum and wampum manufacture. When the material was catalogued in 1988, it was evident that although wampum beads were present in seventeenth-century contexts, all of the wampum production debris was associated with eighteenth-century deposits (Peña 1990:89–133).

The examination of the KeyCorp assemblage revealed two major phases. The first phase of occupation dates to ca. 1650 to 1680, with strata containing such seventeenth-century artifacts as glass trade beads, ceramic sherds from Dutch plates and colanders, and German spechter glass. These seventeenth-century strata were confined to the southern side of the site, which is separated from the northern part of the site by a nineteenth-century wall. Although wampum beads form part of this assemblage, wampum production debris does not (Figure 11.1). Wampum was commonly used at this time, but there is no archaeological evidence that wampum beads were manufactured locally.

The second phase at the KeyCorp site dates to the mid-eighteenth century, based on an artifact assemblage containing early eighteenth-century blue on white delft bowls as well as polychrome Fazakerly delft from the 1760s. Evidence for this phase is restricted to the northern half of the site, on the other side of the nineteenth-century wall that bisects the site. All of the evidence of wampum production at the KeyCorp site, which consists of more than 2,000 fragments of cut clam and conch shell and nearly 200 partially formed wampum beads, was recovered from this northern part of the site, associated with eighteenth-century artifacts (Figure 11.2). Debris from all stages of production is included in this assemblage. The archaeological evidence includes shell fragments, strips, bead blanks, and wasters (beads broken during drilling) (Figure 11.3). Wampum production tools found with this debris include whetstones, awls, and drills (Figure 11.4). A single wampum bead strung on a wire was found, perhaps representing the final stage of production when beads were smoothed on whetstones. In addition, a number of coins were recovered

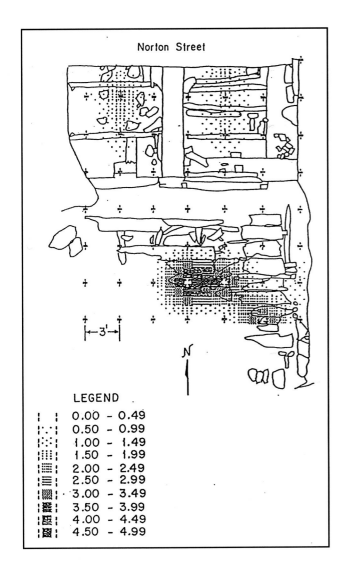

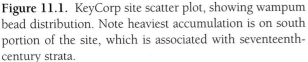

Figure 11.1. KeyCorp site scatter plot, showing wampum bead distribution. Note heaviest accumulation is on south portion of the site, which is associated with seventeenth-century strata.

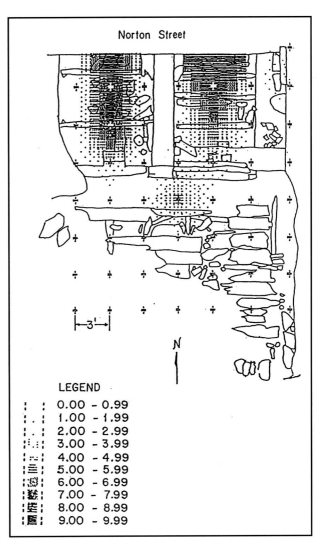

Figure 11.2. KeyCorp site scatter plot, showing wampum debris distribution. Note that debris is largely confined to north part of site, associated with eighteenth-century strata.

in this area, including five examples from the principal wampum debris stratum. All five of these coins were minted between ca. 1729 and 1755, their presence hinting that the specie shortage was no longer so severe by this time.

The fact that this site served as the Dutch Reformed Church almshouse suggests that the almshouse residents made wampum. This group may have included poor people who resided or worked in the almshouse. Historical documents record the names of several rather marginal members of the community who, in the earliest years of the eighteenth century, rented parts of the almshouse to live in with their

families (Munsell 1865:52; Reformed Dutch Church 1978:49–73). For example, one of these renters was Robert Barrett, a British soldier with a Dutch wife and six children. Barrett turns up in the records performing a variety of small jobs—acting as city bellman or night watchman. It is possible that people or families in situations similar to Barrett's may have been responsible for the wampum production debris at the KeyCorp site. It is also noteworthy that the almshouse stood in the first ward of Albany, a quarter characterized by small-time craftsmen working at a variety of trades, such as cordwaining, brick making, weaving, and blacksmithing. Wampum production may have

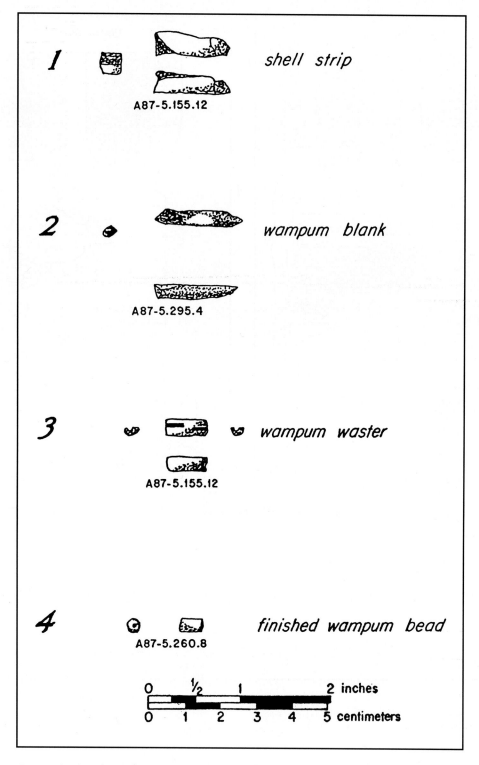

Figure 11.3. Stages of wampum production from the KeyCorp site, collection of the New York State Museum.

fit into this scheme as another marginal, part-time urban craft (Peña 1990:153–154).

State Street and Broadway Sites

The evidence from the KeyCorp site is supplemented by data from other sites in downtown Albany

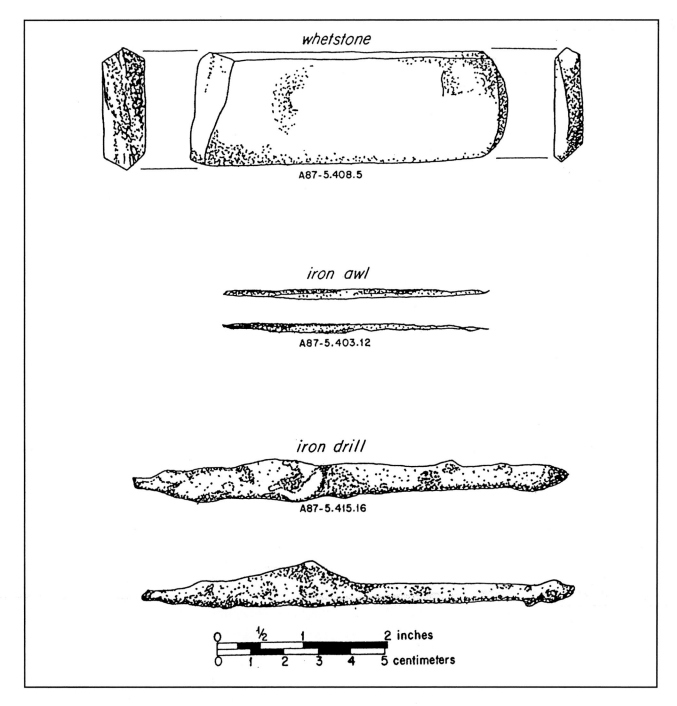

whetstone

A87-5.408.5

iron awl

A87-5.403.12

iron drill

A87-5.415.16

0   ½   1   2 inches
0   1   2   3   4   5 centimeters

Figure 11.4. Wampum production tools from the KeyCorp site, collection of the New York State Museum.

(Peña 1990:133–148). During the installation of an electric line in 1972 and 1973, four wampum production loci were uncovered by the New York State Office of Parks, Recreation and Historic Preservation (Feister 1985:85–86; Huey 1984:67, 73–74; 1987:27–28). The archaeological materials from these sites are very similar to the KeyCorp collection, with the addition of evidence for craft production

such as window glazing and cordwaining. Two of these production loci appear to be on the sites of eighteenth-century blockhouses. A third production site is nearby, though its historical association remains unidentified. Another wampum debris assemblage appears to represent a secondary deposit in the vicinity of the Dutch Reformed Church at the juncture of State Street and Broadway. All of these sites are located within four modern city blocks of the KeyCorp site and are likely to represent part of the same phenomenon. Although the narrow trench cuts preclude the unambiguous association of archaeological deposits with historic maps, the two collections related to British blockhouses appear to be secure identifications. The documentary record contains many references to blockhouse repairs (e.g., Munsell 1850:144, 184, 197–198), but there are few references to soldiers' activities within the blockhouses. The soldiers may have been in a position analogous to the poor at the KeyCorp almshouse site; while on duty, they may have been required to take part in wampum manufacturing, perhaps to bolster the army's coffers. It is also possible that soldiers made wampum for their own profit, as they spent hours waiting, on guard. In addition, a variety of civilians had access to the blockhouses for repair work, lighting the fire, and other tasks (Munsell 1850:171).

Eighteenth-Century Wampum Production in Albany

The evidence from the KeyCorp site and the State Street and Broadway sites led to the question: Why was wampum produced in Albany at this time? Since 1701 wampum had been disallowed as legal tender by the New York government and was by then uncommon in local transactions. The coin shortage that characterized the seventeenth century seems to have abated, as eighteenth-century strata from the Key-Corp site yielded a variety of mid-eighteenth-century coins.

Even after wampum had lost its legitimacy as a medium of exchange among colonists, it retained its other functions, including serving as a "primitive valuable" and "primitive money." Wampum was now a commodity in itself, useful in "wampum diplomacy." There was still a market for wampum beads in the eighteenth century, but it was no longer local; it had spread north and west with the expansion of European dominance. For example, all English trade with the French was prohibited during the Seven Years War from 1756 to 1763. Montreal, however, required large amounts of wampum for its fur trade. Several documentary sources hint that Albany supplied that need, including a series of letters from the trader Robert Sanders, who used coded symbols in his correspondence to hide the identity of his French customers in Montreal (Norton 1974:90, 126). Wampum produced in Albany may have been in-

tended for traders such as Sanders, and the illicit nature of this trade might help to explain the paucity of documentary references to the wampum industry.

It seems likely that a local entrepreneur acted as a middleman, procuring the raw shell, organizing production, and selling the newly made beads to a merchant or trader who exchanged the beads for furs or land with Native American groups on the frontier of colonial settlement. The Loudon List, a document dating to 1756 that lists the dwellings in Albany appropriate for quartering British troops, provides a hint about a possible local entrepreneur (Loudon List 1756). Jacobus Hilton, the owner of one of the houses considered appropriate for lodging troops, is listed as a "wampum maker." Hilton's house, which was very close to the KeyCorp site, is described as being larger than most other houses on the list, and is marked by the additional comment "good house." Assuming that Hilton's large house was a measure of his economic success, it is unclear whether this success was derived from his principal occupation, farming, or his career as a wampum maker. The Loudon List lends some evidence to the notion that there may have been local businessmen involved in the wampum business. Considering that the principal wampum production loci identified in this investigation appear to be the sites of an almshouse and two military blockhouses, it may be that the more marginal members of society, poor people and soldiers, were the actual wampum makers, producing wampum beads to supplement their own incomes or to provide revenue for the church or the military.

In understanding the role of Albany residents in wampum manufacture, it is important to be cognizant of the continuity of Dutch economic behavior. In considering the KeyCorp site, recognizing the insularity of the Dutch "extended town family" (Bradley 1976) is important in understanding that, though the participants in wampum production were New Yorkers of both Dutch and English descent, they seem to have maintained characteristically Dutch capitalistic views and practices that had been established in Beverwyck a century earlier. The fact that eighteenth-century inhabitants of Albany manufactured wampum as a commodity suggests that this distinctly Dutch, entrepreneurial attitude remained an active force with eighteenth-century, second generation New Yorkers, and Dutch economic and cultural behavior persisted despite the establishment of English political and military control.

References Cited

Bradley, J.W. 1976. Christopher Yates and the Logic of Revolution in Schenectady, New York. Unpublished manuscript.

Ceci, L. 1977. *The Effect of European Contact and Trade on the Settlement Pattern of Indians in Coastal New York, 1524–1665: The Archaeological and Documentary Evidence.* Doctoral dissertation, City University of New York. University Microfilms International, Ann Arbor, Mich.

Feister, L. 1985. Archaeology in Rensselaerswyck, Dutch 17th-Century Domestic Sites. *New Netherland Studies, Bulletin KNOB* 84(2–3):80–88.

Huey, P. 1984. Dutch Sites of the 17th Century in Rensselaerswyck. In *The Scope of Historical Archaeology*, edited by D. Orr and D. Crozier, pp. 63–85. Laboratory of Anthropology, Temple University, Philadelphia.

_____. 1987. Archaeological Evidence of Dutch Wooden Cellars and Perishable Wooden Structures at Seventeenth and Eighteenth Century Sites in the Upper Hudson Valley. In *New World Dutch Studies*, edited by R. Blackburn and N. Kelley, pp. 13–35. Albany Institute of History and Art, Albany, N.Y.

Johnson, M. 1970. The Cowrie Currencies of West Africa, Part 1. *Journal of African History* 10(1):17–49.

Loudon List. 1756. Letter to John Earl of Loudon from Albany. New York State Library Manuscript No. 13888, Albany.

Munsell, J. 1850. *The Annals of Albany*, Vol. 4. J. Munsell, Albany, N.Y.

_____. 1865. *Collections on the History of Albany*, Vol. 1. J. Munsell, Albany, N.Y.

Norton, T.E. 1974. *The Fur Trade in Colonial New York, 1686–1776.* University of Wisconsin Press, Madison.

Peña, E.S. 1990. *Wampum Production in New Netherland and Colonial New York: The Historical and Archaeological Context.* Doctoral dissertation, Boston University. University Microfilms International, Ann Arbor, Mich.

Reformed Dutch Church. 1978. *Records of the Reformed Dutch Church of Albany, New York, 1683–1809*, Parts 1–5. Genealogical Publishing Company, Baltimore.

Van Laer, A.J.F. (translator and editor). 1974. *Register of the Provincial Secretary, 1648–1660.* New York Historical Manuscripts: Dutch, Vol. 3. Genealogical Publishing Company, Baltimore.

Williams, L.E. 1972. *Ft. Shantok and Ft. Corchaug: A Comparative Study of Seventeenth-Century Culture Contact in the Long Island Sound Area.* Doctoral dissertation, New York University. University Microfilms International, Ann Arbor, Mich.

CHAPTER 12

New Evidence of Wampum Use and Production From Albany, New York

Matthew Lesniak

Introduction

Several recent excavations in downtown Albany, New York, have provided a wealth of new information about life in colonial Albany or Beverwyck, some of it confirming and some of it conflicting with long-held historical assumptions (Figure 1.1). Many of the Albany archaeological sites relate to the use and manufacture of wampum, a subject that seems to captivate the public imagination as much as it does the imagination of archaeologists and historians (Hagerty 1984). Wampum and evidence for wampum manufacture were found in a variety of contexts at the Picotte–New York Department of Environmental Conservation (DEC) site, which is the focus of this chapter. Excavations at this site are also the subjects of Chapters 5, 10, and 13 in this volume. The historical context for this site is presented in Chapter 10. Because Picotte-DEC contained deposits from both the seventeenth and the eighteenth centuries, it provides a rare opportunity to study the changes and continuities of wampum's role in the colonial economy. The site illustrates important shifts in wampum production and use between the seventeenth and eighteenth centuries, but one thing that stayed the same was that wampum was prized during both centuries, and it remained closely bound with the livelihood of Europeans and native people alike.

The white and purple beads that New England Algonquin speakers called *wampumpeak* and the Dutch called *sewan* or *sewant* had immense spiritual value for the Iroquois and other inland tribes (Hamell 1983). The Iroquois admired shell aesthetically as a material, and the wampum beads woven into belts and exchanged as gifts underscored political and economic relationships for the native people (Ceci 1982:98–99; Slotkin and Schmitt 1949:234). Europeans used wampum to facilitate the highly profitable fur trade (Ross 1902:49-52). Dutch and English traders who had access to Long Island and the Long Island Sound in the seventeenth century, especially, took advantage of wampum in the fur trade (Ceci 1980:845; Grumet 1995:159).

Native groups produced wampum from conch shells and from quahog shells, both of which are plentiful around Long Island. The conch, or channeled whelk, yielded white shell material suitable for beads from its central column. The hardshell clams, or quahogs, however, often have a violet border near the edge; therefore, white wampum beads may have been made from conch or clam, but purple beads always came from clam (Morris 1947:51, 155). It was more difficult to make wampum from quahog shell than to make it from the conch's column, which naturally approximated a bead's cylindrical shape. The quahog shell had to be clipped or cut down into small pieces, then knapped into rectangular strips, followed by shaping into crude wampum blanks (Peña 1990:21–29). Wampum beads were then drilled using metal tools frequently called muxes. Drilling often caused the beads to shatter and break, resulting in partially drilled wampum bead wasters.

Recent Research

The people using this process to make wampum changed in the late 1600s, when the Pequot and Corchaug Indians saw their communities decimated by a series of wars with the colonists (Grumet 1995; Solecki and Williams 1998:3). Wampum production was taken up on a larger scale by European colonists, including many residents of Albany.

Elizabeth Peña's research in the late 1980s began an understanding of this shift. Because Fort Orange's mid-seventeenth-century deposits yielded wampum beads and evidence of wampum production and Dutch colonists in New Netherland used wampum as currency, making wampum in Albany had been considered a seventeenth-century activity only. That was the initial assumption when archaeological work at the KeyCorp site in Albany discovered a wampum manufactory in the basement of a former almshouse (Peña 1990:93; Chapter 11, this volume; Venema 1990). Once the associated ceramics and tobacco pipes were analyzed, however, it was apparent that the wampum production at this site dated to the middle to late eighteenth century.

Peña analyzed four other eighteenth-century deposits where wampum was produced. These deposits were located along the axes of State Street and Broadway and were discovered as a result of utility installations. Based on the KeyCorp site and the four utility installation sites, Peña concluded that wampum making in Albany was a thriving cottage industry in the eighteenth century. Since her work, evidence for wampum production in the eighteenth century has been found at Howard Street (where it seems to date from the *late* eighteenth century) by Hartgen Archeological Associates, Inc., at the Lutheran Church lot on Pearl Street by the Cultural Resource Survey Program of the New York State Museum (Fisher 2000), at the State University Construction Fund parking structure (SUCF) by Hartgen Archeological Associates, Inc., and, of course, by Hartgen Archeological Associates, Inc., at the Picotte-DEC site. The SUCF parking structure site, which was excavated during the summer of 1999, contained literally buckets of wampum and wampum-production artifacts from the soil around the eighteenth-century stockade.

Picotte-DEC Site Seventeenth-Century Deposits

At the Picotte-DEC site, intact seventeenth-century deposits were found in two areas, one referred to as Area 9 and the other as Area 6-7 (Figures 1.1 and 12.1).

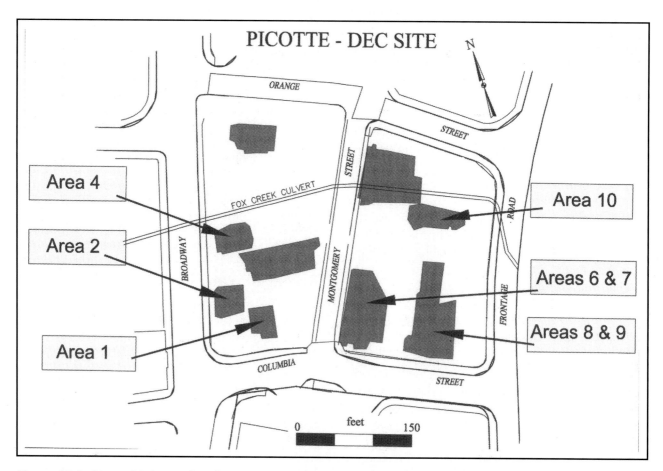

Figure 12.1. Picotte-DEC site plan, featuring excavation areas that yielded wampum beads or evidence of wampum production.

None were found north of Fox Creek (also known as the Vossenkill), indicating that the stream acted as something of a barrier. The eighteenth-century deposits of interest were mostly beneath the nineteenth-century foundations in Areas 4, 2, and 1.

The two seventeenth-century soil levels at Picotte-DEC contained virtually no wampum. The early seventeenth-century habitation in Area 9 left diagnostic seventeenth-century ceramics such as Bartman stoneware, Westerwald, delftware, tubular glass trade beads, and seventeenth-century pipes including Edward Bird pipes and fleur-de-lis pipes, but there was not a trace of wampum either as finished beads or as beads in production. A fragmentary awl was found in the hearth, possibly a part of a thin mux used for drilling wampum beads. The entire mux would have been longer and, commonly, tapered and pointed at both ends (Peña 1990:107). Found without any clipped shell or wampum blanks, however, this awl or mux was more likely to be a trade item in its own right than evidence of wampum production in the location where it was deposited.

It was somewhat surprising to come across a Dutch half duit in the levels that did not have any wampum, because historical consensus has long held that New Netherland was forced to adopt wampum as currency

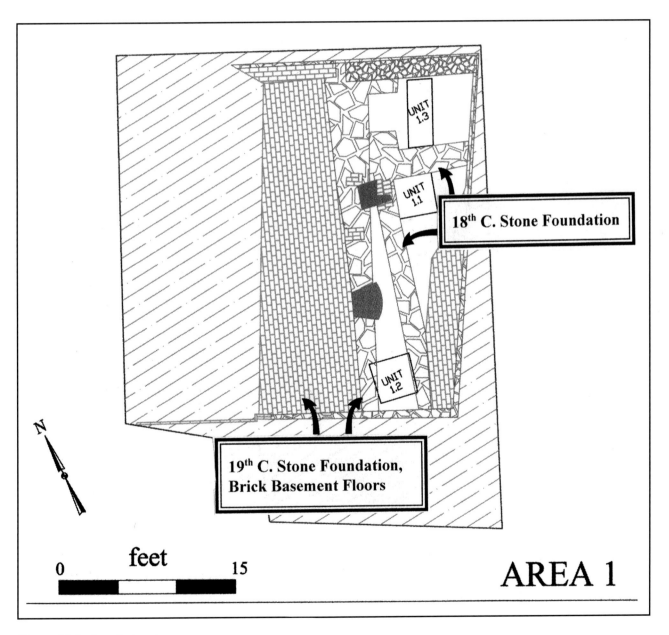

UNIT 1.3

UNIT 1.1

18th C. Stone Foundation

UNIT 1.2

19th C. Stone Foundation, Brick Basement Floors

N

feet

0   15

AREA 1

Figure 12.2. Area 1 site plan.

Figure 12.3. Wampum waster with drill mark, from Area 1.

by the desperate shortage of coinage in the colony (Ceci 1980; Huey 1991:60). Sixteen of these coins were equivalent to a stuiver, or a small string of beads. Between 1650 and 1664, two of these coins would have had the value of a single wampum bead (Huey 1991:60).

The other seventeenth-century deposit at Picotte-DEC was in Area 6-7. It was a large, more than 100-pound, deposit of crown glass scraps, almost certainly dumped by a glazier. Few diagnostic artifacts were found in the glass deposit, but one Tudor Rose pipe dated the deposit to ca. 1650. The soil level deposited over the glass contained a broken wampum blank, apparently undrilled. The bead was weathered and chalky and may have been made from inferior materials.

Picotte-DEC
Eighteenth-Century Deposits

In contrast to the seventeenth-century deposits, many of Picotte-DEC's eighteenth-century deposits

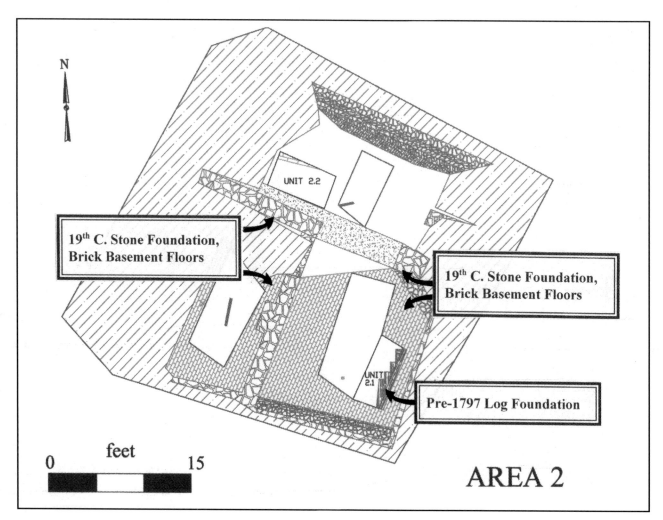

Figure 12.4. Area 2 site plan.

included wampum, both finished and in production. As mentioned above, there are at least eight other sites in downtown Albany with evidence for wampum production in the eighteenth century.

Area 1 was one of the richest for wampum, with wampum in production coming from multiple levels and builders' trench features along eighteenth-century foundations. The pre-1797 alignment of Market Street, or Broadway, was apparent in the stone foundation walls, which were oriented at an acute angle to nineteenth-century stone foundation walls located above them (Figure 12.2). The nineteenth-century foundations were parallel to the current, twentieth-century alignment of Broadway. Conch shell cut into strips was found in one of the builder's trenches, a departure from the recorded use of the central column of the conch. A number of fine wampum wasters were also recovered from the area (Figure 12.3). The wasters were typically hexagonal in cross section and partially polished, with smooth surfaces on the exterior. The wasters displayed a drill mark in the center, often slightly off-center. According to eighteenth-century contemporary accounts of wampum production, wampum makers would drill a hole through a bead blank such as these. If the bead did not break from the drilling (resulting in wampum wasters), the bead maker would grind the bead on a string to reduce its width and create a cylindrical, polished bead (Peña 1990:79).

Area 2 had a pre-1797 board and timber foundation, found beneath nineteenth-century stone and brick floors (Figure 12.4). Wampum beads were found between the boards and in the soil level below them (Figure 12.5). The beads have wide holes and some obvious snags, making it questionable if they would pass the native traders' test of rolling smoothly along their string when rubbed across the nose (Hagerty 1984:104). Poor quality and counterfeit wampum beads in the seventeenth century led to high inflation and contributed to the loss of New Netherland to the English in 1664 (Ceci 1980:847). It seems likely that the variety of wampum producers in eighteenth-century Albany would lead to varying degrees of quality, as well.

Wampum beads and production were also found beneath the floor of an eighteenth-century house in Area 3, and in a barrel in an eighteenth-century shop in Area 4. Area 9's eighteenth-century deposits were also rich in wampum-manufacturing materials, including both conch and cut clam.

Conclusion

It appears that all of the Picotte-DEC contexts that yielded wampum and wampum production dated from the eighteenth century and most could be associated with particular structures. This distribution by buildings recalls that noted by Paul Huey at Fort Orange. Most of the wampum beads found in the mid-seventeenth-century deposits at Fort Orange were located inside of house cellars, rather than scattered around the entranceway where trading was conducted (Huey 1991:60). At Picotte-DEC, likewise, more contexts with eighteenth-century sewant production were near structures than in backyards. This pattern may be best explained by the fact that wampum was widely produced in Albany in the eighteenth century but no longer used as currency among Albany's residents and was actually shipped out for trade with native groups outside the Albany area.

As for the lack of wampum in Picotte-DEC's de-

Figure 12.5. Wampum beads from Area 2, Unit 2.1.

posits dating to the 1600s, the Fort Orange data also shed light. As of this date, the large deposit in Area 9 produced a total of eight glass trade beads but no wampum. Huey recovered six glass trade beads for each wampum bead at Fort Orange; around the entranceway, where the heaviest trading was conducted, the ratio of trade bead to wampum bead was even higher (Huey 1991:60). The Fort Orange data seem to support the hypothesis that the seventeenth-century deposits in Area 9 represent an ephemeral dwelling established as a trading post.

The Picotte-DEC site contributes to a picture of eighteenth-century Albany in which wampum production is widespread in the town. The data from the seventeenth century, in contrast, show much less wampum use than history would lead us to expect. As the contexts from more eighteenth-century deposits are analyzed, we hope to find out more about how wampum was made and used in colonial Albany.

References Cited

Ceci, L. 1980. The First Fiscal Crisis in New York. *Economic Development and Cultural Change*, 28(4):839–847.

———. 1982. The Value of Wampum Among the New York Iroquois: A Case Study in Artifact Analysis. *Journal of Anthropological Research* 38(1):97–107.

Fisher, C.L. 2000. *Archaeology of Social Conflict in Colonial Albany.* Paper presented at Annual Meeting of the Society for Historical Archaeology, Quebec City.

Grumet, R.S. 1995. *Historic Contact: Indian People and Colonists in Today's Northeastern United States in the Sixteenth through Eighteenth Centuries.* University of Oklahoma Press, Norman and London.

Hagerty, G.W. 1984. *Wampum, War and Trade Goods, West of the Hudson.* Heart of the Lakes Publishing, Interlaken, N.Y.

Hamell, G.R. 1983. Trading in Metaphors: The Magic of Beads. In *Proceedings of the 1982 Glass Trade Bead Conference,* edited by C.F. Hayes III, pp. 5–28. Research Records No. 16, Rochester Museum and Science Center, Rochester, N.Y.

Huey, P.R. 1991. The Dutch at Fort Orange. In *Historical Archaeology in Global Perspective,* edited by L. Falk, pp. 91–97. Smithsonian Institution Press, Washington, D.C.

Morris, P.A. 1947. *A Field Guide to the Shells of Our Atlantic Coast.* Houghton Mifflin, Boston.

Peña, E.S. 1990. *Wampum Production in New Netherland and Colonial New York: The Historical and Archaeological Context.* Doctoral dissertation, Boston University. University Microfilms International, Ann Arbor, Mich.

Ross, P. 1902. *A History of Long Island,* Vol. 1. The Lewis Publishing Company, New York.

Slotkin, J.S., and Schmitt, K. 1949. Studies of Wampum. *American Anthropologist* 51(2):223–236.

Solecki, R.S., and Williams, L.E. 1998. Fort Corchaug Archaeological Site National Historic Landmark. *The Bulletin-Journal of the New York State Archaeological Association* 114:2–11.

Venema, J. 1990. "For the Benefit of the Poor": Poor Relief in Albany/Beverwyck 1652–1700. Master's thesis, State University of New York at Albany.

CHAPTER 13

Painted Pearlware from the Picotte Site

Pegeen McLaughlin

Introduction

Excavations at the Picotte–New York State Department of Environmental Conservation (DEC) site in downtown Albany by Hartgen Archeological Associates in 1987 and 1997 uncovered rich deposits of painted pearlware and other early nineteenth-century English ceramics. The deposits, unusual in their density, became one of the focal points of the site mitigation in 1998. The Picotte-DEC site, encompassing two city blocks near the Hudson River, was divided into 12 study areas for the mitigation (Figure 13.1). The objective of Study Area 12, in the northeast portion of the site, was to examine the contents and extent of the ceramic deposits and determine how and why the ceramics were deposited in this particular location. Stratigraphic data from the excavations and documentary information from deeds, maps, and other primary sources have contributed to our understanding of the origins of the deposit. A preliminary analysis of the painted pearlware from the assemblage has suggested that with further study, deposits of this kind can elicit information about ceramic painters that has, until now, been inaccessible.

Area 12 — History and Site Development

Area 12, along with the area adjacent to it on the south, Area 11, went through dramatic change in the early years of the nineteenth century. Areas 11 and 12 represent east-west-oriented lots, which fronted on Montgomery Street during the nineteenth century. In the eighteenth century, however, Montgomery Street ended at the Fox Creek, which flowed through Area

11, bisecting the lot lengthwise (Figure 13.2). A devastating fire in 1797 destroyed both blocks of the Picotte-DEC site, as well as much of the surrounding area, prompting a restructuring of the streets. The construction of a bridge over the Fox Creek and an extension to Montgomery Street were part of this restructuring. The Fox Creek was later covered by a culvert and is now used for overflow in times of flooding.

The 1797 fire was a pivotal event, in its impact on the development of the Picotte-DEC site and on our understanding of the ceramic deposits found in Area 12. An *Albany Centinel* article from August 8, 1797, described the fire and listed the 216 buildings destroyed in the fire, along with the names of owners and occupants. The article groups the buildings by street names, without giving specific addresses. However, the buildings appear to be listed in order, so that if the list is used in conjunction with other documentary sources, it is possible to at least approximate the location of some of them.

Among the buildings destroyed on Watervliet Street (now Broadway) were "two very large crockery and glass ware stores belonging to Mr. John Fonda (sic), jun . . ." (*Albany Centinel* 1797). John Fondey, Jr., was a merchant who, along with partner Jellis Winne, operated a business selling looking glasses, fiddles, glassware, china and earthenware (Albany Institute of History and Art 1992). He also owned a considerable amount of property when he died in 1814 (ACHOR 1830). Judging by the position of the warehouse entry on the *Albany Centinel* list, the crockery and glass warehouses were apparently on the block north of the Area 12 block. Although Fondey's home, store, and warehouse were not located

People, Places, and Material Things: Historical Archaeology of Albany, New York edited by Charles L. Fisher, New York State Museum Bulletin 499, © 2003 by the University of the State of New York, New York State Education Department, Albany, New York.

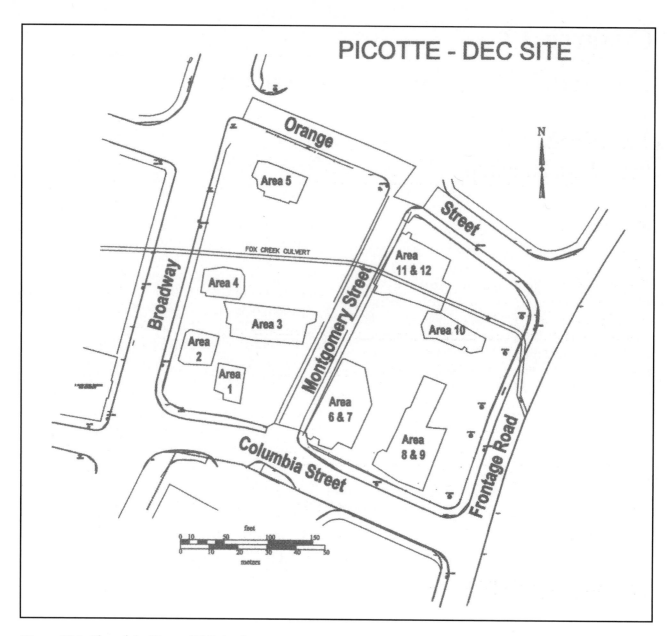

Figure 13.1. Plan of the Picotte-DEC site showing excavation areas.

within the Picotte-DEC site, documentary evidence shows that he held at least partial ownership of the Area 11 and 12 lots.

The primary document demonstrating that Fondey co-owned the Area 12 lot is a 1919 copy of a 1799 survey of the lots between Fox Creek and Orange Street. The survey is an agreement between the property owners as to the size and placement of the lots. The attached contract states that the agreement will not be binding until Montgomery Street has been extended. Nine names are listed on the lot that encom-

passes Area 12 and part of Area 11: "Alida DeForest; Her Right During Widowhood, Philip W. DeForest, Gerulyne & Annatie VerPlank, Lucas & Neltie Hoghkerk, John & Cornelia Fondey, Phil DeForest" (Hailes 1919). Presumably these are the heirs of Alida DeForest's late husband Walter. A lot across Montgomery Street also contains the same list of names, and it is likely that the two lots had originally been one piece of property. A related deed from June 1800 between this group of people and the City of Albany states that they agreed to allow the city to extend

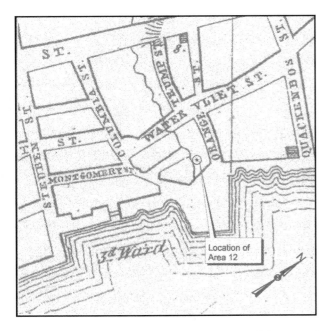

Figure 13.2. Detail of the 1794 DeWitt Map of the City of Albany. Note how Montgomery Street ends at the Fox Creek. Also note the proximity of the site to the riverfront.

The Archaeological Evidence

Backhoe trenches excavated during the Phase I surveys conducted at the Picotte-DEC site in 1987 and 1997 uncovered the first evidence that there were dense ceramic deposits in what would later become Area 12. The Phase III Data Recovery of the site began with the mechanical stripping of each area. The stripping of Area 12 revealed the stone foundation to a small structure, designated 35 Montgomery Street, which had been built after the ceramics had been deposited. Parts of brick walls complete with yellow painted plaster, wood floors, a collapsed wood lathe and plaster ceiling or wall, and a brick fireplace were extant, along with the stone foundation. The building had three rooms and was presumably a two-storied business or dwelling. Artifacts recovered from the builder's trench include creamware, pearlware, and whiteware, suggesting a post-1820 date to the structure.

Five of the six Area 12 units were excavated adjacent to the 35 Montgomery Street foundation, and all of these contained ceramic deposits (Units 12.1, 12.2, 12.4, 12.5, and 12.6) (Figure 13.3). The exact nature and stratigraphy of the ceramic deposits varied in each unit, but the deposits can be divided into two main categories: burned and unburned. The burned deposit is below, and thus earlier, than the nonburned deposits and is essentially a "level" rather than the "pockets" that typify the nonburned ceramic deposits. The burned levels are clay containing a large quantity of ceramics, whereas the nonburned deposits consist of enormous amounts of ceramics with almost no soil matrix.

The predominant artifact of the burned layer is blue painted pearlware, but there were also creamware and other pearlwares, slip-decorated redware, and a small amount of other artifacts such as melted glass and tobacco pipe fragments. The refined earthenwares were extremely charred and fragmented, whereas the glaze on the redware fragments had melted into cracks and along broken edges. Some of the pearlware fragments and many of the redware fragments were fused together in a way that suggests they had been nested or stacked when burned.

The burned level was found in three of the five 35 Montgomery Street units. The other two units were not excavated to a sufficient depth to have encountered the burned level. The burned level extends across the entirety of Units 12.2 and 12.4, which are adjacent (Figure 13.4). The level slopes across the

Montgomery Street through their property for the sum of one dollar, with John Fondey, Jr., acting as power of attorney (ACHOR 1800a).

Over the next 5 years, Fondey and DeForest continued to conduct real estate transactions around Fox Creek in the Montgomery Street block. In October 1800 Fondey, along with Philip DeForest, purchased the large lot to the south of Fox Creek (ACHOR 1800b), and the City of Albany conveyed to Fondey, DeForest, Annatie VerPlank, and Neltie Hoghkerk the bounds of Fox Creek with the right to construct over it (ACHOR 1800c). Later, Fondey and DeForest bought out the VerPlank's interest in the Alida DeForest lots and divided and resold much of the properties they had purchased (ACHOR 1802, 1804a, 1804b, 1805).

Of the heirs of Walter DeForest, only the Fondeys and the Hoghkerks were Albany residents. The rest, including Philip W. DeForest, Fondey's real estate partner, lived in Montgomery County. As the most active and local owner of Alida DeForest properties, Fondey had considerable influence over the Area 11 and 12 lots.

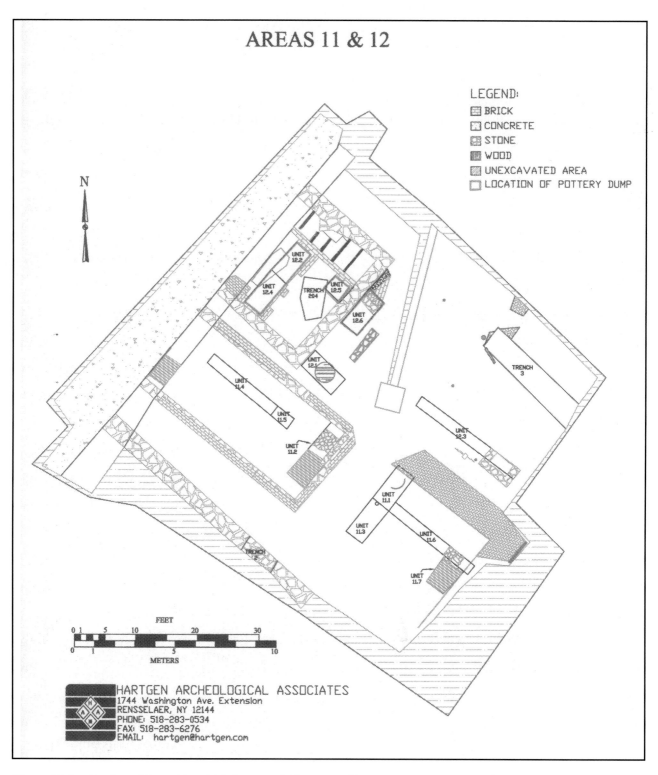

Figure 13.3. Site plan of Areas 11 and 12 showing the location of Units 12.2, 12.4, 12.5, and 12.6 containing ceramic deposits.

two units from the north to the south, toward the Fox Creek Culvert and likely reflects the banks of the creek at the time of deposition.

It is clear that the burned layer represents remains from the 1797 fire. What is less clear is whether the ceramics had been present on the site at the time of

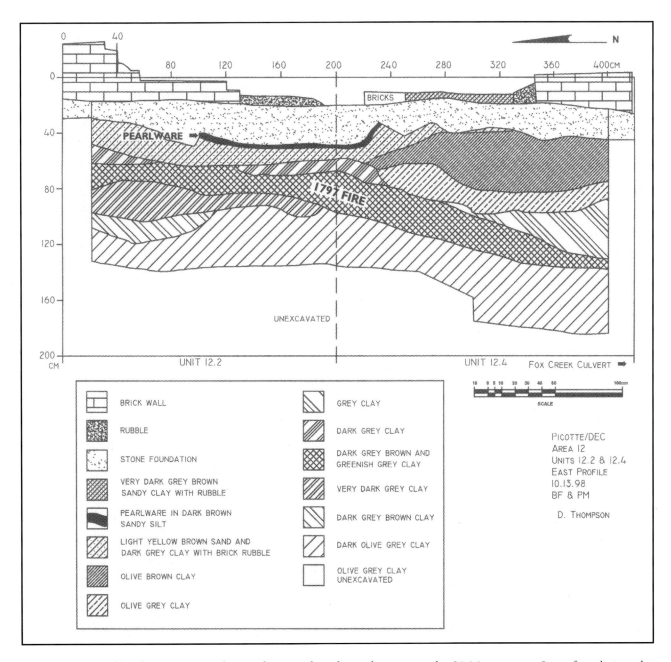

Figure 13.4. Profile of Units 12.2 and 12.4 showing the relationship among the 35 Montgomery Street foundation, the nonburned ceramic (pearlware) deposit, and the 1797 fire level. Note how the burned level slopes toward the Fox Creek Culvert.

the fire, or if they were deposited during the postfire cleanup. There is nothing in the *Albany Centinel* (1797) article that would suggest that significant amounts of ceramics were stored in the vicinity of Area 12 at the time of the fire. Fondey's glass and ceramic warehouses, although located on a different block, were not far away. In 1797 the property that

Fondey co-owned with the other heirs of Walter De-Forest had not yet been divided by Montgomery Street. Therefore, Area 12 was set far back from the main thoroughfare of Watervliet or Broadway and was probably devoid of any substantial buildings. The bank of Fox Creek would have been a convenient place for Fondey to dispose of the ruins of his crockery and glass warehouses.

Unit 12.2 was the only unit from which both burned and unburned ceramic deposits were recovered. The u-shaped pocket of unburned ceramics was about 20 centimeters at its thickest point and was encountered in the level below the wood floor of 35 Montgomery Street. The 1797 fire level was approximately 12 centimeters below the unburned deposit. Two other units (Units 12.5 and 12.6) contained unburned ceramic deposits below the level of the wood floor. In Unit 12.5 the ceramic level was capped by a level of decomposing plant fibers; in Unit 12.6 there were two ceramic levels alternating with two levels of plant fibers. In the higher of these two levels there were engine-tuned redware vessels that had been discarded still nested together. A single fragment of kiln furniture was found in one of the ceramic deposits.

The ceramics from the unburned deposits do not have use-wear marks, suggesting that they were discarded before they had been sold and used. Ceramics shipped from England were packed in straw and shipped in crates or barrels (known as hogsheads), each of which can hold hundreds of vessels. The contents of these crates frequently arrived broken, and it is likely that John Fondey, Jr., dumped the ruined ceramics in Area 12 soon after shipment. The fragment of kiln furniture, the plant fibers, and the nested redware pieces help support this assumption, as do the density and homogeneity of the deposit and the extremely large numbers of fragments. The site's association with a ceramic merchant, its position on the banks of the Fox Creek, and its close proximity to the docks of the Hudson River are all further confirmation of the theory. The unburned ceramics were most likely deposited in the first decade of the nineteenth century, when Fondey co-owned much of the area, and it was still relatively undeveloped.

The Ceramic Assemblage

The unburned deposits of ceramics were so dense that they were not screened; they were simply scooped directly into buckets or bags and brought back to the lab. Because of the enormous number of sherds, many of the smaller, undecorated fragments were simply weighed rather than counted. A single context, from the Unit 12.2 deposit, contained 85 pounds of creamware and pearlware fragments. Ten pounds of these were not counted, and the remaining 75 pounds consisted of approximately 16,500 sherds.

The most prevalent ware types in the unburned

ceramic levels were polychrome painted pearlware and undecorated creamware. Other pearlware types in the deposits were green- and blue-shell edged, and dipped/annular, or mocha. Creamware from the deposits included undecorated hollowware, royal and bath-shaped flatware, and some bat-printed pieces. Also in the assemblage were black-glazed redware, engine-turned redware, and a small amount of overglazed Chinese porcelain. The amount of each ceramic type differed among the deposits. For example, the upper level of ceramics in Unit 12.6 contained large amounts of black-glazed and engine-turned redwares, as well as some table glass. The other unburned deposits, including the lower ceramic level of Unit 12.6, contained very few redware or glass fragments.

The painted pearlware, with its myriad of unique floral and geometric designs in vibrant colors, will be the focus of the ceramic analysis (Figure 13.5). Most of the painted patterns were found on only tea bowls and saucers, while a few patterns were primarily on larger bowls. Two sherds, with a unique pattern, were part of the rim of a small plate. A few patterns came in a variety of vessel shapes, including tea or coffee pots and creamers, as well as tea bowls and saucers.

There are two elements to many of the polychrome painted pearlware patterns, a repeating rim or body design and a single motif on the interior base of the vessel. The base motifs can be elaborate florals or simple crosses. The rim and base designs are dissimilar enough that unless a sherd is found that contains portions of both elements, it may be impossible to match them up. Fifty unique patterns were identified from the Picotte-DEC pearlware assemblage. This includes rim patterns with or without known base motifs and all-over patterns. Base motifs where the rim design is unknown were not counted to avoid pattern duplication. Many of the patterns were represented by a large number of sherds, others by only a few.

Painted pearlware of this type is found frequently at sites dating to the early nineteenth century, and although it seems that the same patterns are seen over and over, that is usually not the case. For this analysis the patterns from four other assemblages with large amounts of polychrome painted pearlware were studied. The assemblages analyzed were from the 7 Hanover Square site, New York City, excavated by Nan Rothschild and Arnold Pickman and housed at Columbia University; Courtland Van Buren's Privy (Feature 18) from the Assay site, New York City, analyzed by Louis Berger and Associates and stored at the

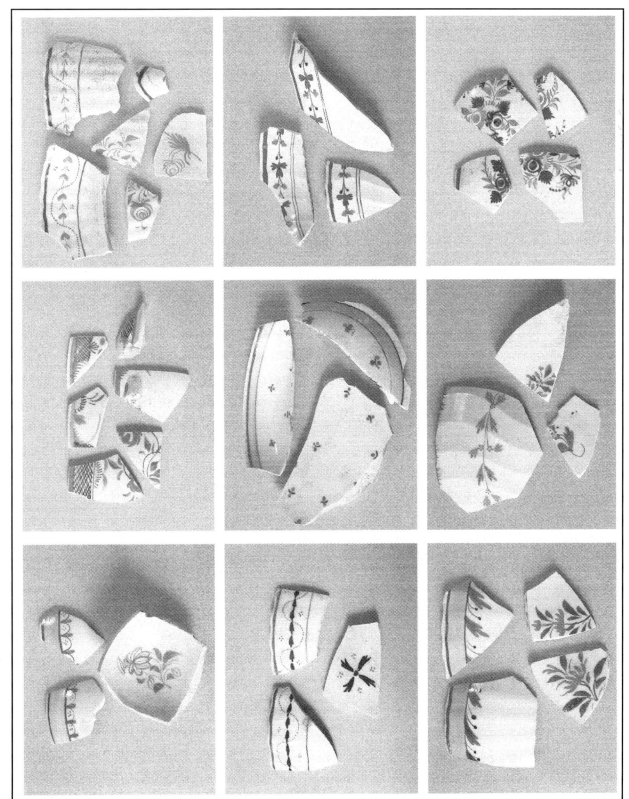

Figure 13.5. A variety of the painted pearlware patterns recovered from the Picotte-DEC ceramic deposits.

South Street Seaport Museum; the dwelling of a general merchant named McKown in Schodack, New York, housed at Eastfield Village; and a collection, stored at the New York State Historic Sites Bureau, from three locations in the block to the south of the Picotte-DEC site in Albany, which were collected by Paul Huey during street repairs. Sixty patterns were identified from these four collections in addition to the 50 patterns from the Picotte-DEC site. Of the 110 patterns, only 24 were found at more than one site. Several of these "duplicated" patterns were actually common motifs, such as the strawberry, tulip, and peafowl, which have countless variations.

The variety of patterns is not entirely surprising. The five Wedgwood pattern books from the years 1800 to 1830 contain approximately 1,950 consecutively numbered patterns (Rockwell 1977). The popularity of printed patterns was short lived, and in most cases a single pattern was not repeated for more than 3 years (Miller, Martin, and Dickenson 1994). It is likely that this was also the case for painted patterns as well.

The sherds in this assemblage were not from first-quality vessels. Defects, such as stray paint marks, are present on some of the fragments (Figure 13.6). A saucer base from a similar ceramic deposit at the 7 Hanover Square site in New York City has an unidentified concretion, about 1 inch in diameter, which fired on in the kiln, and even glazed over, and yet was still exported for sale in the United States. British potters tended to send their inferior wares to the United States (Ewins 1997). According to Ewins, there were several reasons for this. First, the majority of Americans could not afford higher-quality wares. Second, the British potters did not want to risk gaining a damaged reputation by allowing inferior wares to be sold within their own country. Third, the potters did not want the less expensive ceramics competing with the higher-quality wares on the home market. It is interesting to note that workers in the potteries were paid only for vessels that came out of the kiln in first-quality condition, but the poorer-quality wares were still being sold, with none of the proceeds going to the pottery workers (M. Goodby, personal communication 1998).

Some of the painted polychrome pearlwares are marked with simple painted symbols. These painters' marks were used to identify the decorator of the piece, so that if the piece survived the firing in salable first-quality condition, the decorator could be paid for it. Not all of the pattern styles were marked;

marks were found on 12 of the 50 Picotte-DEC patterns. The marks range from simple single or double strokes (the most common mark), to slightly more elaborate shapes, such as a backward pointed 9. It is difficult to determine the exact number of marks represented, because they are made by hand and therefore vary from piece to piece, but there are at least 20 unique marks in the assemblage. Fifteen different marks were found on a single pattern (Pattern 41).

The painters' marks found in an assemblage, although very simple, can elicit some information about the people, often young girls, who decorated the ceramics. The variety of marks found associated with a single pattern shows that the painters themselves were not the designers of the pattern, and it accounts for variations within a design. If you look at a single pattern that is associated with multiple examples of a variety of marks, it becomes possible to see differences in style and technique among painters. The value of this analysis is that it creates a not easily achieved connection to the individual.

Two patterns, designated Patterns 4 and 41, are good examples of how painting styles can be matched up with marks. Figure 13.7 shows six fragments of Pattern 4 with relatively complete base motifs and the corresponding painter's marks on the reverse. The two examples with double stroke marks are remarkably similar, short stems and leaves that are clustered together. The two examples with X marks are also similar to each other with long stems and separated leaves. Figure 13.8 has examples of the base motif of Pattern 41 with five different painter's marks. If you look particularly at the shape of the leaves and the placement of the stems, the technique of each painter becomes evident.

Caution should be used when analyzing painters' marks, particularly when using multiple assemblages or researching distribution. Simple marks, such as a single stroke or an X, were likely used at multiple factories. The widespread use of the double stroke mark in the Picotte-DEC assemblage (it occurred half as often as all the other marks put together and was found on 8 of the 12 marked patterns) suggests the possibility that more than one painter used that mark, even within the same factory. The same mark may have been used by painters working different shifts or during different production runs.

At the Twenty-Second Wedgwood International Seminar, Delhom said about pearlware: "There could not have been a finer canvas for the flower painter" (1977:64), and Rockwell stated that aside from the

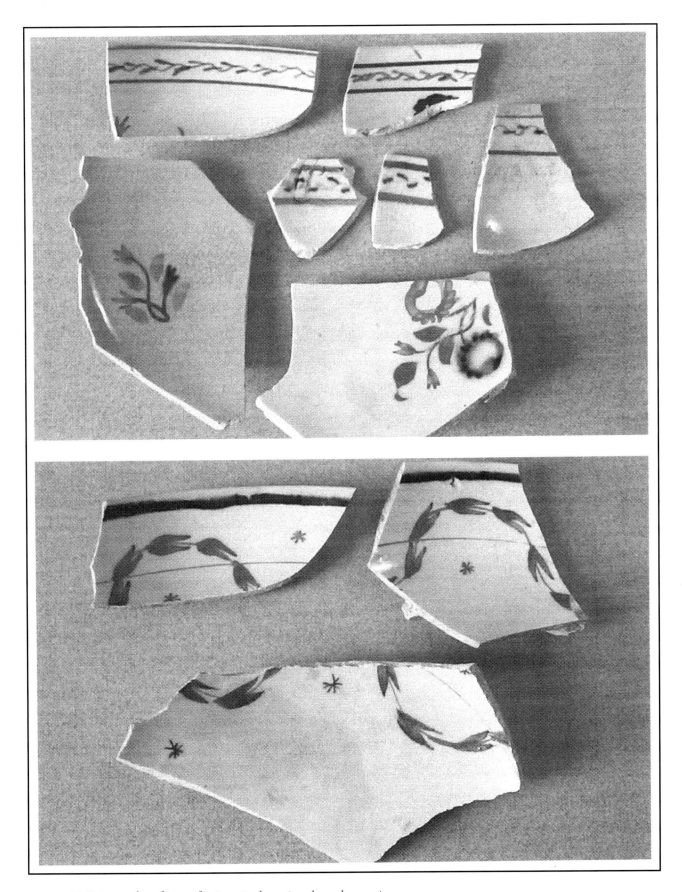

Figure 13.6. Examples of imperfections in the painted pearlware pieces.

Figure 13.7. Pattern 4 base motifs with corresponding painters' marks.

Figure 13.8a. Pattern 41 base motifs with painters' marks.

Figure 13.8b. More Pattern 41 base motifs with painters' marks.

Figure 13.9. Examples of painted pearlware fragments from the 7 Hanover Square site in New York City. Courtesy of the William Duncan Strong Museum of Anthropology, Columbia University.

simple border designs: "one of its most ideal uses was as a medium for some imaginative designers and skilled painters of flowers, foliage, and vines who used the ware to produce bold, colorful and unique patterns on breakfast, dessert, tea, supper and bedroom sets" (1977:246). The patterns found at the Picotte-DEC site are relatively simple. In contrast, examples recovered from a similar ceramic deposition at the 7 Hanover Square site in New York City, excavated by Nan Rothschild and Arnold Pickman, had patterns that were much more complex (Figure 13.9). Were these intricate patterns designed and executed by a single person? Or were they, like the more simple patterns, conceived of by a designer and faithfully rendered by a bevy of painters? It seems unlikely that these complex patterns would be duplicated by more than one individual, and yet, if that were the case, then there would be no need for painters' marks on these pieces. However, one fragment from the 7 Hanover Square site is very elaborately decorated and also bears a painter's mark.

Discussion

The dense deposit of early nineteenth-century British ceramics including brightly colored painted pearlware found during the Picotte-DEC Phase I survey was an intriguing discovery. The mitigation plan called for further excavation of the area surrounding the deposit in order to better understand why and how the ceramics came to be there. Archaeological evidence including nested vessel fragments, plant-fiber packing material, and a fragment of kiln furniture suggests that the ceramics were broken during transit. Documentary evidence shows that the property was co-owned by John Fondey, Jr., a ceramic and glass merchant whose warehouses were destroyed in a large fire. A level of charred ceramics dating to the time of the fire corroborates Fondey's connection to the deposits. The landscape of the site at the time the ceramics were deposited, on the banks of a substantial creek and set far back from the street, seems the perfect setting to dispose of unwanted broken ceramics. The site's close proximity to the Hudson River further substantiates the theory that the ceramics were discarded by Fondey in a convenient location after they arrived at the docks already ruined.

The interest in the ceramics themselves was intensified when it was discovered that individual painting styles and techniques could be studied by comparing the marks on the polychrome pearlware. This re-search is still in its early stages, and whether it will be possible to use this technique to compare multiple assemblages is still unknown. Compiling digital databases of the patterns and marks found at sites with large representative samples may be one way to facilitate analysis.

The pearlware photos in this paper were taken with a digital camera. These images can be stored on a computer and then distributed to other researchers either on CD ROM or printed on paper using a standard printer. The advantages of this method are that it creates a photographic representation of the pattern, which is more easily recognizable than a drawing or written description. The digital photo format allows for the organization and reorganization of the ceramics, from single or multiple assemblages, a nearly impossible task with actual sherds. It is also possible to print multiple images on one sheet of paper, including both the front and back of a single fragment, making the analysis of marks much easier.

References Cited

ACHOR (Albany County Hall of Records). 1800a. Deed between John Fondey, Jr., et al. and City of Albany, June 9. (Book 17, p. 403). Albany County Hall of Records, Albany, N.Y.

_____. 1800b. Deed between Walter Quackenboss (sic) et al. and John Fondey, Jr., and Philip W. DeForest, October 17. (Book 17, p. 433). Albany County Hall of Records, Albany, N.Y.

_____. 1800c. Deed between City of Albany and John Fondey, Jr., et al., October 27. (Book of Conveyances, p. 9). Albany County Hall of Records, Albany, N.Y.

_____. 1802. Deed between John Fondey, Jr., and Philip W. DeForest and John McMilen et al., April 30. (Book 61, p. 309). Albany County Hall of Records, Albany, N.Y.

_____. 1804a. Deed between Gurluyne and Annatie VerPlank and John Fondey, Jr., and Philip W. De-Forest, March 12. (Book 18, p. 537). Albany County Hall of Records, Albany, N.Y.

_____. 1804b. Deed between John Fondey, Jr., et al. and James Scrymser and Peter McNab, July 12. (Book 19, p. 140). Albany County Hall of Records, Albany, N.Y.

_____. 1805. Deed between John Fondey, Jr., et al., and Thomas Harmon, Jr., October 14. (Book 19, p. 206). Albany County Hall of Records, Albany, N.Y.

_____. 1830. Executor's Deed between John Fondey, Jr., deceased, by Executor et al. and Jacob Ten Eyck, June 19. (Book 37, p. 339). Albany County Hall of Records, Albany, N.Y.

Albany Centinel. 1797. Dreadful Conflagration, August 8. American Antiquarian Society, Worchester, Mass.

Albany Institute of History and Art. 1992. Exhibition Text. Unpublished. Family Folders, Fondey Family. Albany Insititute of History and Art, Albany, N.Y.

Delhom, M.M. 1977. Pearlware. In *Wedgwood: Its Competitors and Imitators, 1800–1830*, pp. 61–65. Ars Ceramics, Ltd. The 22nd Wedgwood International Seminar, May 4–6. The Henry Ford Museum, Dearborn, Mich.

DeWitt, S. 1794. *A Plan of the City of Albany.* Reprinted 1968 by Historic Urban Plans, Ithaca, N.Y. From the original in the Library of Congress, Washington, D.C.

Ewins, N. 1997. "Supplying the Present Wants of Our Yankee Cousins . . .": Staffordshire Ceramics and the American Market 1775–1880. *Journal of Ceramic History* 15:1–154.

Hailes, T. 1919. Copy of 1799 John E. Van Alen Survey of Lots North of Market Street. Albany County Hall of Records, Albany, N.Y.

Miller, G.L., Martin, A.S., and Dickenson, N.S. 1994. Changing Consumption Patterns: English Ceramics and the American Market from 1770 to 1840. In *Everyday Life in the Early Republic*, edited by C.E. Hutchins, pp. 219–248. Winterthur Museum, Winterthur, Del.

Rockwell, D.L. 1977. Early Nineteenth Century Borders. In *Wedgwood: Its Competitors and Imitators, 1800–1830*, pp. 245–249. Ars Ceramics, Ltd. The 22nd Wedgwood International Seminar, May 4–6. The Henry Ford Museum, Dearborn, Mich.

Section 5

Battles and Breakthroughs

CHAPTER 14

Archaeology, Historic Preservation, and Albany's Past: The Battle over the DASNY Building Project

Karen S. Hartgen

Introduction

Albany has struggled with its archaeological past since Paul Huey's excavations revealed the remains of seventeenth-century Fort Orange in the early 1970s (Figure 1.1; Chapter 2, this volume). The city has a love-hate relationship with its past: Albany constantly recognizes its heritage in advertising campaigns and street signs, yet has no early Dutch architecture standing. Beginning in 1980 more than a dozen downtown archaeological projects have illuminated the city's rich archaeological past (Chapter 2, this volume). Although public interest swells with each new find, the municipal government has yet to develop an archaeological management plan for the oldest continually inhabited European community in the original 13 colonies.

Since the early seventeenth century, Albany, New York, has been the site of international trade, the center for regional and state governmental administration, the hub of Hudson River valley transportation networks, and, as a result, a place of continuous economic and physical growth. Unfortunately the unique Dutch origins of the city that lie beneath the ground within the center of the modern city have been systematically destroyed throughout the past century. In contrast to Albany—formally established as Beverwyck in 1652 but first settled by the Dutch with the erection in 1614 of a trading fort on Castle Island in the Hudson River—such North American cities as St. Augustine, Jamestown, New York, Plymouth, Montreal, Quebec, and Philadelphia pride themselves on preserving and interpreting the archae-

ological fabric of their past. What happened to the last vestiges of Beverwyck preserved under the nineteenth-century buildings of downtown Albany was just another example of the disregard of the past in Albany.

Possibly the worst example of Albany's disregard for its past was the 1996 destruction of the rich archaeological site at Broadway and Maiden Lane located just inside the stockaded city's north gate (Figure 14.1). What made this incident particularly reprehensible was that the destruction was wrought at the hands of a New York state agency, the Dormitory Authority of the State of New York (DASNY), which was required by law under the State Environmental Quality Review Act (New York State 1987 [SEQRA]) and the State Historic Preservation Act (New York State 1980 [SHPA]) to consider the impact that their projects have on structures and archaeological sites eligible or listed in the National Register of Historic Places. These regulations require that archaeological sites and historic structures be considered in the evaluation of possible impacts that a project can have on the environment. Part of the process requires a report that the public can review and comment on the scope of the investigations and the potential plans for mitigating adverse effects.

DASNY had been looking for a new location for their headquarters for some time. As part of their selection and assessment of alternative sites, state agencies are required by law—both SEQRA and SHPA—to evaluate the potential historic and archaeological sensitivity of each contingent location as well as to

People, Places, and Material Things: Historical Archaeology of Albany, New York edited by Charles L. Fisher, New York State Museum Bulletin 499, © 2003 by the University of the State of New York, New York State Education Department, Albany, New York. All rights reserved

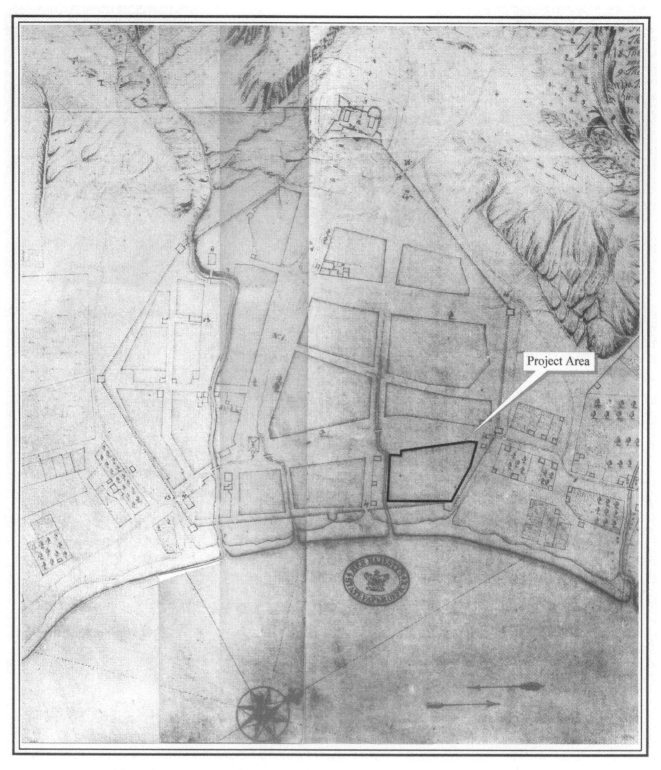

Figure 14.1. Detail from the Römer Map of 1698 showing the location of the DASNY project site.

factor in mitigation procedures, such as archaeological excavation, as part of the overall project schedule and cost. DASNY, however, selected a site in the city of Albany along Broadway, a site that was within the 1652 Dutch West India Company settlement of Beverwyck, without evaluating the archaeological sensitivity of the area. In addition, the construction schedule was fast tracked.

The site that DASNY selected had been the focus of an earlier preservation fight when, in 1992, during the dark of night the city demolished the eighteenth-century townhouse of Abraham Yates, Jr. Yates had been a member of the Albany Committee of Safety during the American Revolution, mayor of Albany from 1790 to 1796, and an ardent anti-Federalist (Bielinski 1975). Yates' house and, in fact, the entire block were located within the boundaries of the National Register Downtown Albany Historic District and also in the city's archaeological district, which is defined by the alignment of the stockade that once enclosed Beverwyck (Munsell 1850, 1865; Römer 1698; Wilcoxen 1981). The National Register District was created to provide protection through the recognition of the area's historic significance. The significance of this district was stated in the National Register of Historic Places Nomination Form as

> the nucleus of Albany's growth for three centuries. The development of the area as a banking, retail, transportation, and political district has created a unique combination of building designs; many were designed by Albany's finest architects. Although the existing buildings date from the early nineteenth century through the twentieth century, the basic street pattern was developed in the late 1600s. Historically, the district has been the site of a Continental Congress, headquarters for armies during the Revolutionary War, and a major transportation center as the United States expanded west. (New York State Office of Parks, Recreation and Historic Preservation 1979:n.p)

Thus the site was clearly located in the heart of a well-known historical district at one time containing both archaeological and structural resources. The site was used as a surface parking lot, and no archaeological investigations had been conducted prior to 1996.

Initial Study of the Property

In June 1996 DASNY solicited proposals for initial archaeological investigations on the site of the proposed DASNY headquarters. Hartgen Archeological Associates, Inc., was selected to complete the study by the beginning of July, a period of less than 4 weeks. The history of the property was compiled in record time using the research of Dr. Paul Huey, a nationally recognized New Netherland scholar and archaeologist, and of John Wolcott, a local historian and

preservation activist (Huey 1988; Wolcott 1987).

Historically the block was situated just inside the north wall of the seventeenth-century stockade near its north gate where Native Americans and European traders entered to conduct the fur trade. In 1652 and 1653 Dutch West India Company Director-General Petrus Stuyvesant granted patents for lots contained on the block to four prominent local men: from north to south, Jan Verbeeck, Frans Barentsen Pastoor, Teunis Cornelissen, and Cornelius Teunissen. Subsequent prominent residents included Jan Baptist van Rensselaer, David Pietersen Schuyler, Dominie Godfridus Dellius, Dominie Eliardus Westerlo, and Abraham Yates, Jr. Early businesses on the property included a horse mill for grinding grain and a brewery, one of the earliest known European breweries in the New World. Obviously this site was a sensitive archaeological area, which was expected to contain extensive archaeological deposits and features relating to the early European settlement of the area where later eighteenth-, nineteenth-, and twentieth-century development and constructions had not already destroyed the archaeological record.

Archaeological Investigation

As soon as archaeological testing of the block was begun, it became obvious that seventeenth- and eighteenth-century materials had been preserved intact in spite of later development. Early seventeenth-century deposits were present in blue and brown clay layers in each of the sets of backhoe tests excavated under the supervision of Hartgen archaeologists (Figure 14.2). The groups of backhoe trenches were placed within each of the original lots owned by Teunis Cornelissen, Cornelius Teunissen, Frans Barentsen Pastoor, and Jan Verbeeck as identified during the documentary analysis of the block east of Broadway between Maiden Lane and Steuben Street. All four of these lots were preserved and could be delineated by the outlines of subsurface remnants of the mortared brick and fieldstone foundations of the buildings erected on them.

Teunis Cornelissen's Lot

Trench 1 encountered the corner of the Yates or Lansing house and what became an important blue-gray clay deposit beneath the concrete floor of the cellar. This layer produced an assemblage of seventeenth- and early eighteenth-century cultural material

Figure 14.2. Seventeenth-century deposits in blue and brown clay located during the initial backhoe testing.

Figure 14.3. Seventeenth- or early eighteenth-century red bricks from the initial testing.

including fragments of a tin-glazed earthenware delft plate, slip-decorated red earthenware, case bottle glass, food bone, oyster shell, a bone knife handle and seventeenth- to eighteenth-century red brick (Figure 14.3). Two red tubular glass trade beads with black interiors (ca. 1650) (Figure 14.4), pan-tiles used for roofing, and a glass vessel base were also found in the very first backhoe test.

Additional finds on this lot included an undisturbed late eighteenth-century privy with fragments of dark green bottle glass, fine engraved glass, red earthenware pan-tiles, unglazed red earthenware, engine-turned red stoneware, shell-edged and transfer-printed pearlware, transfer-printed whiteware, and a chamber pot. A coconut husk was recovered along with oyster shell, late eighteenth-century Chinese export porcelain, and a cut conch shell from a layer of dark gray clay fill resting on the mottled Holocene

brown clay (Figure 14.5). An early nineteenth-century wood-lined privy was found in a second trench on the east side of the Yates or Lansing lot. Artifacts from precontact occupations, in addition to seventeenth, eighteenth, and nineteenth centuries were recovered as well (Figure 14.6).

Cornelius Teunissen's Lot

Trench 3 was adjacent to Maiden Lane and revealed 3 feet of early historic soil deposits beneath the cellar floors of later buildings at 499 and 501 Broadway. Sherds of white salt-glazed stoneware, Rhenish or English stoneware, tin-glazed buff earthenware, and Chinese export porcelain were found along with clay tobacco pipes, Dutch yellow bricks, pan-tiles, oyster shells, shoe leather, a clay marble, and a brass sewing kit that included pins, needles, a clothing fastener, and a thimble (Figures 14.7 and 14.8). A layer of very dark gray clay with matted thin strips of wood and coconut fiber was identified as well. Trade items recovered included a brown to black, round, glass bead, one stone bead, and tubular conch shell beads.

Frans Barentsen Pastoor's Lot

Trench 4 excavated on the Dutch Reformed Church lot, occupied by the Domine Dellius and the site of Bleecker Hall in the nineteenth century, yielded

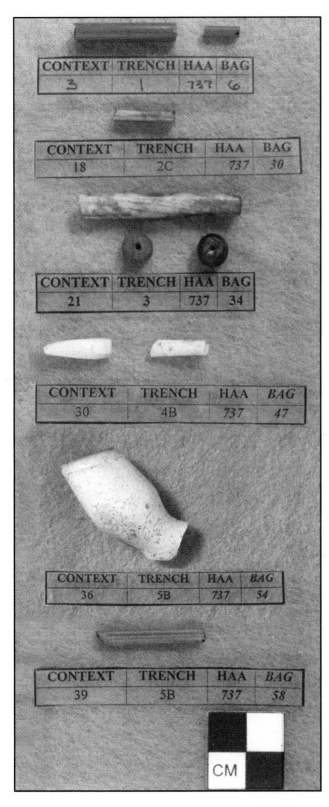

CONTEXT	TRENCH	HAA	BAG
3	1	737	6

CONTEXT	TRENCH	HAA	BAG
18	2C	737	30

CONTEXT	TRENCH	HAA	BAG
21	3	737	34

CONTEXT	TRENCH	HAA	BAG
30	4B	737	47

CONTEXT	TRENCH	HAA	BAG
36	5B	737	54

CONTEXT	TRENCH	HAA	BAG
39	5B	737	58

CM

Figure 14.4. Early trade goods, glass beads, shell beads, and an early English pipe bowl recovered during the initial testing.

artifacts associated with the original occupation of the lot and architectural details of the 1846 Bleecker Hall façade (Figure 14.9). Artifacts from the seventeenth, eighteenth, and early nineteenth centuries were found beneath the cellar floor of Bleecker Hall, which was approximately 7 feet below the existing ground surface.

Jan Verbeeck's Lot

An important discovery in Trench 5 on the Verbeeck or Schuyler lot was a small pit feature that contained seventeenth- and eighteenth-century materials. This feature contained shell, bone, hair, fish bones, tobacco pipe stems and a bowl, wrought iron nails, glazed red earthenware, and case bottle glass fragments. On the east side of this lot, a stone-lined privy with a large quantity of material from 1750 to the 1770s was located. Wine bottle glass fragments, a red earthenware chamber pot, dot- and diaper-patterned white salt-glazed stoneware, creamware, Whieldon creamware, engine-turned red stoneware, porcelain, hand-painted pearlware, shell-edged pearlware, transfer-printed pearlware, and Dutch bricks were retrieved. This feature related to the occupation of David Schuyler and his son Abraham on this property and attests to the wealth and prominence of the families that once lived on this block (Hartgen Archeological Associates, Inc. 1996).

In summary, these remarkable finds in the initial test trenches included glass trade beads, wampum, tin-enameled buff earthenware, Rhenish, English, and Westerwald stoneware, red earthenware pan-tiles, yellow Dutch bricks, and Chinese export porcelains. These dramatic finds demonstrated that even after 330 years, the early vestiges of Beverwyck were preserved under many feet of later historic deposits. Here was an opportunity to open windows to the past and uncover the material culture of the mid-seventeenth-century Dutch settlers and traders, as well as of their Native American counterparts. DASNY decided to fast-track through the regulatory review process.

The Battle Begins

In September 1996, after delaying during the months of July and August, DASNY devised a scope of work for the mitigation of impacts to this extensive and unique archaeological site that was to be completed within seven consecutive days in order to meet

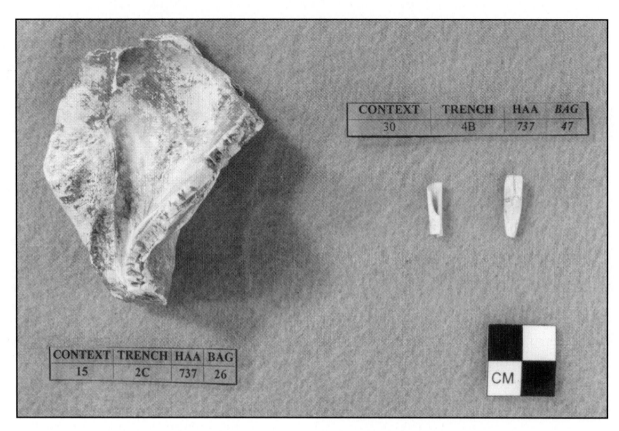

CONTEXT	TRENCH	HAA	BAG
30	4B	737	47

CONTEXT	TRENCH	HAA	BAG
15	2C	737	26

CM

Figure 14.5. Evidence of shell bead production, a cut conch and two shell beads.

CONTEXT	TRENCH	HAA	BAG
17	2C	737	28

CM

Figure 14.6. Native American pitted stone recovered in the initial testing.

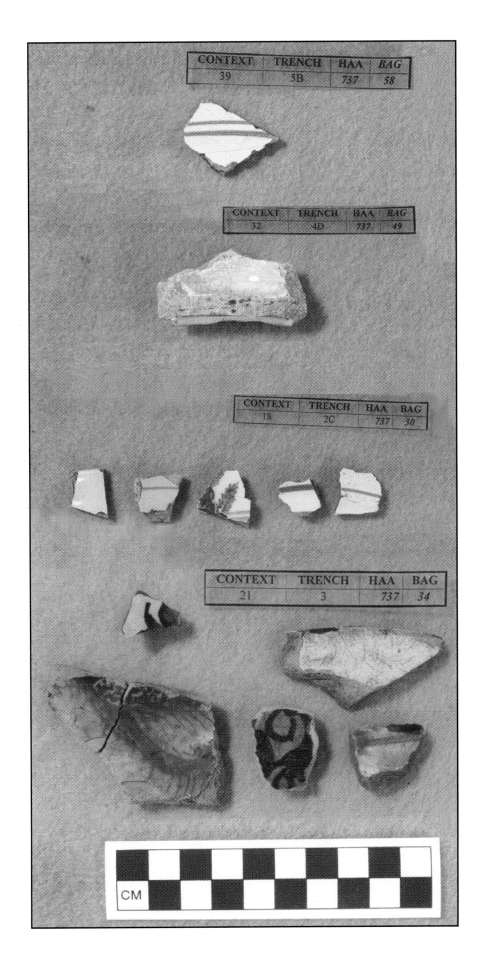

CONTEXT	TRENCH	HAA	BAG
39	5B	737	58

CONTEXT	TRENCH	HAA	BAG
32	4D	737	49

CONTEXT	TRENCH	HAA	BAG
18	2C	737	30

CONTEXT	TRENCH	HAA	BAG
21	3	737	34

CM

Figure 14.7. Tin-glazed enameled-wares recovered in the initial testing.

Figure 14.8. Imported yellow Dutch bricks from Trench 5B.

Figure 14.9. Decorative cut stone from the façade of Bleeker Hall, recorded in initial study.

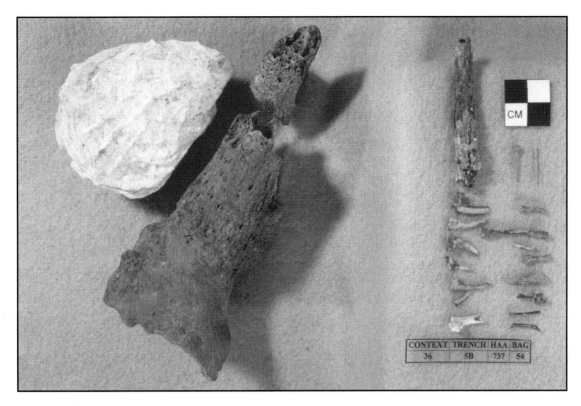

Figure 14.10. Sample of faunal materials from the initial testing, including oyster, cow, bird, and fish remains.

their schedule. The archaeological investigation was limited to Frans Barentsen Pastoor's lot, an area 20 feet by 40 feet, in a section of the site already known to be the least archaeologically productive portion.

Obviously this was not an adequate scope of work or time frame. After meeting onsite with DASNY representatives, Hartgen Archeological Associates, Inc., refused the job because of the inadequacy of the scope of work and the time frame, neither of which met the standard that Hartgen and other professional archaeologists knew was appropriate to the resources. Immediately another archaeological consultant undertook the limited scope of archaeological excavations at the locations selected by DASNY and the ridiculous time frame (Figure 14.11). As the public's interest in the site grew and press coverage increased, additional excavations were authorized by DASNY at various locations in a piece-meal fashion. It was apparent that an adequate research design was not in place and that a systematic sampling plan had to be developed to mitigate the impacts to the site.

In October 1996 the New York Archaeological Council (NYAC) filed a lawsuit in New York Supreme Court claiming that DASNY had not complied with SEQRA and SHPA. The lawsuit requested a stop-work order. Only after a court-imposed stipulation required DASNY to conduct additional archaeological investigations was an adequate work scope prepared. In addition, the archaeological work had to be monitored twice daily by a certified archaeologist designated as the court's representative from the New York State Office of Parks, Recreation and Historic Preservation (OPRHP). NYAC received twice weekly progress reports from the OPRHP during the field investigation and monthly reports during the analysis and report-writing phases. Monitoring was added to the scope and expanded excavations were required in the southeastern portion of the site (Figure 14.12). DASNY was also required to issue regular press releases based on the progress reports.

The court imposed schedule included 3 weeks for the monitoring with all fieldwork to be completed by November 22, 1996. In addition, provisions were made for curation of the collection, a final technical

Figure 14.11. Intact foundations exposed during mitigation, probably from the late eighteenth or early nineteenth century, along Broadway.

report and a popular booklet, and the execution of a Memorandum of Understanding between OPRHP and DASNY addressing DASNY's lack of coordination of its SEQRA process with the SHPA, Section 14.09, compliance. As of January 2003, no draft or final report has been submitted to the OPRHP.

The interpretation and implementation of the con-

ditions of the court-ordered stipulation were less than satisfactory to many in the Albany area. The public sentiment was expressed by Dennis Sullivan in the acknowledgments to his book.

As the finishing touches are put on this volume in preparation for publication, almost daily the Albany-area newspapers carry a story about a

Figure 14.12. Looking south to Maiden Lane showing broad areas of the archaeological mitigation.

showdown between the New York State Dormitory Authority and historic preservations interested in preserving the cultural and material artifacts of Albany's seventeenth-century Dutch community of Beverwijck. At this moment (October, 1996), the Dormitory Authority is in the process of erecting a six-story office building on a site which historians, archeologists, and a wide array of community groups say is a treasure-trove of artifacts that promise inestimable insights into the Dutch beginnings of Albany . . . For those interested in Albany's Dutch heritage, this scenario is déjà-vu all over again, if you will. In the early seventies, as Highway 787 was being built along the Hudson, state and local archeologists were forced to scramble in midwinter to get in a few choice digs before the original site of Fort Orange was buried forever under a cement overpass. Contrast these scenarios with the recent discovery of a seventeenth-century archeological site at Jamestown over which citizens and governmental officials came out in droves to celebrate aware of the site's potential for enlarging our understanding of that early English settlement . . . The present work [*The Punishment of Crime in Colonial New York: The Dutch Experience in Albany During the Seventeenth Century*] is part of this movement to reintroduce ourselves to the new world Dutch culture of the seventeenth century that has been buried for so long. Hopefully it will further communal interest in a forgotten generation of New Netherlanders and indirectly serve as a source of resistance to the kind of riding roughshod over culture-past that the New York State Dormitory has embraced. Perhaps, when the next archeological site is discovered in New York, that state's governor can follow the lead of Virginia's chief executive after the recent Jamestown discovery and break out a bottle of celebratory champagne. (1997:vii–viii)

Professional archaeologists and historians, as well as the public, were denied access to the site and to substantive information. As a result, limited knowledge of the progress of the archaeological investigations on the Broadway and Maiden Lane site was largely garnered from the local media, which has commented in their reports on the lack of information and the secretiveness surrounding the excavation. Moreover, prominent New Netherland scholars,

such as historical archaeologist Dr. Paul Huey, Dr. Charles Gehring of the New Netherland Project, and Stefan Bielenski of the New York State Museum Social History Project, were not formally consulted or allowed onsite during the field investigations.

Nonetheless, according to official DASNY press releases, significant finds include a refuse-filled seventeenth-century drainage channel in the northeast portion of the property, a 14-foot portion of the Domine Godfridus Dellius mansion, a rich eighteenth-century privy, and, in early April 1997, timbers that were tentatively identified as part of the stockade first built in 1659 to protect the community from attacks by warring local tribes (Figures 14.13 and 14.14).

In February 1997 the *Albany Times Union* reported that, during construction, another find of trade beads and other seventeenth-century materials had been made during the installation of a water line in the northern portion of the project in an area newly designated an archaeological preserve by Albany Mayor Jerry Jennings, an area which was not supposed to be affected by the construction of the building (Jakes 1997). Earlier Mayor Jennings was quoted as saying, "The City of Albany will reserve this area for future archaeological investigation. A sign indicating the historic and archaeological significance of the sites will be erected and the area will be maintained as a green space to be disturbed only for future archaeological investigation" (Nelson 1996:B-3).

This breach in the court-issued archaeological protocol in February 1997 resulted in the NYAC filing a petition for violation of, and noncompliance with, the original stipulation and order and to find the Dormitory Authority, the City of Albany, Albany County, and the Albany Local Development Corporation in contempt (NYAC 1997). The state judge refused to accept the petition in a 15-page decision, which clearly indicated his impatience with NYAC and their continuous monitoring of the project (Teresi 1997).

International concern over the proper treatment of the Dutch archaeological remains included inquiries from the Mohican Nation; Tjaco van der Hout, former Dutch Consul General in New York City; Tincke Netlenbos, Netherlands Deputy Minister of Education, Culture and Science; and Wanda Versvest, a reporter from the Dutch newspaper *Noordhollands Dagblad*, who spent a week in Albany covering the story. The public outcry and outrage over the blatant determination of DASNY to destroy the rich archaeological remains of the northern portion of Beverwyck was heartening to the preservation community and was

Figure 14.13. Excavation techniques during the archaeological mitigation. Plastic is obscuring from the public a reputed seventeenth century drainage feature.

absolutely essential to the recovery of the archaeological data from this site (Hartgen 1997).

The saga is not over yet. In 2002, 6 years after the initial field investigations, the consulting firm that conducted the excavations went out of business and a newly formed firm took over the contract. No schedule has been provided for the completion of the artifact processing, conservation, and curation of the materials, preparation of the scientific report, and production of the popular brochure and exhibit. It is hoped that when the final results are presented to the public, the Albany site will gain the national recognition it rightfully deserves and will no longer be clouded by secrecy.

An interesting spin-off from this project was Governor George Pataki's announcement on March 10, 1997, of the establishment of an archaeological fund of $250,000 for archaeological research in the cities of Albany, Schenectady, and Troy, to be paid for by DASNY (DeMasi 1997). This was a one-time-only nonrenewable fund that now has been depleted. The preservation community was pleased that the governor recognized the significance of the state's archaeological sites and provided unprecedented funds for their recovery. However, there is a process already in place that, when followed correctly, results in consideration of historic and archaeological resources in planning and economic development. The DASNY

debacle in Beverwyck is an example of what can happen if existing State Environmental Quality Review Act and State Historic Preservation Act processes are ignored.

Since the lawsuit, an unprecedented number of archaeological projects have received the proper regulatory process. Major excavations have been undertaken by Hartgen Archeological Associates, Inc., at the DEC building site north of the stockade (see Chapters 3, 5, 10, 12, and 13, this volume); the comptroller's building on State Street west of the stockade; and the State University Construction Fund parking structure containing a later eighteenth-century stockade, two eighteenth-century bulkheads and the original river bank (see Chapter 15, this volume). Other field investigations that provided interesting information on Albany's development but did not include data recovery are the Waterfront Bridge at Maiden Lane, the Court of Appeals building, and fiber-optic line monitoring in various locations in the city. Another major archaeological investigation was undertaken by the Cultural Resource Survey Program at the New York State Museum along Pearl Street, where the remains of an eighteenth-century British guard house (see Chapter 4, this volume) and eighteenth-century human remains were discovered and recovered from the Lutheran Church lot (see Chapters 6, 7, and 8, this volume).

Figure 14.14. Archaeological mitigation in the northeast portion of the site exposing a unique seventeenth-century drainage feature.

Was the lawsuit against DASNY a success? The original position taken by NYAC and other professional scholars was that if DASNY could get away with flouting the State Historic Preservation Regulations in the state's capital, Albany, why would these regulations be complied with during the review process of other projects? The number and extent of archaeological investigations in the City of Albany since the lawsuit have dramatically increased. Therefore, in my opinion, it was a success by reinforcing the existing regulations.

Was the data retrieval program at the DASNY site a success? We will have to wait and see.

References Cited

Bielinski, S. 1975. *Abraham Yates, Jr., and the New Political Order in Revolutionary New York.* New York State Museum, Albany.

DeMasi, M. 1997. Pataki Announces Archaeological Plan. *Schenectady (N.Y.) Gazette,* March 10, p. B-4.

Hartgen Archeological Associates, Inc. 1996. Phase IA Literature Review and Phase IB Archeological Investigation of the Dormitory Authority State of New York Office Building, Broadway and Maiden Lane, City of Albany. On file at New York State Office of Parks, Recreation and Historic Preservation, Peebles Island, Waterford.

Hartgen, K.S. 1997. Preserving Albany's Past: The Battle over the Broadway-Maiden Lane Archeological Site. *De HALVE-MAEN: Magazine of the Dutch Colonial Period in America* 70(1):1–6.

Huey, P.R. 1988. *Aspects of Continuity and Change in Colonial Dutch Material Culture at Fort Orange, 1624–1664.* Doctoral dissertation, University of Pennsylvania, Philadelphia. University Microfilms International, Ann Arbor, Mich.

Jakes, L. 1997. Ruling Keeps Dig Site Map Private. *Times Union,* Albany, February 26, p. B-4.

Munsell, J. 1850–59. *The Annals of Albany,* Vols. 1–10. J. Munsell, Albany, N.Y.

———. 1865–71. *Collections on the History of Albany,* Vols. 1–4. J. Munsell, Albany, N.Y.

National Historic Preservation Act of 1966, as amended (NHPA). U.S. Department of the Interior. Washington, D.C.

Nelson, S. 1996. Jennings Makes Preservation Effort. *Troy (N.Y.) Record,* October 11, p. B-3.

New York Archaeological Council (NYAC). 1996. Application Filed in New York Supreme Court for a Judgment Pursuant to Article 78 of CPLR Against Dormitory Authority of the State of New York, The State of New York, The County of Albany, The City of Albany and The Albany Local Development Corporation. Index No. 6303-96 RJI No. 0197ST7484, October. Albany.

———. 1997. Order to Show Cause for Violation of, and Noncompliance with, the Original Stipulation and Order Filed in New York Supreme Court for a Judgment Pursuant to Article 78 of CPLR Against Dormitory Authority of the State of New York, The State of New York, The County of Albany, The City of Albany and The Albany Local Development Corporation. Index No. 6303-96 RJI No. 0197ST7484, February 7. Albany.

New York State. 1980. *Historic Preservation Act,* § 14.09. OPRHPL Art. 114. New York State Office of Parks, Recreation and Historic Preservation. Albany.

_____. 1987. *Environmental Quality Review Act (SEQRA)*. ECL § 8-0101 et seq. New York State Department of Environmental Conservation. Albany.

New York State Office of Parks, Recreation and Historic Preservation. 1979. National Register of Historic Places Inventory Nomination Form: Downtown Albany Historic District. October 10. Field Services Bureau, New York State Office of Parks, Recreation and Historic Preservation, Waterford.

Römer, Col. W.W. 1698. *Plan de la Ville d'Albanie*. New York State Archives. Albany.

Sullivan, D. 1997. *The Punishment of Crime in Colonial New York: The Dutch Experience in Albany During the Seventeenth Century*. American University Studies Series 9, History Vol. 186. Peter Lang, New York.

Teresi, J.C. 1996. Judgment Pursuant to Article 78 of the CPLR, Stipulation and Order, Index No. 6303-96 RJI No. 0197ST7484, signed October 21. Albany, N.Y.

_____. 1997. Decision and Order, Index No. 6303-96 RJI No. 0197ST7484, April 23, 1997. Entered in Office of Albany County Clerk, June 19, 1997, Albany, New York.

Wilcoxen, C. 1981 *Seventeenth Century Albany: A Dutch Profile*. Education Department, Albany Institute of History and Art, Albany, N.Y.

Wolcott, J. 1987. *Succession of Ownership to Property at 513-515 Broadway*. Manuscript on file at Hartgen Archeological Associates, Inc. Rensselaer, N.Y.

CHAPTER 15

From Raritan Landing to Albany's Riverfront: The Path Toward Total 3D Archaeological Site Recording

Joel W. Grossman

Introduction

Karen Hartgen of Hartgen Archeological Associates, Inc., called me Friday evening of the July 4th weekend in 1999. Her message was explicit and urgent. After 3 weeks of excavation along the former riverfront of Albany, New York, her archaeological team had exposed a complex, 300-foot-long matrix of deeply buried log bulkhead structures of the original colonial port settlement (Figure 15.1). The excavation had run out of time, and I was asked to develop a strategy to provide a high-speed recording solution over the weekend and to deploy a team by the following Wednesday. In response, I implemented the dual application of high-resolution single-camera photogrammetry in conjunction with the first use in archaeology of the recently developed three dimensional (3D) laser-radar scanning technology (LIDAR) to produce a 3D record of the site over two 3-day recording sessions in July and August. This chapter presents examples from case studies in archaeological rescue excavations over two decades (1978–1999) to review the precedents and decision-making processes that led me to recommend the dual use of these systems to record a complex archaeological site in record time.

Innovation for Conflict Resolution

These applied technology solutions are deployed to aid in the rapid, accurate, and safe investigation of generally two contexts: emergency rescue excavations of unexpected archaeological discoveries and archaeological discoveries beyond the reach of traditional field approaches, due to contamination or other impediments (Grossman 1978, 1980, 1982a, 1985, 1990a, 1990b, 1995, 1997).

Over the past 20 years, and particularly after a series of high-altitude expeditions in the pre-Inca highlands of Andean Peru, my work has often involved archaeological crisis management, directing projects interrupted because of unexpected archaeological discoveries. These unexpected discoveries have included unknown Native American and colonial burial grounds, which could have precipitated serious ethnic and/or political conflicts, buried historical settlements thought to have been long gone, and on occasion, military secrets that got lost or buried in the physical and archival record.

Regardless of the causes, these situations can be traumatic, expensive, and politically volatile. They require quick and often innovative approaches by all involved. Agencies and corporations have to evaluate and authorize new scopes of work, project schedules, and budgets. Archaeologists need to provide quick and precise answers to difficult questions. How big is the buried site? How deep is it? What are its limits? Is it important? Does it have sufficient stratigraphic integrity to warrant National Register eligibility? How can the project be redesigned to minimize or avoid impacts? If in need of in-depth documentation, can it be cost effectively recorded without causing undue delays in the interrupted construction program?

My use of applied technology to help answer some of these questions has been based on two consistent assumptions. First, that the resolution of environ-

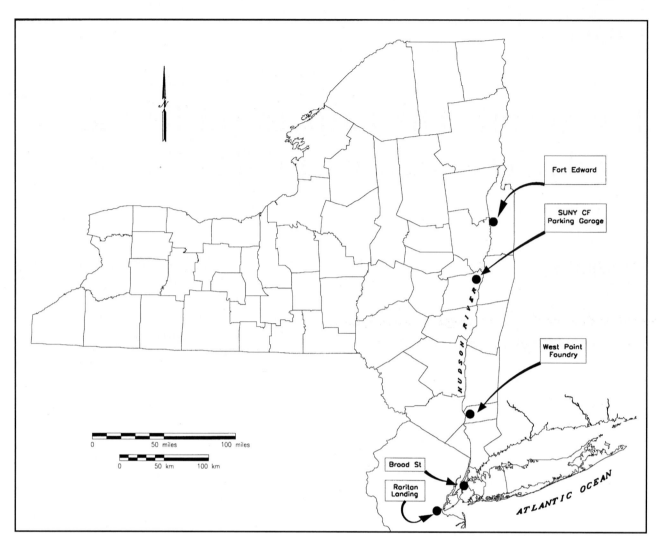

Figure 15.1. Locations of sites discussed in this chapter.

mental conflicts and the ability to quickly develop viable mitigation strategies depends on high levels of definition and data control. Second, that the long-term value of our work depends on the quality, clarity, thoroughness, and precision of our data recording, not on our individual theoretical or interpretative orientations.

Within this high-pressure environment, it was also often necessary to alter the traditional approaches and time frames of archaeology with innovative strategies to increase efficiency or reduce exposure to harmful environments. All of the projects discussed here took place in restricted time frames, and three occurred in adverse deep-winter conditions under heated shelters. All required fresh approaches to meet the challenges of site definition and docu-

mentation in often contaminated settings, which over the past 10 years have included the need to excavate through archaeological deposits laced with cadmium, arsenic, lead, toxic organics, radiation, and unexploded ordnance (Grossman 1990a, 1993, 1994a, 1994b). Instead of random sampling, ground-penetrating radar and other geophysical devices were applied to provide target-specific testing strategies. Instead of traditional fair-weather time schedules, heated steel-reinforced domes with massive heaters and dewatering systems were built to thaw the ground, protect the scientist and artifacts, and permit 24-hour-a-day excavation, even in most severe winter conditions. Instead of laborious measuring tapes, line levels, and rulers, 3D lasers and 3D cameras were employed to provide precise survey and point provenience records in minutes and seconds.

And if the archaeological study was conducted at a contaminated site, usually as part of federally mandated investigations of superfund sites, the large multidisciplinary field and laboratory teams required special training, medical monitoring, protective plastic suits, and daily decontamination after excavation. The handling of contaminated cultural remains in turn mandated the need for building safe onsite decontamination and artifact processing, computer inventory, conservation and documentation laboratories to facilitate concurrent data control and rapid decision making. This discussion is restricted in scope to the applied technology dedicated to enhance the speed and level of definition in site recording.

Precedents and Borrowed Solutions

All of the technologies discussed, single and stereo cameras, metric cameras, electronic transits, geophysical techniques, and, most recently laser-radar scans, were selected and adopted from other disciplines and scientific contexts. Each had met the test of usefulness, field readiness, and potential benefits following 2 to 5 years of demonstrated effectiveness in other fields. Their usefulness as more efficient, precise, or cost-effective than previous archaeological solutions had to be proven. When faced with the real pressures of time and expense, one must choose tried, easily available, and cost-effective solutions or technical aids, rather than the newest or the most advanced, yet untested, technology, which may or may not be reliable.

Overhead bipod systems had been actively under development and deployed by archaeologists since the early 1960s (Whittlesey 1975:258). Computer transit survey and measuring systems had been demonstrated to be faster than optical systems for a Near Eastern mapping expedition a year before they were applied at Raritan Landing in 1978 (Sterud, Strauss, and Abramovitz 1980). Likewise, 2 years before it was first used for archaeological recording in Albany, laser-radar technology had been whole-heartedly applied to replace the more time consuming and less accurate photogrammetry by major oil companies to map existing conditions and complex piping systems on offshore platforms, and by the movie industry. Almost at the same time, Jack W. LeRoy and Associates independently applied the Cyrax laser scanner in May of 1999, 2 months before its use in Albany, to make a 3D map of the National Park Service Oregon Caves National Monument (St. Amand 1999).

Benchmark Case Studies of Applied Technology: 1978–1999

The following case studies focus not on the technical details of how each class of applied technology works, but instead on how and why they were deployed. In each instance, these examples of applied technology were deployed to augment or supersede the limitations of traditional manual and optical field-recording procedures and to do justice to threatened archaeological resources in a timely, feasible, and cost-effective manner.

Five large-scale data recovery excavations spanning two decades will serve to define three phases of development or benchmarks in the quest for faster and more intensive recording systems (Figure 15.1). The first phase or period was marked by the initial use in 1978 of low elevation overhead stereo pair photogrammetry in conjunction with high-speed computer transit equipment to record the pre-Revolutionary War port community of Raritan Landing, a buried colonial site complex belatedly discovered during construction (Grossman 1978, 1980, 1982b). Given its initial success, the same approach was subsequently applied to provide the core recording system for the 1984 winter excavation of the deeply buried Dutch West India Company site found preserved beneath the financial district of lower Manhattan (Grossman 1985). The full power of these new systems with the advent of integrated data collectors with automatic coordinate conversion was fully implemented and tested in 1986 at Fort Edward, New York (Grossman 1990b).

The second phase, which began in 1989 with the excavation of Civil War gun testing facilities at West Point Foundry, was marked by the first archaeological use of single-camera photogrammetric recording and software interpolation systems to overcome the limitations of fixed dual camera setups and to facilitate the first federally mandated archaeological mitigation of a superfund site (Grossman 1990a, 1994a, 1997; Holtzer 1995).

The third phase began in the summer of 1999 with the first archaeological use of 3D laser radar in tandem with computer transit and low elevation photogrammetric systems to help document the 300-foot-long discovery of buried colonial shoreline remains in Albany, New York.

Early Computer Transit and Overhead Stereo Photogrammetry Systems

My initial experience using computer transit systems for rapid grid and 3D data control and low elevation site-specific photogrammetry took place in 1978 with the unexpected discovery of the 1730 colonial remains of Raritan Landing found buried under 3 feet of rock fill in the flood plain of the Raritan River opposite modern New Brunswick, New Jersey (Figure 15.2). The need for high-speed and high-precision recording approaches was driven by the presence of archaeological remains in the construction corridor of a federal sewer line. Scaled historical maps and ground penetrating radar were used to define the location and extent of buried structural remains (Grossman 1978, 1980). A 20-foot-wide by 300-foot-long corridor was fully excavated with wide area exposure techniques to reveal several pre-Revolutionary War structures and two well-preserved, buried, colonial period, ground surfaces with diverse artifact concentrations, building foundations, histori-

cal pit features, and preserved foot prints in the buried mud.

The federally funded construction was stopped, financial and political pressures were building to address the unexpected discovery in the shortest time possible, and the responsible agencies were under comparable pressure to do justice to the important discovery by documenting any impacts to the highest scientific and legal standards. Because of its size and stratigraphic complexity, the wide-area exposure and documentation of the complex multicomponent historic structural remains could not have been done quickly using traditional manual recording techniques. With few options, I proposed to expedite the excavation process with the intensive application of two new recording procedures. One consisted of the use of recently developed high-precision electronic survey equipment for high-speed coordinate and provenience control; the other was an adaptation of a British-developed, bipod suspended overhead photo mosaic and stereoscopic recording system to rapidly capture a detailed record of the site.

(Grossman, 1980)

Figure 15.2. View of Raritan Landing 1979 excavation of the EPA impact corridor showing the derivation of Whittlesey bipod camera support system.

High Precision Computer Transit Systems

Beginning in the mid-1970s, the computerized electronic distance meter first became available to commercial survey and engineering professionals as a cost-saving solution to the tedium and imprecision of traditional optical transit and manual surveying techniques. The new electronic transit systems were capable of measuring the location of survey points, or objects, as angles and distances with a precision of several centimeters in a kilometer (and in millimeters at distances of hundreds of meters). The first models had little or no computing power, were referred to as electronic distance meters (EDM), and were limited in output to measurements of angle and distance. The electronic transit measures the distance in the time it takes the near laser infrared beam to bounce back to the instrument off of a prismatic mirror reflector attached to a stadia rod over a target, provenience point, or artifact. When combined with measurements of the transit's vertical and horizontal angles relative to the target, true coordinates can be computed using standard trigonometric formulas. Each reading takes approximately 4 seconds.

The availability and potential utility of this new technology for high-speed field recording in archaeology was brought to my attention by Dr. Gene Sterud who used an early EDM or electronic transit to map the large site of Sardis, Turkey, in 1977 (Sterud, Strauss, and Abramovitz 1980). He informed me of their successful application at other large urban sites in the Near East and Mayan Lowlands (Miller 1978; Weeks 1978). Based on this precedent, and my need to deploy a high-speed data recovery plan workable under shelter in winter conditions in a matter of weeks instead of months, I recommended the same EDM system for the emergency rescue excavation at Raritan Landing in 1978 (Grossman 1978, 1980, 1982b).

The first challenge to its use as an efficient high-speed field tool came out of the need to automate the data collection and coordinate conversion tasks. Until the mid-1980s, actual coordinates from optical transit systems had to be computed individually with a hand calculator and trigonometric formulas or by linking the EDM to an early portable computer. A mixture of both commercial and in-house software routines was programmed in Basic to link, process, and store the transit readings. At Raritan Landing in 1978, and subsequently for the 1984 excavation of the seventeenth-century Dutch West India site in Lower Manhattan, this hardware interface was ac-

complished with early portable computers, first with a 32k Epson CPM machine with a microcassette data storage unit, and then in 1984 by a ROM-based Radio Shack Model 100 portable (Grossman 1982b, 1985). The task of programming these early onsite data collectors was aided by previous efforts by archaeologists throughout the 1970s to use early scientific calculators for the conversion of optical transit readings to site coordinates in the field (Blakeslee 1979; Hakiel 1980; Rick 1980; Wittlesey 1980). Although functional, these early in-house stop-gap solutions suffered from unreliability, vulnerability to the elements, and to software bugs that made them quirky to operate.

By the mid-1980s, several manufacturers had introduced EDM instruments with built-in or integrated data collectors and computers capable of instantly converting and recording each angle and distance reading into a site-specific set of x, y, z coordinates with typed-in provenience or descriptive data for each record. In the summer of 1986, I deployed one of these early integrated total station systems to record the unexpected discovery of a large multicomponent historic and precontact site complex along the banks of the upper Hudson River in Fort Edward, New York. The deeply stratified site revealed first the bastion of eighteenth century Fort Edward above an extensive 400,000-square-foot Late Woodland site containing more than 900 Native American pit features, burials, and structural remains. A 3000-year-old Transitional Period Broad Spear occupation consisting of cobble platform cooking hearths, undisturbed living floors, and 80,000 chipped stone artifacts was found 5 feet below the Late Woodland Period site (Grossman 1990b).

As was the case with the unexpected discovery at Raritan Landing 8 years earlier, the magnitude and timing of the discovery at Fort Edward threatened the viability of a federally funded public works program, in this instance, a much needed water treatment facility. The challenge was made more acute by the sheer size and complexity of the site. It also underscored the urgent need to define and record the point locations of literally thousands of features and artifacts in a restricted time frame of weeks versus months or years.

The advent of this one category of adapted commercial digital surveying equipment has affected archaeological field strategy in three primary areas: (1) It provides enhanced speed and precision to meet the time constraints of emergency field situations; (2) it increases the archaeologist's ability to provide micro topographic and artifact density and distribution records essential for the identification of behaviorally significant activity and settlement patterns; and (3) it provides the essential data control and precise reference targets for both single camera photogrammetry and LIDAR coordinate scans.

Overhead Stereo Photogrammetry

The idea of low elevation overhead photography in archaeology was not new. Aerial photographic coverage came into use with balloon reconnaissance during the Civil War and World War I. From this foundation, archaeologists experimented using ladders, balloons, model airplanes and helicopters, multilevel mono and bipod suspension systems with varying success (Bevan 1975a, 1975b; Sterud and Pratt 1975). Overhead recording technology involved two major components: first, the recording system itself, and, second and of equal developmental challenge, a system to suspend and support the recording technology over the excavation to provide overhead and 360-degree coverage from a number of different angles, such as near eye level, at 45 degrees, and at nearly overhead vertical coverage.

By the early 1970s, Julian Wittlesey had designed and subsequently patented a ready-to-use lightweight bipod system for archaeologists (Wittlesey 1975). Although the time frame of the Raritan Landing project made it impossible to acquire any available examples,

Wittlesey kindly provided his blueprints to build one for the Raritan Landing dig. The only limitation of the existing design had to do with controlling the orientation of the camera, which, when raised, would often spin. Given the 20-foot by 300-foot area of the Raritan Landing excavation corridor, it was necessary to develop a camera locking system to orient the photographs in line with the grid and thus reduce the number of setups and exposures required to guarantee full coverage with the least number of shots.

My team at the Rutgers Archaeological Survey Office (RASO) designed and built a version of the Whittlesey bipod system with a custom-built beaklike overhead camera mounting mechanism to lock the camera into alignment with the site grid not unlike the docking bay on the International Space Station. When raised by pulley and suspension cables to the apex of the triangular bipod legs, the camera (a Hasselblad with an 80-mm macro lens) was able to capture a flat field image of a 15-foot by 15-foot square of nine adjacent 5-foot excavation units in each view. Several different systems were adopted to trigger the camera remotely while suspended (wire-cable-, air-cable-, and remote-radio-controlled firing devices). By tilting the bipods with cables over a ca. 20-degree arc, the overhead camera system was able to capture stereo coverage with 30 to 60 percent overlap. The resultant coverage provided details of the buried living surfaces, not otherwise visible (Figure 15.3) (Grossman 1978, 1980, 1982b).

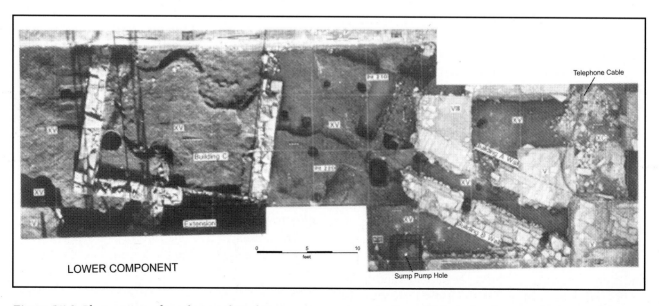

Figure 15.3. Photomosaic of overlapping bipod image segments into single rectified overhead composite image of the earliest eighteenth-century building elements within Raritan Landing construction corridor.

This system needs both height and fair weather. Although much of the excavation occurred during the winter, the bipod worked at Raritan Landing because the air-inflated, steel-ribbed, and plastic-covered, customized "green house" shelters over the site could be moved and slid apart to permit the raising of the camera-mounting system. Although excellent for fair weather, because of its height and the impossibility of moving the fixed 8-foot-high heated winter shelters, this suspension system was not a viable solution 5 years later for the high-speed winter excavation of the mid-seventeenth-century remains of the Dutch West India Company site (Grossman 1985).

Low Elevation Overhead Photogrammetry Under Winter Shelters

In 1983 the large-scale rescue excavation of the former shoreline block of Pearl Street between Broad Street and Whitehall Street in Lower Manhattan led to the discovery of the well-preserved early seventeenth-century remains of the Dutch West India Company, as well as the pre-1650 homes and artifacts of some of its principal residents. The excavation conducted by Greenhouse Consultants Inc., for which I then served as principal investigator, revealed the presence of five periods of early Dutch and British stratified historic deposits (Grossman 1985).

Beneath the basement fill and brick floors of nine-teenth-century buildings, the archaeologists exposed the relatively undisturbed, seventeenth-century fast-land surface, the well-preserved stone foundation re-mains of a number of buildings, some with early sev-enteenth-century cobblestone interior floors and fea-tures of imported yellow brick from Holland. These structural remains included the pre-1651 warehouse of Augustine Heermans, a principal trader of the Dutch West India Company, the wooden barrel cis-tern of Dr. and Mrs. Hans Kierstede, the company's first official surgeon, and the domestic remains of Cornelius van Tienhoven, the secretary of the province under Peter Stuyvesant after 1652 (Gross-man 1985, 2000).

The Manhattan dig took place in deep winter con-ditions under fixed air-inflated and heated shelters with a maximum interior elevation of 8 feet to 10 feet. Because of the low elevation of the shelters and the severe weather conditions that prevented them from being even temporarily moved, the 20-foot-high ele-vated bipod system would not work. An alternative overhead photo recording system had to be devel-

oped. To solve this problem, I worked with a photog-rapher and a metal engineer to design, machine lathe, and build a low-elevation indoor stereo camera sus-pension system that could be easily assembled and maneuvered beneath the winter shelters. After trying many variations on the theme, we designed and built a triangular single-track monorail camera support system suspended between two heavy photo tripods at a height of 7 feet to 8 feet, the allowable clearance at the sides of the shelters. A 3-foot-diameter rotating metal disc was milled from aluminum plate to mount the two cameras, one for black and white and one for color or infrared film. When spun and moved paral-lel to the excavation surface along the triangular sus-pension track, the circular mounting disk provided overlapping 30 to 60 percent stereo and photomosaic coverage at low interior elevations (Figure 15.4).

Figure 15.4. Detail of the 1983 custom-built, overhead-camera suspension system designed to provide low-elevation stereo and photomosaic coverage under winter shelters.

Although elegant and complicated in design and construction, and different in appearance than the 20-foot-tall Whittlesey bipod, it worked on the same principle and had similar drawbacks as the earlier bipod device. It was difficult to lock into place with precise coordinate control, was time consuming to assemble, stopped excavation in the immediate vicinity, and also had a bad habit of falling on people.

Single Camera Photogrammetry at West Point Foundry

Confronting Contamination

The next stage of increasingly more efficient and flexible stereo and photo mosaic recording capabilities began in 1989 with the first large-scale archaeological data recovery effort at a U.S. Environmental Protection Agency superfund remediation site at the

Marathon Battery at West Point Foundry (Figure 15.5). This 5-year multiagency program of terrestrial and underwater archaeology resulted in the discovery of sensitive Civil War era cannon research and testing facilities under 5 feet of modern fill and cadmium deposits at the former site of the West Point Foundry across the Hudson River from the West Point Military Academy. The additional discovery of the elaborate houses and high-quality imported European artifacts and scientific instruments that belonged to well-educated foreign workers, as well as previously unrecorded archival evidence combined to reveal a previously unknown international intelligence and espionage operation within Lincoln's Executive Branch (Grossman 1990a, 1994a, 1994b; Holtzer 1995).

Like the Manhattan dig, the excavation had to be done in winter conditions under heavy shelters with limited access and mobility. Unlike the previous projects constrained only by time, as a superfund site,

Grossman, et. al, 1991, Vol. I, Fig. 1.7)

Figure 15.5. Grossman and Associates 1992 HAZMAT archaeological team excavating under fixed and heated winter shelters at the West Point Foundry.

Marathon Battery was contaminated with heavy deposits of cancer causing cadmium. Something safer than the earlier overhead systems was needed. The added element of having to work in contaminated contexts affected the planning and deployment of archaeological approaches and procedures in two critical ways. First, their presence required the field and laboratory team members to be trained and certified in HAZMAT health and safety procedures, wear somewhat awkward tyvek suits and thick layers of protective plastic gloves, and be medically monitored throughout the fieldwork. Second, the potential health risks mandated the need to limit the proximity and duration of contact with potentially contaminated cultural materials.

In addition to deploying the total station transit system, the solution was provided by a new generation of nonstereo, single-camera, photogrammetric recording systems. Called the Rolleimetric, the new-medium-format metric camera was developed in the mid-1980s by the Rollei Corporation of Germany to record rapidly and remotely crash and disaster scenes for military and police agencies. This system was applied archaeologically for the first time at the Marathon Battery (Grossman, 1990a, 1994a). In 1992 it was also applied to minimize the level of exposure and time for the archaeological recording of a Civil War-era gasholder house remains permeated with toxic organic liquids and fumes found buried beneath the modern Niagara Mohawk Power Corporation facility in Saratoga Springs, New York (Grossman 1993).

The Rolleimetric Single-Camera Photogrammetry System: A Non-Contact Recording Solution

The system is unique because it supersedes the rigid structure and limited recording capabilities of traditional two-camera, stereo photogrammetry configurations. Instead of using fixed, overhead stereo image pairs, the Rolleimetric system uses a single metric camera, and a high resolution, flat field, wide angle, automatic focus macro (90°) lens, which provides a broad range of latitude in the elevation and angle of recording. The metric camera and lens system is associated with a sophisticated computer software package that digitizes, rectifies, and correlates different images or views of the same subject and renders the composite image as a high-resolution, metrically accurate, 2D and 3D plan, profile, or 3D

wire frame image. Unlike traditional photogrammetric systems, this new capability does not require stringently regulated 30 to 60 percent overlapping coverage between adjacent photos, but instead provides coverage with a variable range of perspective views taken from four to six points.

The single camera system reduces field time, enhances the quality of the documentation process, and provides a level of data control that is difficult, if not impossible, to record using traditional procedures. For emergency rescue and contaminated contexts, the single camera Rollei system permits the operator to rapidly document the subject in minutes with minimal contact between the operator and the contaminated remains (Figure 15.6). In addition to making the recording process more accurate, faster, and safer, the resultant photogrammetric prints constitute both a high-resolution visual record, and what essentially amounts to a long-term photographic archive of each subject's coordinates, dimensions, and structural characteristics. This long-term record can be reinterpreted through the computer at any subsequent time to extract additional relevant coordinate information or to render new perspectives, as needed (Figures 15.7 and 15.8).

But the Rollei single-camera photogrammetric system also had some limitations. The early analysis software was expensive, difficult, and time consuming to use. When originally released by the Rollei Corporation in the late 1980s, the relative ease of use and cost of data processing were exacerbated by the fact that each of the images had to be rendered as high-quality, large-format color plates and then processed through manual digital procedures with two different sets of cumbersome and technically complicated software packages that were available only in German.

These limitations have now been superceded by new, high-capacity, desktop computer-based photogrammetric software interpretation programs costing only hundreds of dollars, but considerable time, staffing, and budgets are still needed to computer-process the large sets of photogrammetric data. In addition, although the single-camera Rollei system is effective for rendering computer-assisted design (CAD) drawings of rectangular structural elements, such as cut beams, wooden planks, or masonry walls, it is of limited use for the capture and rendition of a large number of irregular organic forms, such as the large wooden logs and branches exposed on the colonial Albany waterfront site.

Figure 15.6. Single-camera photogrammetric Rolleimetric system over exposed 1863 Civil War gun-testing platform discovered at West Point Foundry.

Laser Radar (LIDAR) and Single-Camera Photogrammetry at Albany

The Challenge

The Rollei system was quick and flexible, but not flexible and fast enough to rapidly document the 3D wooden matrix of large vertical and horizontal log structures that Hartgen's team had exposed more than 12 feet below the streets of downtown Albany in the summer of 1999 (Figure 15.9). In addition to the survival of a buried section of the original shoreline and the eighteenth-century town stockade, the excavation team had exposed a series of parallel, north-south aligned, vertical and horizontal wooden bulkhead structures. Also they had discovered the intact lot of one of Albany's famous merchants, Stuart Dean, which was distinguished by an artificial surface of hundreds of horizontal rough-cut branches and small logs tightly laid in a series of bands to form parallel

working surfaces called ricking behind the eighteenth-century bulkhead wall (Figure 15.10). In this, and other lots, the density and irregularity of the exposed wooden elements suggested that traditional manual recording and field photography would not be sufficient to do justice to the complexity and magnitude of the 3D matrix of vertical and horizontal log structures in the available time frame.

As usual, time was short. The call had come on July 3, 1999, on the eve of the July 4th weekend. The challenge was exacerbated by the need to complete the recording task within seven calendar days, the time remaining before construction was to begin. Three of the days were holidays across the country, and Tuesday would be the first work day for most of the nation.

Against this backdrop, and following discussions with the New York State Historic Preservation Office, Hartgen Archeological Associates, Inc., requested that

I develop, mobilize, and implement a high-speed 3D recording solution by the Wednesday following the holiday weekend that would record the entire site complex. The New York State officials had asked that I develop and deploy an applied technology recording solution as I had used first in 1989 at the Marathon Battery. I was also asked not to immediately say no, but instead to think it over, hopefully with a solution over the weekend. The conditions were clearly stated. There was no lead or mobilization time.

The Solution

At first I was not optimistic. Nothing I had done in the past 20 years would be sufficient to meet the complexity and time frame of the Albany challenge. So, as

Figure 15.7. (left) Near-overhead Rolleimetric perspective image of an exposed iron and wood cannon-testing platform discovered at West Point Foundry.

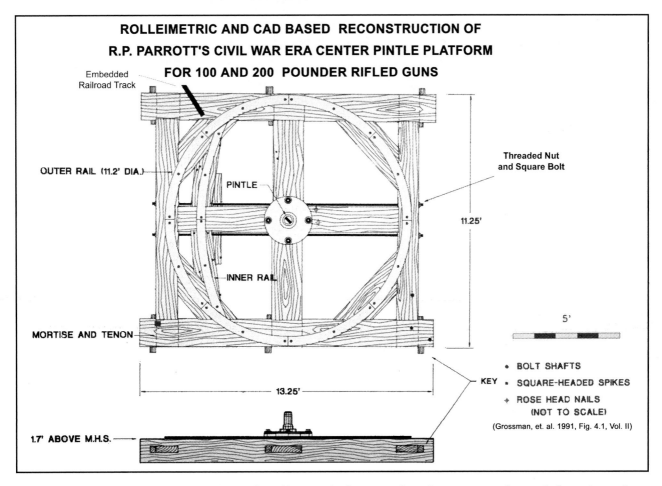

Figure 15.8. Final-scaled AutoCAD plan and profile record of excavated Civil War cannon-firing platform drawn from Rolleimetric photos.

Figure 15.9. Rolleimetric view looking southeast toward the Hudson River showing two-block-long excavation in Albany, New York.

I had done in previous challenging situations, I borrowed a new, but proven, high-speed recording technology from unrelated disciplines, the oil and movie industries. In addition to the previously used Rollei system to record hundreds of high-resolution, medium-format overhead and photogrammetric color images of the site, I recommended the first archaeological use of the Cyrax large-format 3D laser scanner (the Cyrax 2400 Mark-1) to capture an almost infinite series of millimeter-precise laser point clouds of x, y, z coordinate points for each log and beam of the Albany wharf and bulkhead complex.

Although untried in an archaeological setting, this recently developed 3D capture technology had been applied with enhanced precision over the best of pho-

togrammetry to map complex structural details on oil platforms at sea, to develop realistic special effects and sets for the science fiction film *Star Ship Troopers* (where it helped giant flying bugs land on virtual reality interplanetary battlefields), and to guide robotic welding systems. It had also been used for a range of unspecified military and police applications (Ashley 1999; Cullison 1998; Cyra Technologies 1998). If it was good enough to help map intergalactic flying bugs, I made the determination that it was good enough to help record the large and complex historic archaeological matrix of the Albany excavation.

Photogrammetry has some severe limitations that affected my decision to augment its capabilities with the laser scanner technology. The relative merits of

Figure 15.10. View toward the southern section of excavation. LIDAR scanning in progress.

this new capability over the time and manpower constraints of traditional and even single-camera photogrammetry systems had been clearly defined in a scientific paper by Ashley (1999). It takes a trained specialist time and numerous steps to extract coordinate measurements. For complex structures, adequate coverage requires that a large number of metric views be taken, manually correlated, referenced to one another, and evaluated to extract detailed representations of the subject. The process is labor intensive and expensive, in terms of both film and processing costs and human hourly costs. Finally, while photogrammetry works fine for rectangular structural elements, such as a building, or the relatively limited number of square cut beams exposed in association with the Civil War cannon testing facilities at West Point, the Rolleimetric camera alone would become excessively time consuming and costly for a site consisting of thousands of irregularly rough cut logs uncovered in Albany.

I had been tracking the developmental progress of this and comparable large format 3D recording systems in the United States, Canada, and Europe for the past several years. A number of small laser scanner systems for small objects within a 1-foot to 5-foot range had been available from a variety of sources for some 5 years, but the first large-scale systems to be made commercially available on the open market dated only to 1998. The Cyrax system was still undergoing rapid developmental refinements, only 18 units were available worldwide, and it was still housed in a wooden box of dubious all-weather durability. If operational, available, and capable of doing for archaeology what it had provided the oil and movie industries, this new technology promised radically to alter how archaeologists could and would record their excavations with a potential for vast increases in detail and resolution, in a fraction of the time.

Over the weekend, I placed a call to the Cyra Corporation in California, the makers of the LIDAR laser scanner technology, and quite simply left a message with their answering service asking them to drop everything they were doing and fly their best people and equipment to Albany, New York, by the following Wednesday. On Sunday, a senior executive from Cyra called me back at home and, after a moment of guarded skepticism, agreed to do just that. Assuming the availability of immediate funding, he said yes, and so did I. The Cyra Technologies Corporation representative saw this as an ideal opportunity to test the

rapid-response capability of their new systems. By Wednesday, the directors of the project, representatives of the New York State Historic Preservation Office, and senior administrators of the State University Construction Fund authorized and funded the deployment of the laser-radar team.

Looking like a large box-shaped transit on a tripod, this new large-scale, and highly portable, laser scanner is capable of capturing details of a three-dimensional structure with an accuracy of millimeters over a distance of 600 feet (Figure 15.11). In essence, the high-resolution 3D laser scanner developed by Cyrax can produce an extremely dense series of scans or point clouds, which in turn can be computer-rendered to create a mesh model of the subject. Officially known as LIDAR, the laser-radar technology can scan more points than either integrated total stations or photogrammetric reduction in a fraction of the time and cost. Each scan of a 50-foot portion of a site or grid matrix can typically contain 300,000- to 500,000-millimeter precise x, y, z coordinate points. When seamed together using software to georeference the various scans relative to the precisely measured coordinate control targets measured with the onsite computer transit, the multiple scans can be rendered into a CAD-compatible 3D mesh model from which accurate dimensions and locations can be extracted. Laser-based radar is not harmful to humans, and can work in full daylight or in total darkness.

The time frame for this rapidly mobilized, high-technology recording solution is only half the story. The 150-foot by 300-foot site was recorded in tandem with both systems. One major variable affecting the time frame hinged on how the two recording technologies would be raised and positioned to provide full coverage from all necessary angles. Given the lack of mobilization time to deploy both, a dedicated suspension system was out of the question. Instead of developing and building a system to provide wide area coverage of the two-block-long excavation, a 100-foot-high movable electronic lift or cherry picker provided unlimited 360-degree perspective views and near overhead coverage from the air for both the laser scans and hundreds of photogrammetric images (Figure 15.12).

The site was divided into eight 50-foot-square quadrants, four along the eastern side and four along the western side of the wide area exposure. Each quadrant was recorded from ground height, and then from the lift at 45 degrees, then 60 degrees, and finally with vertical and near overhead views from

Figure 15.11. Three-dimensional Cyra LIDAR scanner equipment and technical support team mapping exposed bulkhead features.

eight side and corner positions within each quadrant. For each 50-foot by 50-foot recording quadrant, a total of between 24 and 30 Rolliemetric images were recorded to provide flat-field planar overhead and overlapping perspective views adequate for photogrammetric reduction and 3D reconstruction of each structural element exposed at the site.

The two teams, the Cyra staff manning the laser and I taking the overhead metric images, worked in tandem. When one was recording from the ground, the other was taking shots from the lift and vice versa. The eastern half of the site was fully recorded and cleared for construction in 6 days, between July 7 and 12. The western half of the site was recorded in 42 hours over a 3-day period from August 8 to 10. The first 4-day recording session was undertaken with one Cyra LIDAR unit and a single operator. However, because of problems of hardware and software inter-

face on the first day of the initial effort in July, for the second phase, I pulled in the equipment and technical expertise from two sources across the country: one from a Cyra representative in New Hampshire and a second instrument and team from 3D Engineering of Florida, permitting two scanners and operator teams in the air and on the ground both day and night for the last 3-day recording effort. A total of 900 metric Rolleimetric images and 600 megabytes of multiple 3D laser-point cloud scans were recorded. The project began construction on schedule without undue delays and costs.

Discussion

The two technologies are not redundant but provide independent processes for remotely recording the context and coordinates of excavated features and

Figure 15.12. Field view of portable LIDAR scanner and technicians suspended over the wooden bulkhead structures.

artifacts. Whereas LIDAR provides dense records of point coordinate information, the single-camera photogrammetry system exemplified by the Rolleimetric camera and software systems provides a long-term visual archive of frozen provenience and metric information. Images can be retrieved and reanalyzed via the computer coordinate software components to extract specific points and dimensions of any visible objects or surfaces. The high-resolution, metrically precise, medium-format images produced by the single-camera photogrammetry can be enlarged and studied in detail to reveal minute elements and surface details of exposed archaeological features. What may have been exposed but overlooked during excavation can be reevaluated at any time in the future.

The two recording technologies are also complementary. The point-cloud data of the LIDAR scans can be interpolated in the computer into actual coordinates and as an interpolated or triangulated matrix to form a metrically accurate framework or skeleton rendition of the recorded features. These frameworks can be computer processed in varying degrees of resolution from a simple 3D matrix of connected points to a high-resolution computer image, which simulates the form and surface details of the objects or structures being recorded. But this computer-processed LIDAR imagery is not yet photo-realistic in its detail (Figures 15.13 and 15.14).

In essence, the high-speed LIDAR produces a metrically accurate point cloud or skeleton record of the

Figure 15.13. Detail of one section of the vertical eighteenth-century wooden log bulkhead with control targets for reference to laser-radar scans. An example of a laser-radar scan may be seen in Figure 15.14.

archaeological surfaces and structural elements (Figure 15.14). In contrast, the high-resolution color imagery produced by the Rolleimetric single-camera photogrammetry, produces a precise, metrically accurate, high-resolution color image of the surface, or skin, of what is being recorded (Figure 15.13). The current technological challenge is to seamlessly blend the two, to fit the photogrammetric skin over the skeleton of precise LIDAR coordinate records.

Currently available software can readily surface-map or laminate digital images onto simple geometric forms. But the ability to precisely match or surface-map the thousands of points that make up an irregular hand-cut wooden form or irregular stone-building element with the minute visual details of a high-reso-

lution metric photograph is still being developed. Current computer systems can produce or simulate the appearance of realistic-looking surface mapping of images over digital frameworks, but the level of precision is at best still crude. The ability to accurately surface-map the 900 metric images of the hundreds of wooden elements recorded in Albany onto the dense 3D point clouds recorded by the LIDAR scanners is still probably 2 to 5 years off.

Conclusion

What are the implications for the future of these recording technologies for archaeological project management and planning? In the first place, it is im-

Figure 15.14. A computer "screen shot" of a raw 3D laser-radar scan of vertical wooden bulkhead elements. Each scan line represents thousands of millimeter-precise coordinate points across the surface slice of exposed log elements.

portant to reiterate that these systems are new, still under development, and by no means perfected. Any recommendation for their use is not a slam dunk. Hardware and software are constantly being upgraded. The photogrammetric and laser data sets are generally massive and difficult to process with standard office computer systems, and they require a concerted effort and budget allocation to integrate and control. Nevertheless, the potential exists for this technology to have a significant impact on archaeological excavation and documentation procedures.

From the project management perspective, the speed, flexibility, precision, and near total coverage provided by the LIDAR scanning technology together with high-resolution color imagery of single camera photogrammetry gives the profession the ability rapidly to document unexpected finds or sites difficult to access. The availability of the current generation of powerful portable computers, in turn, gives the archaeologist in the field the means to transform this cloud of scanned point records into a database of recorded site-specific artifact provenience and feature coordinate points. Instead of 300 readings per day made possible beginning in the mid-1970s with the advent of computerized total-station electronic surveying instruments, this new LIDAR scanner technology in conjunction with computerized photogrammetry provides the field archaeologist with the ability to record literally millions of data points in a matter of hours.

The implications of these emerging technologies are profound from legal, policy, scientific, and public interpretative perspectives. For the archaeologist and planner faced with the challenge of needing to record a complex archaeological discovery unexpectedly encountered in the path of ongoing construction, this technology can become a tool of conflict avoidance.

This evolving capability in turn gives both the scientist and the planner the means of responding to unexpected discoveries in a feasible, practicable, and cost-effective manner that serves to reduce or even negate past arguments against doing justice to our dwindling record of unwritten history and precontact evidence. The specter of dire fiscal constraints posed by the popular paradigm of "history versus progress" may no longer hold.

Finally, from the perspective of our ability to create public interpretations, these new recording capabilities also suggest that the field archaeologist will be able to provide the educator and museum curator with almost ready-made visual data sets capable of being transformed into dynamic public interpretative programs in a fraction of the traditional time frame.

As recently demonstrated by the extraordinary public theater installations in Israel, Canada, Europe, and Japan, large-scale photo-realistic interactive and total immersion virtual reality simulations of ancient archaeological sites are now becoming the norm at major national tourist centers around the world. Up to now, these projects have been both costly and time consuming, largely due to the nature of traditional archaeological data recording and rendition. Much of the effort to simulate "walk-through" reconstructions of ancient monuments and sites has involved the often laborious process of transforming traditional manual and paper archaeological field and publication records into computer-compatible formats suitable for rendering into 3D simulated, computer-rendered models. These time and cost factors could change significantly if and when the archaeological community readjusts traditional field strategies to incorporate the newly available computer-compatible digital point-data and image-recording systems.

It is not unreasonable to project that in the near future archaeologists will be able to concurrently record 3D digital records of what they excavate with near total accuracy. Images of excavated structures and features can be reviewed on the computer screen in the field, and any point can be zoomed in to reveal the dimensions, coordinates, surface texture, and accurate color qualities of what is being excavated during, instead of long after, the objects are discovered and/or destroyed. The day may not be too far off when proforma archaeological reporting and interpretative efforts will include millimeter-precise virtual reality reconstructions of archaeological sites.

References Cited

Ashley, P. 1999. New 3D Scanner Zaps Sci-Fi Movie Set. *Professional Surveyor* 19(3):n.p.

Bevan, B. 1975a. *Aerial Photography for the Archaeologist.* Museum Applied Science Center for Archaeology, University of Pennsylvania, Philadelphia.

———. 1975b. An Introduction to Stereo Photography. Appendix to J.H. Wittlesley in *Photography in Archaeological Research*, edited by E. Harp, Jr., pp. 259–264. University of New Mexico Press, Albuquerque.

Blakeslee, D.J. 1979. Mapping with an Electronic Calculator. *Journal of Field Archaeology* 6:321–329.

Cullison, A. 1998. A Technological Leap in Robotic Programming May Be on the Horizon. *Welding Journal Magazine*, July, n.p.

Cyra Technologies, Inc. 1998. *Cyrax TM System Overview: 3D Laser Mapping System for Complete, Accurate, Fast Visualization and Modeling for Large Structures and Sites.* Product Bulletin, Oakland, Calif.

Grossman, J.W. 1978. *The Ground Penetrating Radar Survey of Raritan Landing: Archaeological Findings, Documentary Evidence, and Data Recovery Options.* Prepared for the U.S. Environmental Protection Agency, Region II, New York.

———. 1980. Defining Boundaries and Targeting Excavation with Ground-Penetrating Radar: The Case of Raritan Landing. *Environmental Impact Assessment Review* 1(2):145–166.

———. 1982a. *Seeing Underground: The Feasibility of Archaeological Remote Sensing in Coastal and Highland Peru.* The Instituto Nacional de Cultura, Lima, Peru. Conducted under the auspices of UNESCO, the OAS, and the Andres Bello Fund.

———. 1982b. Raritan Landing: The Archaeology of a Buried Port. Rutgers Archaeological Survey Office, New Brunswick, N.J. Prepared for the U.S. Environmental Protection Agency and the Middlesex County Sewer Authority, Region II, New York.

———. 1985. The Excavation of Augustine Heerman's Warehouse and Associated 17th Century Dutch West India Company Deposits, Vols. 1–3. The Broad Street Financial Center Mitigation Final Report. Prepared by Greenhouse Consultants, Inc., for New York City Landmarks Preservation Commission, New York. On file at New York Office of Parks, Recreation and Historic Preservation, Waterford.

_____. 1990a . The Archaeological Discovery and Excavation of R.P. Parrott's Civil War Era Gun Testing Facility at West Point Foundry. Prepared for Malcolm Pirnie, Inc., and the U.S. Environmental Protection Agency, Region II, New York. On file at New York Office of Parks, Recreation and Historic Preservation, Waterford.

_____. 1990b. The Excavation, Analysis and Reconstruction of Transitional Period, Late Woodland Period, and Colonial Occupations at the Little Wood Creek Site, Fort Edward, Washington County, New York. Prepared for the U.S. Environmental Protection Agency and the Washington County Sewer Authority. USEPA Project No. C 36-1305-01, Region II, New York. On file at New York Office of Parks, Recreation and Historic Preservation, Waterford.

_____. 1993. Stage II Archaeological Data Recovery and Mitigation Results of the Investigation of Historic Coal Gassification Works at the Niagara Mohawk Power Corporation Site, Saratoga Springs, Saratoga County, New York. Prepared for Niagara Mohawk Power Corporation, November. Saratoga Springs, New York. On file at New York Office of Parks, Recreation and Historic Preservation, Waterford.

_____. 1994a. High Caliber Discovery [The Historical Archaeology of West Point Foundry] *Federal Archaeology* 7(2):38–43 .

_____. 1994b. The Role of Espionage and Foreign Intelligence in the Development of Heavy Ordnance at the West Point Foundry, Cold Spring, New York. In *Look to the Earth: The Archaeology of the Civil War,* edited by C. Geier, pp. 215–255. University of Tennessee Press, Knoxville.

_____. 1995. The Archaeology of Civil War Water Control Systems on the Lower East Side of Manhattan. Data Recovery and Mitigation Within Lots 58 and 59, PSA 4 Project, New York, New York (CEQR No. 95CHA001M). Prepared for the New York City Housing Authority. New York. On file at New York Office of Parks, Recreation and Historic Preservation, Waterford.

_____. 1997. *Applied Technology in Archaeological Investigation.* U.S. Army Environmental Center, Aberdeen Proving Ground, Maryland.

_____. 2000. Mrs. Kierstead's Rear Yard: The Archaeological Discovery and Ethno-botanical, Cartographic and Archival Reanalysis of the 17th Century Dutch West India Company Remains in Lower Manhattan, New York. Paper presented at the 1st Annual *Regia Civitas* Conference Medieval Towns and Its Citizens. Institute of Archaeology of the Hungarian Academy of Sciences, Budapest, Hungary. June 1–4.

Hakiel, N.E. 1980. Note on Mapping with an Electronic Calculator. *Journal of Field Archaeology* 7:264–265.

Holtzer, H. 1995. Lincoln's Secret Arms Race. *Civil War Times* 34(4):32–39.

Miller, J.M. 1978. Archaeological Survey of Central Moab. Paper presented to the Joint Annual Meeting of the American Academy of Religion and the Society of Biblical Literature, New Orleans.

Rick, J.W. 1980. *Prehistoric Hunters of the High Andes.* Academic Press, New York.

St. Amand, B.W. 1999. Out of the Dark Ages: New Laser Technology Brings Cave Mapping into the 21st Century. *Point of Beginning,* Business News Corporation, July. Reprint n.p.

Sterud, E.L., and Pratt, P. 1975. Archaeological Intra-Site Recording with Photography. *Journal of Field Archaeology* 2:151–167.

_____, Strauss, L.G., and Abramovitz, K. 1980. Annual Review of Old World Archaeology. *American Antiquity* 45(4):759–786.

Weeks, K.R. 1978. *The Berkeley Map of Thebian Necropolis: Preliminary Report.* University of California, Berkeley.

Wittlesey, J.H. 1975. Elevated and Airborne Photogrammetry and Stereo Photography. In *Photography in Archaeological Research,* edited by E. Harp, Jr., pp. 223–258. University of New Mexico Press, Albuquerque.

_____. 1980. Commentary on Mapping with an Electronic Calculator. In *A Complete Manual of Field Archaeology: Tools and Techniques of Field Work for Archaeologists,* edited by M. Joukowsky, pp. 540–547. Prentice-Hall, Englewood Cliffs, N.J.

Contributors

J.W. Bouchard
Hartgen Archeological Associates, Inc.
1744 Washington Avenue Ext.
Rensselaer, NY 12144

Nancy Davis
Cultural Resource Survey Program
New York State Museum
Albany, NY 12230

Lois M. Feister
New York State Office of Parks
Recreation and Historic Preservation
Peebles Island
P.O. Box 219
Waterford, NY 12188-0189

Charles L. Fisher
Cultural Resource Survey Program
New York State Museum
Albany, NY 12230

Joel W. Grossman
520 West 218th Street
New York, NY 10034

Karen S. Hartgen
Hartgen Archaeological Associates, Inc.
1744 Washington Avenue Ext.
Rensselaer, NY 12144

Paul R. Huey
New York State Office of Parks
Recreation and Historic Preservation
Peebles Island
P.O. Box 219
Waterford, NY 12188-0189

Matthew Kirk
Hartgen Archeological Associates, Inc.
1744 Washington Avenue Ext.
Rensselaer, NY 12144

Matthew Lesniak
Hartgen Archeological Associates, Inc.
1744 Washington Avenue Ext.
Rensselaer, NY 12144

Pegeen McLaughlin
Hartgen Archeological Associates, Inc.
1744 Washington Avenue Ext.
Rensselaer, NY 12144

Kevin Moody
Hartgen Archeological Associates, Inc.
1744 Washington Avenue Ext.
Rensselaer, NY 12144

Elizabeth S. Peña
Buffalo Museum of Science
1020 Humboldt Parkway
Buffalo, NY 14211-1293

Shawn Phillips
Department of Geography
Geology and Anthropology
Indiana State University
Terre Haute, IN 47809